PRINTED TEACHING MATERIALS: A NEW APPROACH FOR LAW TEACHERS

Richard Johnstone
B Bus Sci (Hons) (Cape Town); LLB (Hons); PhD (Melb)
Associate Professor
Faculty of Law
The University of Melbourne

Cavendish
Publishing
Limited

First published in Great Britain 1996 by Cavendish Publishing Limited,
The Glass House, Wharton Street, London WC1X 9PX.
Telephone: 0171-278 8000 Facsimile: 0171-278 8080

Johnstone, R
Printed teaching materials: a new approach for law teachers
1.Law – Study and teaching – England
I.Title
344.2′007

ISBN 1-85941-233-5

Printed and bound in Great Britain

FOREWORD

The future for higher education in the next decade will be marked by unprecedented turbulence and change. Two important challenges face universities in many countries.

The first of these challenges is the rapid shift to mass higher education, a phenomenon which is most apparent in the developed Asian countries, the United Kingdom and Australasia. Twenty years ago, the classes I taught comprised a tiny hand-picked intellectual élite; today's lecturers often face hundreds of students of highly variable ability and background. By any yardstick, university teaching is a more exacting occupation than it used to be.

The second hazard amplifies the first – the pressure from stakeholders, employers and students to deliver better quality university education. This customer and client-driven drive for higher quality has introduced a new competitiveness into higher education. It has meant a demand for graduates who not only possess a wider range of technical skills and academic knowledge, but who are also continuing learners with a broader repertoire of workplace and social skills. They need to be more adaptable, more independent, more able to communicate, more used to working in teams, and more attuned to a dynamic and uncertain working life.

Neither challenge is going to go away. How can we meet them? Both imply the use of methods of teaching and learning which are better adapted to students' and employers' needs, combined with the selection and continuing professional development of a more broadly skilled academic workforce. To achieve the learning outcomes required of today's graduates requires the highest standards of innovative teaching and course design. To deliver these things reliably will need large scale organisational and staff development.

More flexible learning methods are probably the only way to reach and motivate today's larger and more diverse student population and to provide the quality of education they now expect. 'Flexible learning' is not the same thing as distance education, or using high technology methods of teaching, or saving money by replacing lecturers with computers. Flexible learning takes many forms, but it typically incorporates greater freedom in location and time of study, greater student control over learning goals and style, less lecturing and transmission of knowledge in large classes (together with more time for interactive group work), and the use of high quality resource materials such as printed study guides or their computer-based equivalents. Practised well, flexible learning fits education more closely to the needs of students, and has the potential to enhance the quality of outcomes through closer and more active engagement with the subject matter. The application of flexible learning methods to professional subjects, where strong integration between theory and practice is an indispensable part of a student's training, is particularly appropriate.

To use this approach effectively will require substantial investment in people. Most academics will need to acquire an array of new skills and to adopt a different way of thinking about teaching and planning courses. If universities seek to deliver a excellent education to more students, they will need a faculty whose professional teaching skills are more finely honed and are practised more consistently. In turn this will mean that they must find ways of building on the enduring values of academics – including their commitment to embedding practice in theory and empirical research – in order to overcome their understandable resistance to radical change.

It is precisely the challenges of flexible learning and higher quality that Richard Johnstone addresses in this book. His credentials for the task are faultless. I know him from my own work at The University of Melbourne to be an exemplary teacher and an inspiring leader of other teachers. Difficult as it is to teach today's university's students well, it is even harder successfully to develop academics' professional teaching skills. Richard Johnstone is one of the small number of Australian academics to have achieved distinction in both fields, as well as in the profession he teaches. The present book is of special value to practitioners because its examples are imbued with the author's own well-articulated knowledge of educational principles. Richard Johnstone has been able to do for legal education what academics in all disciplines more often aspire to do than actually achieve – to link research and teaching so that they mutually reinforce and inform each other.

The theory of teaching and learning in law on which he bases his advice is anchored in the substantial literature on student learning and teaching in higher education which has been established in the last 20 years. Undoubtedly the best thing about this theory is the fact that it works. People have been able to use it, and have derived benefit from using it.

Richard Johnstone's own application of this theory, in his work with the outstandingly successful Australasian Law Teachers Association (ALTA) Law Teaching Workshop and in his earlier book (*The Quiet (R)evolution*, co-authored with Marlene Le Brun) has amply confirmed its value as a basis for more effective professional education in our universities. It engages with the real needs of law teachers – especially those who will shape the future of legal education. It is practical, without being dogmatic or merely a list of recipes (the trouble with recipes in teaching, as in cooking, is that they are useless without a knowledge of basic principles and some solid experience; better to know how to produce three dishes reliably than to 'know' a hundred recipes that no-one can eat). The book's style and argument is in harmony with law teachers' requirements for rigorous standards of evidence and their warrant to give their best to their clients and their profession.

This book is modestly presented as a book about how law teachers can use printed teaching materials. Using print-based resources effectively is a specially relevant topic in legal education, since written documentation plays such a substantial part in legal practice. Richard Johnstone's advice on how to compile materials and how to use them as valuable adjuncts to (but never replacements for) interaction between teachers and students is precise and useful. The principles listed in Part 3 relating to comprehensiveness, access, readability, varied objectives, different voices, signposting, dialogue, personal experience, authenticity, assessment, and monitoring are critical for all effective resource-based learning. The illustrations of actual materials will bring the ideas vividly to life for all law teachers.

But Richard Johnstone's book contains much more than this. It is a primer in skilful university teaching: much of its advice applies to all subject areas and most teaching and learning methods. If you read it carefully, you will not only learn how to write educationally valuable teaching materials. You will also come to realise how the fundamentals of effective flexible learning methods are also the fundamentals of all good teaching, and that the change to more flexible learning is not so great a leap as you might at first have feared.

You will also, I hope, acquire a desire to find out more about university teaching and how to make your own teaching more effective and more personally satisfying. As the pressure for quality in higher education inexorably increases, so good university teaching will become increasingly important in advancing academic careers, and its practice will be more systematically recognised and rewarded. Tomorrow's academics in professional subjects will need to learn a second profession: the profession of university teaching. This book will provide them with an idea of the knowledge and standards they will need to achieve if they aspire to full success as professional teachers of law.

As organisations outside higher education have discovered, the key to helping staff embrace the challenges of a changing external environment is to be found in effective leadership. Turbulent times demand convincing leaders. Competent leadership in higher education invariably embodies many of the principles of good teaching which Richard Johnstone articulates so well. Good academic leaders are credible, inspiring, and positive. They have experienced what they exhort others to experience, and learned from it. They are good communicators and they use varied, well-chosen management strategies. They know the importance of appealing to the heart as well as the head. They constantly reflect on and improve their own performance. They get things done.

This book represents good academic leadership in action, and it points the way to a more secure and confident profession of teaching in the unsettled but exciting university environment of the 21st century.

Paul Ramsden
Professor of Higher Education
Griffith University

PREFACE

This book has been written at a time when the focus in education is increasingly falling on teaching technologies far more sophisticated than printed materials. While I have no doubt that in future years law teaching will make more use of a broad array of electronically-based educational media to improve student learning in law, I am confident that there will always be a place for printed materials. What is more, to be effective in helping teachers to facilitate improvements in student learning, all forms of educational media must be developed in the context of what we know to be sound principles of learning and teaching. This book is a very modest contribution to the debate about learning and teaching in law that has established some momentum in Australia over the past decade. The book's principal focus is on the use of printed teaching materials in tertiary law teaching, although I hope that the principles discussed in the book will provide some sort of educational framework for law teachers seeking to use computer-based technologies as part of their teaching strategies.

In writing this book I looked at many casebooks prepared by law teachers. None adopted the approach to teaching that is developed in the following pages, although I traced in a few of them a movement towards some aspects of the model developed in this book. This book offers a new approach to the use of instructional materials in law teaching. Its central premise is that we law teachers cannot develop more effective classroom teaching methods unless we make imaginative and creative use of instructional materials to motivate students to learn outside and inside the classroom. As I have argued in the book, however, the suggested approach draws on what we know about teaching and learning in higher education. In that sense, at least, the book is simply an application of well established educational principles. My greatest hope is that the book will play a part in provoking law teachers to rethink their teaching, and in particular the manner in which teaching materials, and other educational media, are utilised in law teaching. It puts an argument about one way of teaching law. It does not claim to be the only way, or even the best way. It is up to the reader to develop or modify the ideas set out in the following pages. Of one thing I am certain, that this book is not the last word on its subject. The principles espoused in its pages can be developed, improved and adapted by other law teachers.

The ideas and arguments in this book are not just the product of my own work, but have been heavily influenced by members of the community within which I work. The research towards this book was originally supported by a 1991 grant from the Commonwealth Department of Employment, Education and Training's National Priority (Reserve) Fund, which was administered through The University of Melbourne's Centre for the Study of Higher Education. I am grateful to Agnes Dodds and Jeannette Lawrence for the part they played in the achievement of that grant, and for their advice and comments at the outset of this project. An early, and fairly rudimentary, draft of my research was published by the Centre in 1993. Since that time I have continued to rethink the basic model of learning and teaching which underpins this book, based on my experience as a teacher, my reading of the educational literature, and my work with colleagues in the ALTA Law Teaching Workshop and at The University of Melbourne Law School. My colleagues have provided many comments and suggestions which have shaped the contents of this book. In particular thanks go to Gordon Joughin and Sarah Biddulph for their very detailed and thoughtful comments on earlier drafts, and for their encouragement and support during this project. I also thank Paul Ramsden for his support and encouragement over the past six years, and for writing the very generous Foreword to this book. Most of my ideas on law teaching have been forged in collaboration with Marlene Le Brun, whose expertise, energy and enthusiasm for law teaching is awesome. I am also indebted to Andrew Kenyon, Fred Ellinghaus, Les McCrimmon, Frances McGlone, Anthony O'Donnell, Jenny Morgan, Glen Patmore, Veronica Taylor and Mary Hiscock for their comments and suggestions on earlier drafts of this work. It goes without saying that I am fully responsible for all the misconceptions and errors that remain in the book. I am grateful for the support of the staff at the Centre for the Study of Higher Education at The University of Melbourne for assistance in wordprocessing at the early stages of this project. My Dean, Professor Michael Crommelin, provided all the support and encouragement for the project that I could possibly ask for. Finally, I acknowledge the contribution of Jo Reddy of Cavendish Publishing, and in particular her enthusiastic support of this project which has resulted in the publication of this book.

The book is dedicated to my parents, Alan and Jennette – may they enjoy their well earned retirement.

ACKNOWLEDGMENTS

The Commonwealth Department of Employment, Education and Training's National Priority (Reserve) Fund funded the early part of the research towards this book in 1991.

Thanks to:

- The Department of Justice, Victoria, for permission to use extracts from the Law Reform Commission of Victoria, Discussion Paper No 10, *Liquidated Damages and Penalties*.
- The *Melbourne University Law Review* for permission to extract parts of an article by Andrew Ham, 'The Rule Against Penalties in Contract: An Economic Perspective' (1991) 17 MULR 649, 654-670.
- The Law Book Company for permission to use parts of the following cases: *O'Dea v All States Leasing System (WA) Pty Ltd* (1983) 152 CLR 359; *Esanda Finance Corporation Ltd v Plessnig* (1988) 166 CLR 131; *Pigram v Attorney General for New South Wales* (1975) 132 CLR 216.

CONTENTS

PART 1

NEW DIRECTIONS FOR LAW TEACHING

1.1 INTRODUCTION

The practice of the law, by its very nature, relies heavily on the analysis of documents and other texts. So too, has law teaching come to rely on reading done by students. 'Learning the law' involves reading about the law, finding its rules and principles, discovering how it operates 'in action', providing a critique of legal rules, their assumptions and operation, and theorising about the nature of law and its place in society. We law teachers base much of our teaching on the assumption that our students have read, or will read, a statute, the law reports, a casebook, our own compilation of teaching materials, a book, an article or some text detailing the operation of the law in action. In most law subjects we use specially prepared materials or published books of cases and materials prepared for the purposes of teaching basic legal principles to law students.

It is appropriate that law teaching place special attention in its teaching methods to the use of printed teaching materials. Lawyers[1] need to be able to absorb, comprehend, apply, analyse, synthesise and evaluate huge amounts of new information which has its source in the written word.[2] The independent absorption, comprehension, application, analysis, synthesis and evaluation by students of written material should, therefore, be an integral part of their legal education. Our students will gain as much, if not more, from a good text as they will from listening to a well presented lecture. Students can read material several times faster than they can absorb aurally, and have the opportunity to work at their own pace, browse, skip to another part of the text to make connections between concepts, reflect on interesting material, or re-read sections of the material they initially did not understand. Students may also find it easier to engage critically with a text than a lecture, and have a greater opportunity for judicious note-taking. It is widely acknowledged[3] that lecturing is an inefficient means of achieving what its adherents believe to be one of its purposes – the passing of information from teacher to student. Printed material is a far more accurate medium for the transmission to students of a teacher's conception of a topic. This book seeks to go beyond these advantages of using printed materials in law teaching, and to develop means to enable teachers to develop printed teaching materials which engage students in more active (even interactive) and

1 I use the term 'lawyers' in this book to include lawyers engaged in the different aspects of legal practice, lawyers involved in formulating legal policy, and lawyers who teach and research in educational institutions.

2 Lawyers who are visually impaired face enormous disadvantages in their attempts to deal with the written word. Law schools can play a part in helping these students to develop the skills to deal with 'reading', and to sensitise all law students to the difficulties experienced by visually impaired lawyers.

3 See, for example, Gibbs, G, 'Twenty Terrible Reasons for Lecturing', Standing Conference on Educational Development, Occasional Paper No 8, Birmingham, 1982; Bligh, D, *What's the Use of Lectures*, Penguin, Harmondsworth, 1972; Le Brun, M and Johnstone, R, *The Quiet (R)evolution: Improving Student Learning in Law*, Law Book Company, Sydney, 1994, 257-60.

reflective learning, and which play a part in a better quality classroom interaction between teachers and students.

This book is concerned with the preparation and the use of printed teaching materials in law teaching. It is written for law teachers who wish to develop their teaching around their own printed teaching materials and for the compilers of commercially published casebooks. Throughout the book I will use the term 'teaching materials' to mean printed teaching materials, rather than materials utilising more complex technologies going beyond the printed medium,[4] and to include what have traditionally been referred to as casebooks.

The underlying philosophy of the book is that teaching materials can provide a means for independent learning, and enable teachers to adopt a variety of classroom teaching methods which stimulate active student learning through self-instruction, rather than passive note-taking. The basic assumptions of the book are:

(i) that current law teaching practices rely to a large extent on printed teaching materials, and that despite the rapid developments taking place in educational technology, for most of us printed teaching materials will play an important role in our teaching strategies at least for the remainder of this decade;

(ii) that these existing teaching materials tend to be fairly 'static' in their conception, and narrowly focused in their vision, of law and law teaching, and that current approaches to law teaching have failed fully to explore the full potential of teaching materials;

(iii) that teaching materials provide an important vehicle to broaden, diversify and enrich law teaching;

(iv) that basic principles and frameworks for the development of exciting and challenging teaching materials can be communicated in a book such as this; and

(v) that these principles can also be of assistance to those of us who are exploring ways of using more sophisticated educational technology, such as computer-based media, in our teaching strategies.[5]

The broad aims of the book are twofold: first, to provide law teachers with a 'way of thinking' about appropriate ways of developing and using printed teaching materials; and, second, to provide examples of the ways in which we law teachers can develop printed teaching materials to stimulate students to learn about the practical and theoretical dimensions of law in their own private study and in our classes. The book anchors teaching practice in educational theory. While I do not believe that there is any one way of teaching, in this book

4 For an outstanding discussion of the potential use of more sophisticated educational technology in university teaching, see Laurillard, D, *Rethinking University Teaching: A Framework for the Effective Use of Educational Technology*, Routledge, London, 1993.

5 In particular, these principles will be useful for teachers using computer technologies such as hypertext to present their teaching materials to students: see O'Connor, P, 'Teacher Bids Good-bye to the Book' (1993) 24 (No 13) *ANU Reporter* 1; Richardson, J, 'Computers Mooted Ready to Lecture – the Law Students Set to be the Precedent' (1993) 3 *Campus Review* No 34, 1; and Laurillard (1993) ch 6.

I set out basic broad principles for those of us who are compiling printed teaching materials and casebooks for use in law teaching. The focus is at all times on producing imaginative teaching materials which enable our students to optimise their learning through interesting and challenging private study outside class, so that we can use class time for more participatory and reflective methods of learning.

The book is divided into five parts. Part 1 examines the context surrounding the development of teaching materials for law teaching. This entails a brief discussion of traditional law teaching, and the need to develop a new paradigm for law teaching. This starting point is important because I argue in the book that the creative and effective use of teaching materials in law teaching requires an approach to legal education with more of a critical and interdisciplinary focus, and which is more in line with contemporary research into student learning.

Part 2 of the book sets out a model of teaching and learning which provides a framework for the development of teaching materials. This model is built upon recent research on the nature of student learning, the basic aims and objectives of legal education, the purpose and principles of assessment, and the range of available teaching methods. This part also emphasises how important it is that we constantly evaluate our teaching to ensure that our curriculum design, materials, assessment and classroom teaching methods enhance our students' learning. Part 3 outlines principles for developing teaching materials which promote active learning. Principles are illustrated with practical examples. Part 4 provides an example of teaching materials designed to promote independent learning inside and outside the classroom. Part 5 gives a very brief conclusion.

1.2 DEVELOPING A NEW PARADIGM FOR LAW TEACHING[6]

In my experience law teachers have difficulty envisaging new ways of using teaching materials because they are locked into a particular view of learning and teaching. This section provides a thumb-nail sketch of the way in which law has traditionally been taught in Australian law schools. I will argue that the optimal use of teaching materials in law teaching depends on moving away from this traditional approach and developing a different framework for law teaching. In the following sections I will outline aspects of this new paradigm as it affects the development and use of teaching materials.

1.2.1 The traditional approach to law teaching in Australia

While it is indisputable that since the 1960s Australian law schools have moved away from a 'trade school' model towards the classic liberal model of university

6 This part of the book is an abbreviated and modified version of part of an earlier article: see Johnstone, R, 'Rethinking the Teaching of Law' (1992) 3 *Legal Education Review* 17-59, especially 17-30, and 38-42. For a much fuller discussion of the changing paradigm of Australian law teaching, see Le Brun and Johnstone (1994) ch 1.

education,[7] there has nevertheless been much recent criticism of legal education in Australia,[8] and of at least two aspects of Australian law teaching. The first is its narrow focus on the study of legal rules, and a basic reluctance to question what is constituted by 'law' and to locate substantive and procedural law within practical, theoretical and critical frameworks,[9] so that there is a simultaneous failure to provide a critical legal education and to develop practical legal skills. The second is the very limited and unimaginative use of teaching methods. A much favoured approach is to focus on teaching students 'what the law is', largely through the lecture method,[10] in the hope that they will be able to then 'apply' the law so learnt to a set of facts in an examination. Some teachers have modified this style by interspersing their lectures with questions to students, or by using a casebook method.[11] One consequence is that law students may engage in passive and uncritical learning of abstract legal rules in an abstracted university environment, and find it difficult to use what they have learnt.

This book is primarily concerned with the second criticism. It is impossible, however, to ignore the first criticism, and much of the book will be informed by issues relating to the need in law teaching to examine what law is, and to place legal rules and practices within broader critical and theoretical frameworks.[12]

The traditional approach to law teaching gives an important, but narrowly defined, place to teaching materials. This is largely due to the influence of the casebook method, where students are expected to have read material (generally cases) before class, and classroom activity is centred on questions aimed at drawing out important points in the reading.[13] At its best, this method involves students exploring the concepts, reasoning and assumptions behind the legal rules in the materials, applying the rules and principles to new situations, and critically evaluating the content and consequences of these rules. At its worst,

7 Chesterman, M and Weisbrot, D, 'Legal Scholarship in Australia' (1987) 50 *Modern Law Review* 709, 718.

8 In particular, see Parliament of the Commonwealth of Australia, Senate Standing Committee on Employment, Education and Training, *Priorities for Reform in Higher Education*, AGPS, Canberra, 1990; Pearce, D (chairman) *Australian Law Schools: A Discipline Assessment for the Commonwealth Tertiary Education Commission*, AGPS, Canberra, 1987 (the Pearce Report); Chesterman and Weisbrot (1987); and Le Brun and Johnstone (1994) ch 1. For a recent discussion of developments in Australian law schools since the Pearce Report, see McInnis, C and Marginson, S, *Australian Law Schools after the 1987 Pearce Report*, AGPS, Canberra, 1994.

9 See Duncanson, I, 'Broadening the Discipline of Law' (1994) 19 *Melbourne University Law Review* 1075.

10 For a definition of the lecture method, see p 52 below, and Gibbs, G, Habeshaw, S, and Habeshaw, T, *53 Interesting Things To Do In Your Lectures*, Technical and Educational Services Ltd, Bristol, 1987, 9.

11 The case method of legal education was fostered by Langdell in 1871. See, for example, Langdell, C C, *Preface to a Selection of Cases on the Law of Contracts*, Boston, 1871.

12 See Duncanson (1994). There are now a number of Australian books exploring these broader critical and theoretical frameworks: see generally Davies, M, *Asking the Law Question*, Law Book Company, Sydney, 1994; Berns, S, *Concise Jurisprudence*, Federation Press, Sydney, 1993; Bottomley, S, Gunningham, N, and Parker, S, *Law in Context*, 2nd ed, Federation Press, Sydney, 1994; and Hunter, R, Ingleby, R, and Johnstone, R, *Thinking About Law: Perspectives on the History, Philosophy and Sociology of Law*, Allen & Unwin, Sydney, 1995.

13 For a discussion of this method, see Le Brun and Johnstone (1994) 282-6.

the casebook method can be an ill-directed assortment of aimless but aggressively asked questions, often to students who have not read the designated material, where the students' main concerns are to avoid being asked a question, and where the principal product is frustration and distrust.

The quality of teaching materials varies greatly from teacher to teacher, subject to subject, and law school to law school. Some teachers use reading guides which are little more than lists of headings and cases with no commentary or guiding questions. The reading guide might be accompanied by a set of photocopied cases. At the other end of the spectrum, and far less common, are materials and published casebooks which include detailed introductions to topics, commentaries on cases, statutes or relevant principles, and which sometimes include theoretical and empirical observations about the legal principles, and questions to guide students through the material, or to assist them to think reflectively about the material. Very few teachers use teaching materials or casebooks designed to promote activity-based learning in and out of the classroom. Student reading is, more often than not, not very well directed, nor focused on any kind of activity. Consequently, students often find their required reading abstract and meaningless. Casebooks are often shrouded with an ambiguity as to their purpose. Commercial pressures require authors to aim their casebooks both at students for use in learning the law, and at practitioners.[14] Casebooks have not principally been seen as learning and teaching tools.[15]

Most teachers would be familiar with students who appear disinterested in learning, or hostile to working for and during class. I would argue that one of the reasons for this frustration is that teaching methods fail to motivate students to learn. Many law students are bewildered by the nature of the subject matter they are expected to learn. They feel that they are not given enough guidance as to how to go about learning the law on their own outside class, and often prefer to read materials after the lecture rather than before it. Class time is a time of anxiety and frustration, where students fear being called upon to enter class discussion, and at the same time find it difficult to follow class activities because they are inadequately prepared.

A modern approach to printed teaching materials needs to focus on designing materials to stimulate and facilitate student learning by enabling students to do the kinds of things that lawyers do, and at the same time critically reflect on their activities within sound theoretical frameworks. Learning must be activity based, contextualised and critical.[16] In Part 2 I examine a framework for thinking about teaching and learning and in Part 3 use this framework to outline principles for developing teaching materials which promote this type of learning.

---

14 See Chesterman and Weisbrot (1987) 713-14 .

15 Indeed, I suspect that most law academics would categorise their published casebooks as research output, not as part of their teaching activity.

16 See generally Le Brun and Johnstone (1994) chs 1-3.

PART 2

THE EDUCATIONAL FRAMEWORK FOR DEVELOPING TEACHING MATERIALS

A discussion of the development and use of printed teaching materials must be based on a teaching model or framework for teaching law. This part of the book outlines a framework within which we can think about how we design printed teaching materials which promote critical and contextualised student learning through activities. The framework seeks to integrate factors which we may sometimes see as unrelated or unconnected: the characteristics of our students; the ways in which our students go about learning our subjects; the manner in which our students make sense of the subject matter; the learning objectives we set for our students; the assessment for the subject; the content of the subject; the teaching methods we select; and the evaluation of our subjects and our teaching.

In section 2.1 I discuss recent research into the way in which students go about learning, and constructing knowledge in, academic subjects, and the implications of that research for our teaching strategies. In section 2.2 I argue that we need to consider the characteristics of our students so that we can design our teaching strategies in line with their interests and past educational experiences. In section 2.3 I examine a range of aims and objectives for student learning in our subjects, and in section 2.4 I outline principles that govern the assessment of student learning. Section 2.5 briefly discusses how we might decide upon the content of our subject, and the way in which it might be sequenced. Section 2.6 outlines the range of teaching methods (including the use of teaching materials) which we can draw from when we develop our teaching strategy. Part 2 concludes with a reminder that we should constantly evaluate our teaching to ensure that our teaching is improving student learning. Part 2 thus provides a context for an examination, in Part 3, of principles governing the design of printed teaching materials. The factors discussed in Part 2 are not disparate, but are interconnected and must be integrated in a model of learning and teaching. We can only develop our teaching materials once we have determined the aims and objectives of our subject, its assessment regime, its content, and its teaching methods. Figure 1 (see page 8) provides a very simple flow chart to illustrate how these elements fit together in a model for developing printed teaching materials for law teaching. Readers looking for a more complex and dynamic representation of the model should consult Figure 4 on page 64.

2.1 HOW DO STUDENTS LEARN?

Any attempt to develop a model or framework for developing and using printed teaching materials in law teaching must begin with a discussion of basic principles of learning and teaching. In this section I engage in a brief examination of the theories of student learning upon which I have based the framework for the development and use of teaching materials which is outlined in this book.

1. Consider: Who are our students?
How do they learn?
↓
2. Determine aims and objectives for teaching and learning
↓
3. Determine assessment
↓
4. Select and sequence the content of the subject
↓
5. Choose teaching methods
↓
6. Structure materials
↓
7. Evaluate teaching
↓
8. Modify 2–6

Figure 1: Steps involved in developing teaching materials

In this book I start from the assumption that the aim of teaching is simply to make student learning possible.[1] The way we teach is heavily dependent on what we understand or assume about student learning.[2] If we believe that our task as teachers is to transfer information from our minds into the heads of our students, we will use expository teaching methods such as lecturing.[3] But if we know that learning occurs in other ways, we will have to design our teaching methods to accommodate these ideas of how learning takes place.

Teaching and learning are intimately related. As teachers, we need to find out about student learning and what makes it possible. Good teaching involves a continuous process of learning about student understanding and the way it is affected by teaching. In this book I assume that learning is more than simply an increase in the amount of knowledge that students acquire. Rather, learning involves a process of change, in which learners move to a greater understanding, experience or conceptualisation of a subject or discipline.[4] Learning builds on the learner's background and previous learning, and can only be carried out by the learner. Yet, as Laurillard reminds us, it 'is the teacher's responsibility to create the conditions in which understanding is

1 See Ramsden, P, *Learning to Teaching in Higher Education*, Routledge, London, 1992, 5; and Laurillard (1993) ch 1.

2 This discussion of student learning is built on a previous paper: see Johnstone, R, 'Improving Student Learning in Labour Law' in R Mitchell (ed), *Redefining Labour Law*, Centre for Employment and Labour Relations Law, The University of Melbourne, 1995.

3 Biggs, J B, 'Teaching for Better Learning' (1991) 2 *Legal Education Review* 133.

4 See Ramsden (1992) ch 1.

possible, and the student's responsibility is to take advantage of that'.[5] As we increase our understanding of how student learning takes place, we will change our teaching to facilitate student learning.

Research into the quality of students' understandings in academic disciplines and professional subjects suggests that most students are able to perform complex routine skills, absorb huge amounts of detailed knowledge, at least for a short period, regurgitate large amounts of factual information when required, and pass examinations, but that they are unable to deal properly with simple but searching questions which test their real understanding of the subject. They do not seem to learn how to analyse the unfamiliar, to assess critically proposed solutions to problems or proposed theories about reality, or to apply ideas learned in the classroom to the outside world. They often retain erroneous or naive conceptions, fail to pick up self-critical awareness in their subjects, and are unaware that they do not know.[6] This suggests that we can do much to improve student learning if we have a better understanding of how that learning takes place.

There is no single theory of student learning. Research into student learning has been conducted from a range of perspectives.

> 'Some focus on cognitive processes, thus investigating human cognition, memory, and information processing. Some investigate approaches to learning, thus examining issues of personality, motivation (intention), learning style and their relationship to study strategy or to type or depth of learning. Others emphasise autonomous academic study. A few take elements of each and combine them.'[7]

This section does not attempt to survey all research into learning.[8] It does, however, draw on key ideas and concepts which can enhance the development and use of teaching materials in law teaching. In particular it discusses four influential, but different, though not necessarily irreconcilable, schools of thought about learning:

- the relational theorists (for example Ramsden, Marton and Säljö, Biggs and others) who focus on the ways (motives and strategy) in which students approach learning tasks;
- cognitive theories (the psychology of learning) which examine situated learning or cognitive apprenticeship, and the nature of expertise;
- Perry's theory of students' cognitive and ethical development; and
- problem-based learning.

---

5 Laurillard (1993) 1-2.

6 See the discussion in Ramsden (1992) 31-37; McKeachie, W J, 'Research on College Teaching: The Historical Background' (1990) 82 *Journal of Educational Psychology* 189, 190.

7 Le Brun and Johnstone (1994) 53.

8 For more detailed discussions of theories of learning and of cognitive development, see Ramsden, P (ed) *Improving Learning – New Perspectives*, Kogan Page, London, 1988; Ramsden (1992) chs 1-7; Le Brun and Johnstone (1994) chs 2 and 3; Entwhistle, N, *Styles of Learning and Teaching*, David Fulton Publishers, London, 1988; Bereiter, C and Scardamalia, M, *Surpassing Ourselves: An Inquiry into the Nature and Implications of Expertise*, Open Court, Chicago, 1993; Laurillard (1993) chs 1 to 3; Jacques, D, *Learning in Groups*, 2nd ed, Kogan Page, London, 1991, ch 3.

In this section I also outline some basic principles of self-regulated learning. I should emphasise at this point that although the various theories of student learning have different theoretical and methodological underpinnings, there are, as readers will see, many points of overlap, and I believe that each theory contributes to a rounded picture of the way in which our students go about learning our subjects. To illustrate this point, at the end of this section I draw the threads together with a discussion of a contemporary model of a teaching strategy.

2.1.1 Relational perspectives: the approach to learning

A key aspect of improving the quality of students' understanding has to do with their 'approach to learning', based on their descriptions of the way in which they experience learning about phenomena.[9] This perspective on learning is metacognitive, in that it is built up from students' descriptions in open interviews of how they approach the learning task, how they think about it, why they do what they do when they learn, and so on.[10] Relational theory examines students motives and strategies when they engage in learning.[11]

When students learn, they relate to different tasks in different ways – sometimes memorising facts, arguments or procedures for the purposes of an examination, at other times immersing themselves in an idea, or re-working material until they are satisfied with it. A number of studies have identified at least two approaches to learning: a surface approach and a deep approach to learning.[12] These approaches are not characteristic of different learners, because everyone is capable of deep or surface learning approaches. Rather they describe the relationship between the student and the learning she or he is doing, in response to different circumstances.

Surface approaches to learning focus on the constituent parts of the task rather than on trying to make sense of the whole. The learner is not personally involved in the task, but rather sees the task as something to be completed for an external purpose; for example, 'playing the law school game'[13] to achieve good enough grades to be employed by a prestigious law firm. Learners limit their target to the essentials of completing the task requirements. For example, they will memorise a lot of information for examinations, or focus unthinkingly and unreflectively on the words of the text or on the elements of a legal rule in solving a legal problem. Consequently they distort the structure of the task and

9 Biggs, J B, 'Approaches to the Enhancement of Tertiary Teaching' (1989) 8 *Higher Education Research and Development* 7, 12; Biggs, J B, 'Individual Differences in Study Processes and the Quality of Learning Outcomes' (1979) 8 *Higher Education* 381-394; Biggs (1991) 138-140; Marton, F and Säljö, R 'On Qualitative Differences in Learning – I: Outcome and Processes' (1976) 46 *British Journal of Educational Psychology* 4; Van Rossum, E J and Schenk, S M, 'The Relationship Between Learning Conception, Study Strategy and Learning Outcome' (1984) 54 *British Journal of Educational Psychology* 73; Watkins, D A, 'Depth of Processing and the Quality of Learning Outcomes' (1983) 12 *Instructional Science* 49; Ramsden (1992) ch 4; Laurillard (1993) ch 3.

10 See Ramsden (1992) 51-55 and Laurillard (1993) 34-37.

11 Biggs (1989) 12.

12 Some studies include a 'strategic' approach.

13 Some would classify this as a strategic approach to learning.

focus on the unrelated concrete and literal aspects of the task.[14] They are less likely to remember the ideas and facts and more likely to reproduce lecture or text book material. Their knowledge is cut off from the reality of everyday life.

By contrast, deep approaches to learning are based on interest in the subject matter of the task. The learner aims to maximise understanding and sees the task as interesting and personally involving. Learners organise and structure the content into a coherent whole, and focus on the task's underlying meaning, rather than on its literal aspects. They seek to integrate the components with other tasks and subjects, and to relate the new material to their personal experiences, interests and previous knowledge. They relate theoretical ideas to every day experience and real life situations, and distinguish evidence and argument. Whereas surface approaches are just about a quantitative increase in knowledge, without any change in understanding, deep approaches are about learning facts in relation to the concepts and changing understanding.[15]

In this book I work on the assumption that the best way for students to *really understand* teaching materials is through a deep approach.[16] This is because the research shows that deep approaches to learning result in high quality, well structured and complex outcomes, an enjoyment of learning, a commitment to the subject and the imaginative and adaptive skills envisaged by teachers in higher education.[17] Consequently, teachers should do all they can to engage students in ways that encourage the use of deep approaches to learning. How can this be done, and what are the consequences for the development of teaching materials?

The approach students take to their learning depends on the learning task and on the educational environment, which is created through students' past and present experiences and perceptions of the curriculum. Students bring with them habits based in deep or surface approaches to learning. Other factors include the curriculum, the teaching and assessment methods, the quality of interaction with teachers, and the atmosphere or 'ethos' of the program of study, or of the institution.[18]

The crucial point here is that it is students' perceptions, not teachers' intentions, of these things that count.[19] If students get the message from the educational environment that surface approaches are all that is required, they will use such approaches, even if frameworks are provided to encourage deep approaches to learning. For example, one way of encouraging students to use

14 Biggs (1989) 13; Ramsden (1992) ch 4.

15 Ramsden (1992) ch 4.

16 Marton, F and Säljö, R, 'Approaches to Learning' in F Marton, D J Hounsell and N J Entwhistle (eds) *The Experience of Learning*, Scottish Academic Press, Edinburgh, 1984, 46.

17 Ramsden (1992) ch 4; Biggs (1991) 140. Unfortunately there is not much research into the way in which Australian law students learn about law: but see Mullins, G, Whittle, J and Mack, K, 'Law Students' Perceptions of Learning', paper presented at the Annual Conference of the Australian Association for Research in Education, Adelaide, 1989; and work currently being undertaken at the Griffith Law School.

18 Ramsden (1992) 65; Ramsden, P, 'Student Learning Research: Retrospect and Prospect' (1985) 4 *Higher Education Research and Development* 51-69.

19 Ramsden (1992) 62-3.

deep approaches in reading teaching materials might be to insert questions that encourage students to relate different parts of the text to each other. Yet Marton and Säljö report that this can have the opposite effect, and can actually encourage extreme forms of surface learning where students take the answering of the questions to be an end in itself, and try to find parts of the text to answer the questions, without engaging with the text as intended.[20]

Deep approaches to learning will be encouraged:[21]

- if students have an intrinsic interest in and identification with the subject matter, and see the relevance of the subject matter, so that they develop an interest in the task for its own sake;[22]
- if students have a well developed base of knowledge in the area they are studying, so that they can build on previous learning;
- if our requirements, expressed through the method and amount of assessment, encourage, and do not impede, deep approaches to learning. Deep approaches to learning will not be encouraged by assessment methods which emphasise recall or trivial problem solving, or which create undue anxiety;[23]
- if the learning task involves students in active and long term engagement with the subject matter, involves them in actively thinking about the subject matter, and in creating personal meaning from the activity;
- if students are not expected to cover too much material in too little time.

This suggests that deep approaches will be promoted:

- by a teacher who is stimulating, who communicates an interest in and enthusiasm for the subject matter, who uses clear explanatory skills, who shows respect for students, who develops rapport with students, and who interacts with students in a manner which encourages involvement, commitment and interest;
- by a teacher who works at the level of students, who encourages student independence in the learning process, and who explains requirements and expectations clearly and fully;
- where students are able to exercise reasonable choice in the method and content of study;
- where we teachers provide good and timely feedback on how students are progressing in class, and help to overcome student misconceptions which may impede learning;
- where we are at home with our subject, at least in the sense of having structured knowledge of the area to be taught and of its culture, and having an ability to solve the kinds of problems that arise within the discipline;
- if we encourage students to learn and to take risks in learning, without fear of being put down by us, or their classmates; and

20 Marton and Säljö (1984) 47.

21 See generally Ramsden (1992) chs 5 and 6; Biggs (1991) 16.

22 See the discussion of situated learning later in this section.

23 I discuss assessment in section 2.4.

- if the teaching policies and practices of the institution do not encumber students with a high workload, a low level of student independence, and perceived low quality teaching.

The relational model of learning and teaching therefore has profound implications for law teachers. It reminds us that we need constantly to examine the way in which students are responding to the messages about desired forms of learning put out by our institutions and by our own cues in our design of our curricula, our materials, our assessment, and in our classroom teaching.

2.1.2 Cognitive theory: situated learning and cognitive apprenticeship

Rather than examining this relational approach to understanding learning (the relationship between the student and the learning she or he is doing, in response to different circumstances), cognitive psychologists focus on our knowledge of competence, and on what happens within our students when they learn. 'Thus, learning is said to be based on competence, accumulated knowledge about cognition, the human mind, and on research into their application to problems in the real world.'[24]

In the past decade or so, developments in cognitive theory have undermined the traditional, classical model of academic knowledge which envisaged knowledge 'as an abstract Platonic form'[25] with a stable conceptual structure abstracted from the context in which the concept is experienced. According to the traditional model, this knowledge is imparted by the teacher to the student. As a consequence, traditional legal education has been based principally on teaching students a coherent, generalised but abstract body of legal doctrine, transmitted to students by lectures or case-based discussion. The attraction of this model has been bolstered by the development of information processing models of cognition, which base themselves on computational models of cognition.

Recent work in cognitive psychology has begun to challenge this mainstream view of academic knowledge. These recent developments envisage learning to be a process of constructing knowledge, rather than merely transferring or absorbing knowledge. Knowledge is built on previous knowledge, and depends on the situation in which it takes place. '[T]eaching as envisaged by this school of thought is not about giving students information *per se*. Rather teaching is an act of intervention in the student's construction of knowledge.'[26]

For example, in a very influential article, Brown, Collins and Duguid suggest that the perceived gap between learning ('knowing that') and use ('knowing how') may be the product of the structure and practices of our

24 Le Brun and Johnstone (1994) 71.

25 Laurillard (1993) 15.

26 *Ibid.*

education system.[27] Many methods of didactic education, including traditional legal education, 'assume a distinction between knowing and doing, treating knowledge as an integral, self-sufficient substance, theoretically independent of the situations in which it is learnt and used'.[28] The primary concern of legal education has appeared to be the transmission of abstract, decontextualised formal concepts, with the activity and context in which learning takes place regarded as secondary.

Brown, Collins and Duguid report that recent investigations into learning challenge this separation of what is learned from the way it is learned and used. Far from the activity in which knowledge is developed and deployed being separable from or ancillary to learning and cognition, or in any way neutral, they argue that it is an integral part of what is learnt. Situations and activities structure the process of gaining knowledge. Concepts are not abstract, self-contained entities, but continually evolve each time they are used. Brown, Collins and Duguid suggest that rather than teaching abstract knowledge (the classical model of academic knowledge) we should encourage students to learn by generalising knowledge which they have constructed for themselves through different activities in different situations – what Laurillard refers to as abstraction from multiple contexts. For example, instead of telling students about the basic legal rules which govern a particular area of law, we might require students to engage in activities in which they have to look up the rules and use them to resolve a series of situations we have created for them. If we then engage students in activities which require them to reflect on the rules which they have found and used, our students will develop an understanding of the relevant legal principles which is grounded in the different situations in which they have used the rules.

By ignoring the situated nature of cognition, Brown, Collins and Duguid argue that education defeats its own goal of providing useable, robust knowledge,[29] and instead will produce only inert book knowledge. They suggest that conceptual knowledge is similar in many ways to a set of tools.[30] It is possible to acquire a tool but to be unable to use it. Similarly it is possible to acquire decontextualised knowledge, and even carry out exercises with that knowledge, but to be unable to use it in a truly practical sense. People who use tools actively build an increasingly rich understanding of the tools, and a knowledge of the world in which they use the tools. Learning how to use tools

27 Brown, J S, Collins, A and Duguid, P, 'Situated Cognition and the Culture of Learning' (1989) 18(1) *Educational Researcher* 32 (1989a). The following discussion of situated learning is drawn from this article. See also Brown, J S, Collins, A and Duguid, P, 'Debating the Situation: A Rejoinder to Palincsar and Wineburg' (1989) 18(4) *Educational Researcher* 10 (1989b); Collins, A, Brown, J S and Newman, S E, 'Cognitive Apprenticeship: Teaching the Craft of Reading, Writing and Mathematics' in L B Resnick (ed) *Knowing, Learning and Instruction: Essays in Honour of Robert Glaser*, Lawrence Erlbaum Associates, Hillsdale, New Jersey, 1989; and Laurillard (1993) 16-23.

28 Brown, Collins and Duguid (1989a) 32.

29 Brown, Collins and Duguid (1989a) 32; Clanchy, J, 'Improving Student Writing' (1985) 7 *HERDSA News* 2.

30 Brown, Collins and Duguid (1989a) 33.

31 Glaser, R, 'Education and Thinking: The Role of Knowledge' (1984) 39 *American Psychologist*

or concepts involves far more than just receiving a set of explicit rules for use.[31]

> 'The occasions and conditions for use arise directly out of the context of activities of each community that uses the tool, framed by the way members of that community see the world. The community and its viewpoint, quite as much as the tool itself, determine how a tool is used.'[32]

In short, activity, concept and culture are interdependent. Learning must involve all three. Academic disciplines and the professions are communities with cultures, bound by intricate, socially constructed webs of belief, which are essential to understanding what they do.[33] Students in law school can be shown legal, critical, philosophical, economic, feminist, historical or sociological tools, but do not observe, or participate in, these cultures. The university culture can actually impede learning in a particular discipline because the way that universities use the tools of these disciplines can be different to the way that practitioners (in the broadest sense) use them. This is not to suggest that all students learning legal philosophy, the sociology of law, law and economics, or the rules of substantive law will become 'practitioners' or theorists in those disciplines. Rather, to learn those subjects, instead of just learning about them, students need much more than fixed, abstract and decontextualised concepts and self-contained examples. They need 'to be exposed to the use of ... conceptual tools in authentic activity – to teachers acting as practitioners and using these tools in wrestling with problems of the world'.[34] Such activity can tease out the way lawyers, historians or legal theorists look at the world and solve emergent problems.

So what is 'authentic activity'? Authentic activities are simply defined as the ordinary practices of the culture,[35] and involve the genuine application of knowledge. There is a danger that in the university context students may come to rely on factors which are wholly absent from and alien to authentic activity. For example, law students can learn to solve 'problems' by looking for key words in the description of the problem, or the position of the problem in the particular section of the book, rather than understanding properly the issues and what is required to resolve the issues. This, of course, is a surface approach to learning.

Brown, Collins and Duguid call this process of situated learning in authentic activities '*cognitive apprenticeship*'.[36] They outline the following steps as being part of a structured framework for cognitive apprenticeship.

First, we should embed the learning task in activity familiar to our students. This will show students the legitimacy of their implicit knowledge and its availability as scaffolding in apparently unfamiliar tasks. For example, in the law of contract we can require our students in their first class to negotiate the

31 Glaser, R, 'Education and Thinking: The Role of Knowledge' (1984) 39 *American Psychologist* 93, 99; Mitchell, J B, 'Current Theories on Expert and Novice Thinking: A Full Faculty Considers the Implications for Legal Education' (1989) 39 *Journal of Legal Education* 275, 291.

32 Brown, Collins and Duguid (1989a) 33. For example, carpenters and cabinet makers use chisels differently; physicists and engineers use mathematical formulae differently.

33 See Geertz, C, *Local Knowledge*, Basic Books, New York, 1983.

34 Brown, Collins, and Duguid (1989a) 34.

35 *Ibid.*

36 *Ibid* 37. See 37 onwards for two examples of this kind of learning in the field of mathematics.

drafting of a contract to protect the interests of their client or to look closely at a contractual clause which is part of a contract in every day use. Further examples appear in Part 4 of this book.

Second, by pointing to different approaches to the problem, we can show that problem solving principles are not absolute, but assessed with respect to a particular task.

Third, by allowing students to generate their own solutions, they are given a chance to be conscious, creative members of the culture of problem solving lawyers, law and economics practitioners, sociologists of law or feminist legal theorists. Through this activity, they acquire some of the culture's tools – a shared vocabulary and the means to discuss, reflect upon, evaluate, and validate relevant procedures in collaboration with other students.

By this method, students develop abstract concepts from the many contexts in which they have used the knowledge they are learning. The process begins when we provide:

> 'modelling ... and scaffolding for students to get started in an authentic activity. As students gain more self-confidence and control, they move to a more autonomous phase of collaborative learning, where they begin to participate consciously in the culture. The social network within the culture helps them to develop its language and belief systems ... Collaboration also leads to articulation of strategies, which can then be discussed and reflected upon. This then fosters generalising, grounded in the students situated understanding. From here, students can use their fledgling conceptual knowledge in activity, seeing that activity in a new light, which in turn leads to the further development of the conceptual knowledge.'[37]

As this description of cognitive apprenticeship indicates, group learning is an important part of the process because it enables students to pool their knowledge to provide individual students with insights they would not otherwise have obtained; allows students to learn from playing a number of different roles; provides students with feedback so that they can identify their misconceptions and inefficient problem solving strategies; and gives students opportunities to learn how to work with others.[38] Even though the process of situated learning through cognitive apprenticeship may appear informal, full-blooded and authentic activity can be deeply informative in a way that textbook examples and declarative explanations are not. Students will see teachers question their own values in the classroom, and will have an opportunity to explore their own values.

If we follow the arguments espoused by Brown, Collins and Duguid, we will need to shift the traditional focus of legal education from concentrating primarily on conceptual exposition and assuming that this is the starting point for all student learning. The theory of situated cognition suggests that activity and perception are epistemologically prior to conceptualisation. Accordingly, we should expose our students to the ill-defined problems of real life, in contrast to the well defined exercises typically found in text books and

37 *Ibid* 39. See figure 3 on page 40.

38 *Ibid* 40. For a detailed discussion of group learning, see Jacques (1991).

examinations. We should talk about cases as we would to practising lawyers, referring to facts, statutes, tactics and so on as the discussion unfolds.[39]

For example,[40] we should encourage our students, in a contracts class, to bring contracts problems to class so that the class can try to solve the problems as if they were practising lawyers. Alternatively, we can ask students to choose an interesting aspect of the law of contract, and try to develop a law and economics, feminist, or socio-legal research framework to examine the issue. The students can then witness and participate in thinking within the particular discipline. Part 4 of this book provides a number of examples of this kind of framework for learning.

Also crucial is that we analyse the solution to help reveal to the class the way in which a person in the particular discipline looks at problems. For example, the class can work collectively through a number of strategies to provide a 'solution' to the 'problem'. On reflection, they may recognise some of the solutions as more general or more useful legal, sociological or other theoretical ideas. We should not stop at the traditional end point: the answer.[41] The problem should not just be an exercise, but rather the objective should be to understand the legal and theoretical issues involved. By exploring other possible approaches and solutions to the problem, we can help our students to discover general principles. All strategies should be illustrated in action, developed by the class in conjunction with the teacher, and not declared by the teacher.

This description of situated learning raises at least two issues for us as teachers. The first is that we face a number of practical problems in trying to implement a framework for cognitive apprenticeship. We may have to choose between trying to cover a large amount of material, and reducing the amount of material while ensuring that it is properly contextualised and learnt through activities. It may not be possible to use a pure cognitive apprenticeship model for each topic in our subjects, and we may prefer to deal with key topics, particularly those early in the subject, using this model, and then resort to different teaching models with other topics.

It is rare that law schools will be able to teach students in situations that are totally authentic, in the sense used by Brown, Collins and Duguid. Totally authentic activity would involve basing teaching on a clinical model with reflective discussion about the internal logic of legal practice and the role of the lawyer an integral part of such learning. In the legal theory area, authentic activity would comprise supervised research. Nevertheless we can involve students in hypothetical situations that closely approximate the kind of work that legal practitioners and legal theorists engage in. We can begin topics with concrete examples and problems, and work through appropriate examples in detail. We can construct learning environments which enable students to learn contextualised descriptions of the world and to reflect on these descriptions.

39 Mitchell (1989) 294.

40 See Schoenfield, A H, *Mathematical Problem Solving*, Mathematical Press, Orlando, Florida, 1985.

41 Brown, Collins, and Duguid (1989a) 38.

Part 4 of this book shows how hypothetical situations set out in teaching materials can be used for that purpose.

The second issue is that we may fear that Brown, Collins and Duguid's strong emphasis on learning through activities in specific situations may lead to knowledge that is only pertinent to the specific situation, and not tansferable to other situations. Or we may fear that Brown, Collins and Duguid are effectively requiring law schools to adopt a 'trade school' model of legal education. Neither of these concerns need undermine the usefulness of the cognitive apprenticeship model.

In a critique of situated learning Laurillard argues that 'the point of an academic education is that knowledge has to be abstracted, and represented formally, in order to become generalisable and therefore more generally useful'.[42] The issue is rather how to teach students to develop knowledge that is abstracted, without it being taught directly as an abstraction. She argues that multiple contexts are necessary, but they are not sufficient to ensure appropriate academic knowledge. We need to ensure that our students do engage in a process of generalising from these multiple contexts to 'obtain an abstraction, a description of the world that does not consist in doing the activity alone'.[43] Laurillard argues that there is a difference between everyday knowledge and academic knowledge, between 'natural environments which afford the learning of "percepts" and unnatural environments which are constructed for learning "precepts" in education'.[44] In addition, we want students to learn more than that 'which is already available from experiencing the world'.[45] In law schools, we want our students to learn by experiencing the world at one remove, through exposition, argument and interpretation, and going beyond experience and reflecting on it. In describing what she calls 'mediated' learning, Laurillard pithily argues[46] that:

> 'Everyday experience is located in our experience of the world. Academic knowledge is located in our experience of our experience of the world. Both are situated, but in logically distinct contexts. Teaching may use the analogy of situated learning of the world, but must adapt it to the learning of descriptions of the world ... Teaching as mediated learning involves constructing the environments which afford the learning of descriptions of the world ...'

Consequently our teaching, according to Laurillard, should address both 'the direct experience of the world', and 'the reflection on that experience',[47] so that students understand the symbolic representation which is the medium through which the world is known and acquire knowledge of the way in which others experience the world.

One final point in relation to situated learning. In exploring a new discipline, students are bound to experience a significant degeneration of their existing

42 Laurillard (1993) 19-20.

43 *Ibid* 23.

44 *Ibid* 24.

45 *Ibid* 25.

46 *Ibid* 26.

47 *Ibid* 29.

writing and problem solving skills,[48] and to lose confidence in their abilities, as they try to assimilate a huge amount of knowledge. We need to support students through this process, and to encourage students to experiment with their thought processes, and to take risks, without fear of failure.

2.1.3 Cognitive theory: the nature of expertise

Another way of looking at improving students' learning in a discipline is to consider the characteristics which distinguish experts and novices within that discipline. Robert Glaser argues that educational practice should be based on the accumulated knowledge about human competence, cognition, and the human mind, and on research into their application to real world problems.[49] 'The more complete our descriptions of competence, the more accurately we should be able to design the conditions that help attain them.'[50]

One approach taken by cognitive psychologists is schema theory. It revolves around 'schemata', which are interpretive frameworks, built out of past knowledge and experience, which allow people to make sense out of information in particular situations.[51] An experience or text is incomprehensible, and of little benefit as a basis to learning, unless there is a schema into which it can be assimilated. Importantly, the schema itself supplies elements that are not included in the experience or text.[52]

Highly instructive studies have examined the difference between experts (persons highly competent in a discipline) and novices in different activities.[53] In one sense, experts are people who have accumulated certain types of experiences and knowledge, which give them an expert schema from which to approach a problem, processing information in ways that a novice cannot.[54] Chi and Glaser[55] have summarised the typical features of expert or proficient performance:

48 Mitchell (1989) 289, 292.

49 Glaser, R, 'Learning, Cognition, and Education: Then and Now', unpublished seminar paper, Centre for the Study of Higher Education, The University of Melbourne, 24 April 1991.

50 *Ibid*. See also Newell, A and Simon, H A, *Human Problem Solving*, Prentice Hall, Englewood Cliffs, New Jersey, 1972; and Greeno, J G 'Cognitive Objectives of Instruction: Theory of Knowledge for Solving Problems and Answering Questions' in D Klahr (ed) *Cognition and Instruction*, Erlbaum, Hillsdale, New Jersey, 1976.

51 Anderson, R C, 'The Notion of Schemata and the Educational Enterprise' in Anderson, R C, Spiro, R J and Montague, W E (eds) *Schooling and the Acquisition of Knowledge*, Lawrence Erlbaum Associates, Hillsdale, New Jersey, 1977.

52 *Ibid* 422. See also Mitchell (1989).

53 Glaser, R and Chi, M T H, 'Overview' in M T H Chi, R Glaser and M J Farr (eds) *The Nature of Expertise*, Lawrence Erlbaum and Associates, Hillsdale, New Jersey, 1988, xv-xxxvi. See also Bereiter and Scardamalia (1993).

54 Mitchell (1989) 278.

55 Chi, M, and Glaser, R, 'The Measurement of Expertise: Analysis of the Development of Knowledge and Skill as a Basis for Assessing Achievement' in E L Baker and E S Quellmetz (eds) *Educational Testing and Evaluation: Design, Analysis and Policy*, Sage Publications, Beverly Hills, 1980, 37-47. See also Mitchell (1989).

- Experts have *structured, principled knowledge*. They rapidly see patterns and shapes in a problem, and visualise a problem differently to the way a novice would see the problem. In legal education, emphasis should be on the principles underpinning the rules, and the way in which the principles relate to each other, not only within the traditional subject divisions, but between these subject divisions.
- Experts *represent the problem effectively*. They qualitatively assess the nature of a problem and build a mental model from which they can make inferences and add constraints to facilitate the solution. In contrast, novices tend to try to solve the problem too quickly.
- Experts have *proceduralised knowledge*. They know when to use (the conditions of applicability) and how to use (the procedures for its use) what they know. For example, experts can say that certain factors are important, and that when certain conditions occur knowledge should be used in a certain way.
- Experts have *skilled memory*. They do not have to search for information, but draw on their knowledge in ways that circumvent the limits of short term memory capacity. Experts do not necessarily have a different memory capacity to novices. Rather their memory is developed in larger configurations or patterns thereby facilitating the ability to remember detail.
- Experts display *automaticity*. They execute basic skills automatically, almost 'without thinking', so that they can focus their attention on the complex and less usual aspects of the task, and on comprehending, thinking, and considering strategies for problem solving and decision-making.
- Experts have *self-regulatory skills*, which they use to monitor or control their performance. Experts are able to give themselves good critical feedback.

This growing understanding of expertise has important implications for legal education. Even though this body of work only tells us how experts differ from novices, rather than how novices become experts, it does show us what we should aim for when we develop a teaching strategy. We can focus on the different skills and competences we desire to inculcate in students, and then design teaching environments and methods to produce these characteristics. Teaching should be directed towards helping students to understand legal phenomena and solve legal problems the way experts do. Legal education should utilise self-assessment and develop self-regulatory skills.

2.1.4 Students' intellectual and ethical development

In contrast to relational theories of learning and situated learning, which do not account for the ways in which individual students change as they progress through their studies, William Perry and colleagues conducted a longitudinal study of Harvard undergraduates and analysed their intellectual and ethical development over time.[56] Perry argued that students develop intellectually and ethically by moving through recognisable positions and transitions. For

56 Perry, W G, *Forms of Intellectual and Ethical Development in the College Years*, Holt Rhinehart and Winston, 1970. See Le Brun and Johnstone (1994) 83-87.

example, a student's intellectual journey begins with basic dualism, where he or she envisages knowledge as facts that are right or wrong (the cognitive component), and sees an authority figure as being responsible for what is known (the ethical component). Both these cognitive and ethical components develop through transitions to a position where the student conceives of many possible correct explanations (cognitive) and where each explanation is equally correct (ethical); to a position where everything is relative (cognitive) and not necessarily valid (ethical); to a position where the student recognises that he or she will have to make a commitment (ethical) to certain positions (cognitive); to a recognition that he or she must be wholehearted but tentative (in the sense of being open minded and ready to learn) in her commitments to positions.

While this explanation suggests parallels between cognitive and ethical development, this need not be the case. Older students may already have developed a system of personal values and may resist being told what to think, while at the same time beginning their learning with the belief that there are right and wrong facts.[57] Not all students work through all the stages, nor do students proceed through the stages at the same pace. A student may postpone his or her development, or may seek to escape responsibility, or may retreat from complexity into an earlier stage. We should not be surprised, therefore, to observe substantial differences between students. Perry exhorts us to pay close attention to the way our students make meaning, and not to try to force students into later stages of development, but rather to provide students with opportunities to grow. We should teach 'dialectically', by introducing students to 'the orderly certainties' of the subject matter, and to its 'unresolved dilemmas'.

Säljö has also identified a developmental progression in the way students conceive of learning, which make explicit what was implicit in Perry's framework. He suggests that students conceptualise the process of learning as:

- a quantitative increase in knowledge, acquiring information;
- memorising, in the sense of storing information that can be reproduced;
- the acquisition of facts, skills and procedures for use in practice;
- the abstraction of meaning, or making sense by relating parts of the subject matter to each other and to the real world;
- an interpretive process for understanding reality in a new way, by reinterpreting knowledge.[58]

A knowledge of these stages provides us as teachers with an important understanding of the way in which students might conceive of their own learning, so that we can develop a strategy to make useful interventions to facilitate student learning. We should ensure that we provide students with opportunities to develop their conceptions of what knowledge is and their ethical beliefs.[59]

57 Laurillard (1993) 44-46.

58 Säljö, R, 'Learning in the Learner's Perspective: Some Common-sense Conceptions', Internal Report, University of Gothenburg, No 76, 1979; Ramsden (1992) 26.

59 Laurillard (1993) 47.

Much of the discussion thus far in this section has been concerned with fairly complex theories of student learning and intellectual development. Many of the principles outlined in these diverse theories are implemented in two closely related modes of learning, problem-based learning and self-regulated learning. Both have much to offer law teachers.

2.1.5 Problem-based learning

Problem-based learning has emerged as an important approach to professional education, and emphasises the importance of student engagement with the subject matter.[60] Problem-based learning enables us to help students develop the intellectual skills to acquire knowledge for themselves, process information, solve problems and evaluate results.[61] We should distinguish problem-*based* learning from the problem *method*, in which we give our students hypothetical problems to solve by drawing on their knowledge and subject materials, and then discuss their solutions in class.[62] In problem-based learning students learn in the very process of solving the problem.[63] Its underlying principle is that the starting point for learning should be a problem, a query or a puzzle that the student wishes to solve. We only introduce organised forms of knowledge when the problem demands it.[64] Professional practice, for example, is organised around problems which may draw on a number of subject areas and skills.[65] Students learn at their own pace and at their own initiative, conduct their own research, and make their own observations and conclusions to solve problems.

The form taken by problem-based learning depends on the discipline and the learning objectives. Barrows and Tamblyn[66] set out a typical list of six stages in the process:

(i) Students encounter the problem first in the learning sequence, before they have undertaken any preparation or study.

(ii) We present the problem situation to students in the same way that the problem presents in reality.

60 For general discussions of problem-based learning in legal education, see Le Brun and Johnstone (1994) 92-97; and Kurtz, S, Wylie, M, and Gold, N, 'Problem-Based Learning: An Alternative Approach to Legal Education' (1990) 13 *Dalhousie Law Journal* 797. For an example of problem-based learning in nursing education, see Alavi, C, 'Quality in Problem Based Learning' in Sachs, J, Ramsden, P and Phillips, L, *The Experience of Quality in Higher Education*, Griffith Institute of Higher Education, Brisbane, 1995.

61 Kurtz, Wylie and Gold (1990) 816.

62 See Le Brun and Johnstone (1994) 93; and Ogden, G L, 'The Problem Method in Legal Education' (1984) 34 *Journal of Legal Education* 654.

63 Le Brun and Johnstone (1994) 93.

64 Boud, D, 'Problem-Based Learning in Perspective' in D Boud (ed) *Problem Based Learning in Education for the Professions*, Higher Education Research and Development Society of Australasia, Kensington, 1985, 13.

65 At the heart of problem-based learning is the maxim that 'the most effective learning occurs through our individual explorations of the ever changing environments we experience through our lives': Bawden, R J, 'Problem-based Learning: An Australian Perspective' in Boud (1985) 44.

66 Barrows, H S, and Tamblyn, P, *Problem-based Learning: An Approach to Medical Education*, Springer, New York, 1980. See also Kurtz, Wylie and Gold (1990) 809-814.

(iii) The student works with the problem in a manner that permits her or his ability to reason and apply knowledge to be challenged and evaluated, appropriate to her or his level of learning.

(iv) Students identify areas of learning in the process of working with the problem and use these areas as a guide to individualised study.

(v) Students apply the skills and knowledge acquired by this study back to the problem, to evaluate the effectiveness of learning and to reinforce learning.

(vi) Students summarise the learning that has occurred in work with the problem and in individualised study, and integrate this learning into their existing knowledge and skills.

For example, we can initiate learning by giving our students a legal problem in which they are required to advise a hypothetical client, or give them a socio-legal research problem in which they are required to specify the project aims, assumptions and methods that they would develop in researching a particular phenomenon. As far as possible we should give our students exactly the same information that a legal practitioner or socio-legal researcher, for example, would be given in the same situation. The problem must be authentic, and not just an artificial 'exercise'. We could give our students a copy of the contract to interpret, or the client's instructions to draft the contract.[67] But it is important that we pitch the problem at a level appropriate to student's experience, previous learning and ability, and give them enough time to work on the problem and to reflect on their efforts. Working together, students identify what they need to know or do to solve the problem. Our role as teachers is to facilitate this process by helping students to formulate questions, and by providing access to required information. Students will generally become motivated to engage in a lot of private study to solve the problem, and can then apply the material learnt to the problem situation. This requires skills in goal setting and self-assessment.[68] The student should get feedback from fellow students and from us. The feedback can then be used to develop our students' learning and to refine the solution. The final debriefing stage is important to enable students to see the importance of academic learning in solving real world problems.[69]

There are many advantages of this approach.

- It emphasises student centred learning,[70] where students determine what they need to know, and how they will go about learning it.
- It requires students to take responsibility for their own learning, and to plan, organise and evaluate their learning.[71]

67 See the materials set out in Part 4 of this book.

68 See the discussions of self-regulated learning in this section.

69 See generally Boud (1985) 14-15, and Pearson, M, and Smith, M, 'Debriefing in Experience-based Learning' in D J Boud, R Keogh and D Walker (eds) *Reflection: Turning Experience into Learning*, Kogan Page, London, 1985.

70 Boud (1985) 15.

71 See generally Boud, D (ed) *Developing Student Autonomy in Learning*, 2nd ed, Kogan Page, London, 1988.

- Problem-based learning requires multi-disciplinary learning, because the problems will require approaches which transcend specific disciplines.
- Problem-based learning breaks down the artificial division between theory and practice,[72] concepts and applications.
- Problem-based learning places an emphasis on the processes of acquiring knowledge, rather than on the product of the process. Students need to work out how to approach the problem, and to reflect on the nature of the process.[73]
- We teachers become facilitators of the process, rather than presenters of information.
- Students learn communication and interpersonal skills, in addition to technical legal skills. Students' feelings, attitudes and values are developed, not just their cognitive skills.[74]

In short, problem-based learning in legal education provides a vehicle for the achievement of a variety of learning objectives. I will discuss learning objectives later in section 2.3. If student autonomy is to be one of the objectives of legal education, we need to provide students with opportunities to solve genuine problems and to learn how to regulate their own learning.[75]

2.1.6 Self-regulated learning

Teaching materials can provide students with opportunities for self-study, where they can engage in problem-based learning, by working through the material at their own pace, and managing their own learning. This section focuses on how students can monitor or regulate their own learning.

Zimmerman and Martinez-Pons describe self-regulated learners as people who plan, organise, self-instruct and self-evaluate at various stages during the process of acquiring knowledge.[76] Self-regulated learning involves a student controlling her or his own learning, through planning, monitoring and checking.[77] Students will need to apply and evaluate their own conceptual and strategic knowledge. They will have to check their progress in learning, judge problem difficulty, apportion additional resources, allocate time, ask questions to elaborate their knowledge, and predict the outcomes of their performance.[78] Brown, Bransford, Ferrarra and Campione argue that:

72 See the above discussion of situated learning earlier in this section at pp 13 to 19.

73 Boud (1985) 15; Schon, D, *The Reflective Practitioner*, Basic Books, New York, 1983.

74 Boud (1985) 16.

75 But see the cautionary words of Phil Candy, 'Evolution, Devolution or Revolution: Increasing Learner Control in the Instructional Setting' in D Boud and V Griffin, *Appreciating Adult Learning from the Learners' Perspective*, Kogan Page, London, 1987.

76 Zimmerman, B J and Martinez-Pons, M, 'Construct Validation of a Strategy Model of Student Self-Regulated Learning' (1988) 80 *Journal of Educational Psychology* 284-290.

77 Brown, A L, Campione, J C and Day, J D, 'Learning to Learn: On Training Students to Learn from Texts' (1981) 10 *Educational Researcher* 14, 15. See also Washbourne, M, Lawrence, J, and Kurzeja, D, 'Training Problem Solving Skills in Children: Two Approaches to Adult Intervention', paper presented at Annual Meeting of Australian Association for Research in Education, Hobart, November, 1985.

78 See Glaser (1991).

'Effective teachers are those who engage in continual prompts to get [students] to plan and monitor their own activities and model many forms of critical thinking for their students, processes that the students must internalise as part of their own problem solving activities if they are to develop effective skills of self-regulation.'

It should be apparent at this stage that learning through problem solving has a very close relationship with self-regulated learning. Problem solving promotes deep approaches to learning through activities which require and enable students to plan, check and monitor their learning and performance.

As teachers we have an important role in modelling the kind of thinking that we would like students to internalise. As a first step we must analyse the components of the task and both the specific and general skills necessary for its successful performance, taking into account the differing teaching needs of students. We should ascertain which knowledge and skills from previous learning students will use when learning the new material and skills. We must make students aware of the new learning tasks, and the importance of monitoring their skills in the new situation. We may need to teach them basic skills to regulate their own learning, as well as other skills such as summarising, reading and self-interrogation.

We must also ensure that each student has a very clear idea of the nature of the task she or he is expected to perform. There are direct links between problem solvers' mental representations of tasks and their solution processes and outcomes. This includes the mental imagery and constructions with which problem solvers approach and structure their operations, their initial interpretations and expectations and the mental models they use to guide behaviour on a particular task.[79] A student's knowledge of what is required in a particular learning situation influences the activities that she or he undertakes. Students need to know whether the task requires them to understand the gist of the issue, apply the material to new situations, or whether they should be capable of factual recall. The more the student knows about the end requirements of the task, the better the outcome of studying.[80] Also important is the student's perceptions of her or his own characteristics and capabilities. The ability to compare what one brings to a task with what is required, and to judge where the discrepancies lie, are important for deciding how to tackle the task.[81]

For students to be able to regulate their own learning, we must teach them how to plan and set goals for their learning. Goals give direction, meaning and focus to learning activities.

Once the goals of learning have been established, we should provide scaffolding by giving students prompts, frameworks and guiding questions to enable students to see how to approach the material to be learnt. It may be necessary initially to simplify both the number and complexity of tasks required

79 Volet, S E, *The Significance of Goals in Management of Academic Study*, unpublished Ph D thesis, Murdoch University, 1988, 3-4.

80 *Ibid* 5.

81 *Ibid*. Scheier, M F and Carver, C S, 'Cognition, Affect and Self-regulation' in J M Levine and M C Wang (eds) *Teacher and Student Perceptions: Implications for Learning*, Lawrence Erlbaum and Associates, Hillside, New Jersey, 1983, 157-183.

in any particular activity, and then to build up the level of complexity as the subject progresses. For example, it may be useful to start with a familiar hypothetical situation, without any cases, so that students are not lost in the complexity of unravelling the legal rules. Students can be encouraged to reason through the situation, using their existing knowledge, common sense and imagination. Gradually legal doctrine and other factors can be introduced, so that students build up their schemas and gradually immerse themselves into the topic.[82] This to a large extent is what the agreed damages materials in Part 4 of this book attempt to do.

The basic objective is for students to internalise the framework for learning that is being modelled by the materials. The student should then begin asking the same kinds of questions that have been used in the materials, thereby anticipating the questions we are likely to ask in class.[83] Over time the student acquires competence in the area under study and internalises the required approach to the topic or skill. We then gradually withdraw the scaffolding, leaving the student to monitor her or his own performance.

Self-regulated learning is inconsistent with the teacher being the sole source of power or control, and involves us passing control of, and responsibility for, the learning process to our students once we have modelled the process and provided appropriate scaffolding.[84] Vygotsky[85] argued that the most natural learning occurred in social interaction. It involved a gradual transfer of executive control from an expert to a novice. Self-control is instilled in the student with the help of the supportive teacher. The student first experiences active problem solving activities in the presence of others, and then gradually comes to perform these functions for herself. First, the teacher performs the cognitive activity, sensitive to students' level of functioning. Students then actively participate in the activity and attempt to perform it with guidance and support. Gradually the student internalises the desired activity, and takes over, performing it without help.[86]

Self-regulated learning depends on students generating reliable feedback on their performance. In particular, we need to provide students with as much feedback as possible on their performance, and need to provide them with every opportunity assess their own work. I will discuss this issue in section 2.4, which deals more specifically with assessment.

82 Mitchell (1989) 292-3.

83 Boud, D J and Tyrie, A L 'Self-and Peer Assessment in Professional Education: A Preliminary Study in Law' (1980) 15 *Journal of the Society of Public Teachers of Law* 65 at 66.

84 See Higgs, J, 'Planning Learning Experiences to Promote Autonomous Learning' in Boud (1988) at 55.

85 Vygotsky, L S, *Thought and Language*, John Wiley, New York, 1972; Vygotsky, L S, *Mind in Society: The Development of Higher Psychological Processes*, M Cole, V John-Steiner, S Scribner and E Souberman (eds and trans), Harvard University Press, Cambridge, 1978.

86 See also Brown, A L, Bransford, J D, Ferrarra, R A and Campione, C, 'Learning, Remembering and Understanding' in J H Flavell and E M Markman, *Carmichael Handbook of Child Psychology*, Vol 1, John Wiley, New York, 1983.

2.1.7 From theories of student learning to developing a teaching strategy

In this section of the book I have briefly outlined some of the different theories which help us to understand the way in which students learn, and I have tried to draw out the implications of these theories for teachers writing teaching materials. I have emphasised that the different theories about student learning have different assumptions and methodological underpinnings, and are difficult to reconcile on a theoretical level. At a practical level, however, they all appear to emphasise the importance of providing students with appropriately structured opportunities to work with the subject matter, and to make their own meaning from material, to reflect on what they know, and to get feedback so that they can monitor their own learning.

While it is well accepted that learning and teaching are intimately related, educationalists have struggled with the link between theories of learning and teaching practice.[87] Many educationalists have attempted at develop a teaching strategy from the accumulated knowledge of student learning. A recent example is to be found in Diana Laurillard's work. Working from a relational view of knowledge,[88] and emphasising the situated nature of all learning,[89] she argues that a teaching strategy has to address the different aspects of what students bring with them to learning a new topic. These include:

(i) *developing a knowledge of our students' conceptions of the topic.* We need to develop descriptions of the ways our students think about or conceptualise topics, so that we come to know of the fundamental misconceptions they develop in learning about law, and can intervene to challenge and correct these misconceptions. This is a labour intensive project, but must be done before we can develop a sound teaching strategy.[90]

(ii) *developing students' representational skills.* The aim of academic learning in law is not the same as the real world task of acting as a legal practitioner. Rather academic learning is intended to introduce students to the language, concepts and skills of law and lawyering, so that students will be able to describe legal rules and their operation in practice. We need to give students opportunities to interpret and discuss the law, its practice and its theoretical models, in language, symbols and so on. Students need to learn the language and conventions of the law and the legal way of thinking.[91]

(iii) *enabling students to develop their understanding of what knowledge is, their ethical beliefs, and their conceptions of learning.*[92]

We need also to consider what goes on when students learn. Laurillard suggests that we teachers need to encourage student activities that will result in high quality learning. How do students come to an understanding of a new

87 For a thoughtful discussion of some of these attempts, see Laurillard (1993) ch 4.

88 See pp 10 to 13 above.

89 See pp 13 to 19 above.

90 Laurillard (1993) 43, 187-94.

91 *Ibid* 47.

92 See the discussion of the work of Perry and Säljö at pp 20 to 22 above.

idea? She suggests that there are five aspects of learning that combine content and action, and which encompass the essence of the learning process.[93] Students must address all of these interrelated aspects of learning to learn successfully.

(a) To use Laurillard's terminology, students must *'apprehend the structure of the discourse'*.[94] As we saw earlier in this section, Laurillard argues that academic learning focuses not on the world itself, but on others' views of the world. The academic structure of a subject is usually more complex than an everyday conception of the same thing. When we teach a subject, we try to convey to students an alternative way (that is a perspective framed around the law and its operation) of looking at a world that they already know through their own experience. To learn or grasp the specific intended meaning that we give the subject, students must be able to interpret a complex range of new technical words and concepts. To enable students to do this properly, we need to give our students 'the big picture' of our subject. We must provide students with a structure within which to understand the subject, explain phenomena and negotiate learning goals for the topic, so that students can use deep approaches to learning. For example: what are the principal purposes of the criminal law? What are its central concepts? How do these concepts fit together? As we know from the earlier discussion of deep and surface approaches to learning, we should map out a structure for the subject so that students can focus on the central argument and concepts; relate and distinguish evidence and argument; and organise and structure the content into a coherent whole. Students must look for the goals and structure of the topic, so that they focus on the main arguments of the subject and the way in which these arguments unfold. We want them to put together the different parts of the subject into the coherent whole that we have conceptualised for the subject, rather than coming up with a series of unconnected points or an inappropriate structure of the subject. If students fail to see the original structure of the subject, they will resort to simple formulae to solve problems, without being able to appreciate the meaning of the solution they have produced.

(b) Students must *'integrate the sign with the signified'*.[95] All academic disciplines use special forms of representation. Physicists, for example, use mathematical diagrams and equations, symbols and so on to represent and convey concepts. Part of studying a subject involves learning how to represent concepts using these forms of representation, and how to decode the forms of representation to understand the concepts. Lawyers have their own language which they use to represent ideas. We teachers need to help students to interpret and make sense of these representations and to express underlying meanings in accepted language and using accepted concepts. As Laurillard[96] notes:

93 These are discussed in detail in Laurillard (1993) ch 3, and summarised here.

94 *Ibid* 50-56.

95 *Ibid* 56-58.

96 *Ibid* 58.

'This is a non-trivial and persistent problem throughout higher education: students need help in practising the mapping between world and formalism, the ways of representing academic ideas and their interrelations.'

In learning about law our students need opportunities to understand and practise the language of the law and the forms of representing legal ideas and concepts, and to represent legal ideas as a coherent whole, as well as its constituent parts.

(c) Students need opportunities *to act on the world and on descriptions of the world*.[97] This involves learning by doing, by applying theory to practice. But we know that academic knowledge of law is different from experiential knowledge, because much academic knowledge of law involves theories, descriptions and viewpoints. So in law, learning activities should include not just clinical work and simulations of clinical work such as moots, role plays and simulations, but also theorising, relating theory to practice, relating knowledge to experience and so on. We should enable our students to solve problems, test hypotheses, and engage in other activities (discussions, debates, essays and so on) to produce descriptions of the subject matter. We should also compare student descriptions with our desired outcomes.

(d) Students need opportunities to *receive meaningful feedback*, and to use that feedback.[98] If students are to learn through activities they must receive timely feedback which indicates whether their actions or representations of knowledge are correct or misconceived, and which shows how they can improve their performance to achieve their goals for learning.

(e) Students need opportunities to *reflect on the relationship between the learning goals, the activities and representations of knowledge involved in learning, and the feedback* the student has received in relation to these activities and representations of knowledge.[99] Has the student, through the activities, achieved the goal? Should the goal be modified in the light of the feedback? Have we, as teachers, adequately explained the goals of the learning process to our students so that they share our perception of what the goals are? Are the goals appropriate to ensure that student learning is focused on the desired structure for learning, and so on.

These five aspects of learning are not independent of each other – rather they are closely related to one another and interdependent. Laurillard argues that when we teach we should create a learning environment in which students can engage in all of these aspects of learning, in a manner which integrates goals, conceptual structure, activities, and feedback.

From her research of the literature on learning, Laurillard concludes that a teaching strategy should not focus on what we should do as teachers, but rather on how we should set up interactions between us, our students and the content of our subject.[100] In general, 'the learning process must be constituted as a

97 *Ibid* 58-61.

98 *Ibid* 61-64.

99 *Ibid* 64-68.

100 *Ibid* 84.

dialogue between teacher and student, operating on the level of descriptions of actions in the world, recognising the second-order character of academic knowledge',[101] and should have the characteristics outlined in Table 1.

This is a useful 'conversational framework' for envisaging teaching as a dialogue between us and our students, rather than as a process which we inflict on our students. It should result in better quality student learning because it

Table 1: Laurillard's Model of A Teaching Strategy[102]

Discursive

- the teacher and students must agree on learning goals for the topic and on task goals;
- the teacher and students must each reveal their different conceptions of the topic, and ensure that these conceptualisations are accessible to each other, so that they can be compared and contrasted. In other words, we teachers should describe to students the main points in the topic, the definitions required, key concepts, the relationships to be drawn, the structure of the argument, and illustrative examples. Students can provide their descriptions of the topic in class discussions and activities, written work, etc;
- the teacher must provide an environment within which students can act on, generate and receive feedback on descriptions appropriate to the topic goal;
- the teacher must be able to reflect on student descriptions and modify her or his own descriptions to be more meaningful to students.

Adaptive

- the teacher has the responsibility to use the relationship between her or his own and the student's conceptions to determine the task goals and focus of the continuing dialogue. The teacher asks students to compare their conceptions with the teacher's conceptions. Continuing dialogue and interactions focus on steps to clarify and remove student misconceptions or other shortcomings in students' descriptions of the topic;

Interactive

- the students must act to achieve the task goal set by the teacher in the adaptive stage above;
- the teacher must provide meaningful feedback on the actions that relates to the nature of the task goal;
- something in the world must change observably as the result of student actions.

Reflective

- the teacher must support the process by which students link the feedback on their actions to the topic goal for every level of description within the topic structure. Students must be able to control the pace of the learning process so that they have adequate time for reflection.

encourages deep approaches to learning and engages students in reflective, situated learning. This framework will help us to design appropriate teaching materials and to choose suitable teaching methods. Laurillard goes on to examine what different teaching media and methods have to offer education, and in particular the way in which different types of teaching media can play a role in her conception of teaching as a conversational framework.

I have discussed Laurillard's model of a teaching strategy in some detail because it will give readers an insight into the link between learning theory and the development of a teaching strategy. In this book I will develop a model for developing and using teaching materials which borrows in many respects from Laurillard's model, but I make no claim to anything as sophisticated as a 'Laurillardian model' for the development of teaching materials in law. I will concentrate on examining printed teaching materials and classroom methods which do not involve anything more than simple technology such as overhead slides and whiteboards. Readers interested in working with more sophisticated technology should consult Laurillard's work.

In the rest of this section I outline the basic model of teaching and learning which underpins the principles for developing printed teaching materials in Part 3. I have outlined the model in Figure 1 on page 8. In short, the model requires us to:

- determine the characteristics of the students who will be using the materials;
- determine the aims and learning objectives of the subject;
- determine the assessment tasks;
- determine the structure of the subject;
- select appropriate teaching methods;
- design printed teaching materials; and
- evaluate the materials to ensure that they play a role in improving student learning.

The next section considers ways in which we can find out who our students are so that we can pitch our subject and our teaching methods at an appropriate level to facilitate student learning.

2.2 KNOWING OUR STUDENTS

When we plan a subject and set about developing materials for that subject we need first to profile the students who will be doing the learning.[103] When we write teaching materials we need to have in mind real people whose learning needs we are trying to address. Do our students have similar characteristics, or will we need to build up a range of student profiles? What are the interests,

101 *Ibid* 94.

102 *Ibid* 94-95, 100-103, 194-205.

103 See generally Rowntree, D, *Teaching Through Self-Instruction. How to Develop Open Learning Materials*, Kogan Page, London, 1990, 39-43; Rowntree, D, *Preparing Materials for Open, Distance and Flexible Learning*, Kogan Page, London, 1994, 41-48; Race, P, *53 Interesting Ways to Write Open Learning Materials*, Technical and Educational Services Ltd, Bristol, 1992, 19-22.

feelings, past experience, strengths and weaknesses of our students? Race suggests that it is most helpful 'to think of an individual learner and try to imagine what would interest, confuse or help such a person'.[104] If there is likely to be a range of different student profiles in the class it is best to think of students one at a time. Even if we have no idea of who our students might be, it is worth making an educated guess as to their characteristics. We might be able to rely on our previous experience (or the experience of colleagues) of teaching students in the same subject. We may want to meet a small group of the students and discuss with them their expectations of the subject and what they already know, or send a questionnaire to prospective students to elicit the basic information. Some writers suggest that teachers address a set list of questions in compiling a profile of their students.[105] These should cover:

- demographic factors (age range, gender breakdown, background etc);
- motivation (why are students taking our subject, what are their hopes and fears etc);
- learning factors (prior educational experiences, level of ability etc); and
- subject background (knowledge, skills and attitudes that students already have about the subject).

Whatever method we use, we need to have a clear idea of who our students are, so that we can write teaching materials that are appropriate for them. The purpose of profiling our students is to develop an understanding of how we should design our subject, and pitch our materials and classroom teaching. Will our students have any educational or life experiences that we can build on to improve their learning in our subject? What aspects of the subject are likely to be meaningful to them? What do our students already know about our subject? What relevant prior knowledge, skills and interests do they bring to the subject? Are our students likely to have any preconceptions about our subject, which we can build on, or which we need to alter? What concepts or technological terms have common, everyday equivalents that could distort our students' understanding of our subject? Our past experiences of teaching the subject will tell us what aspects of the subject are of particular interest to students, and what are the common misconceptions of students when they engage with the concepts in the subject. Once we work out what these common misconceptions are we can design our curricula to expose and correct these misconceptions. If we are aware of difficulties that students are likely to have in making logical connections in our subject, we can anticipate these difficulties and address them explicitly and proactively.

In conclusion, when we develop teaching materials we need to keep firmly in mind the characteristics or profile of our students, and, as we saw in section 2.1, the ways in which they are most likely to learn effectively, and the stages they may go through in their intellectual development. Once we have examined the individual and group characteristics of our students, we need to consider how to go about establishing the aims and learning objectives that will guide the development of teaching materials so as to facilitate student learning.

104 Race (1992) 19.

105 See Race (1992) 19-21; Rowntree (1990) 39-43; Rowntree (1994) 42.

2.3 SETTING GOALS AND LEARNING OBJECTIVES

Laurillard's model of a teaching strategy reflects the emphasis in most theories of student learning on the importance of goal setting. Once we have considered the characteristics of our students ('where they are when they begin our subject'), and the way in which they will best learn the subject matter, we need to determine the aims and objectives of our subject ('where we wish them to be at the end of the subject'). By establishing aims and objectives for student learning, we and our students are able to establish whether our students have engaged in the kind of learning in which we have intended to involve them.

In this book an 'aim' is a general statement of our educational intent, either in terms of what our students might learn or what we will do. For example, an aim might be 'learn about drafting and interpreting agreed damages clauses'; or 'to introduce students to the commercial context in which agreed damages clauses are used'. An objective is a more specific statement of what a student will be able to do, or do better, as a result of engagement in a learning environment.[106] For example:

'At the end of this topic the student should be able to:

1. Summarise the commercial considerations and policy issues involved in the drafting of agreed damages clauses;
2. Describe the legal principles developed by the Australian courts to distinguish between agreed damages clauses and penalty clauses; and
3. Draft an agreed damages clause.'

Setting learning objectives for a law-related subject is not as straightforward an exercise as it may at first appear. Law teaching occupies an uneasy position between two poles.[107] On the one hand the legal profession relies on university law schools to provide the basic legal training to future barristers and solicitors, and it specifies requirements for recognition of subjects and degrees. It is difficult to argue that law schools should not teach basic skills such as how to analyse and reason from cases and statutes; legal research skills; problem solving skills; interviewing, counselling, negotiating, mediating skills; litigation skills; skills in gathering information; and organisational/managerial skills.[108] Future lawyers should also have an understanding of the basic elements of civil and criminal procedure, and of the core substantive areas of the legal system, such as contract, tort, criminal law, constitutional law, administrative law, property law, company law and so on.

On the other hand, many of us argue that legal education should be just that – a liberal education devoted to rigorous scholarly inquiry within a

---

106 Le Brun and Johnstone (1994) 153; Rowntree (1994) 50.

107 See Thornton, M, 'Portia Lost in the Groves of Academe Wondering What to Do about Legal Education' (1991) 34 *The Australian Universities' Review* 26 at 26.

108 For a general discussion of the range of possible skills to be taught in law schools, see American Bar Association Section on Legal Education and Admissions to the Bar, *Legal Education and Professional Development – An Educational Continuum*, Report of Task Force on Law Schools and the Profession: Narrowing the Gap, American Bar Association, Chicago, 1992; and Le Brun and Johnstone (1994) 170-173.

university environment.[109] Consequently, the study of law needs to do more than expound legal rules, and train lawyers in the skills for legal practice. Many of these skills are better taught in professional practice courses or during articles of clerkship, rather than in universities. The study of law in universities should be reflective and critical, examining the problem of what law is, locating law within its societal context, and within other disciplines in the humanities and social sciences which enrich an understanding of the nature of law and its operation in society.[110] It should be restlessly exploring the socially constructed nature of law,[111] an activity at loggerheads with the notion that legal education is professional training. University educated lawyers need to be well schooled in important debates, issues and methodologies within the broad field of legal theory. These issues, debates and methodologies need to be properly integrated into substantive subjects, not left to specialist subjects later in the degree.[112] They assist lawyers to research and to understand the shape that the law (statutes and cases) takes in practice out in the community.

In sum, a university course should do more than train lawyers in the professional skills required for practice in the legal profession. While legal education has to have, as part of its focus, the lawyer's 'pragmatic rationalisations of legal rules into more or less systematic form',[113] it should never lose sight of the fact that law and lawyers operate in a complex society, which is governed by non-legal as well as legal norms. Learning about law in a university context should involve seeing law as a socially constructed phenomenon located in society and history, interconnected with other political and cultural institutions, and the subject of philosophical theories and debates. University legal education should produce students who are thinking individuals, not just catalogues of knowledge.

Another way of conceptualising this is to examine what students should learn in terms of a series of qualitatively different levels.[114] At the first level law schools should be requiring students to develop intellectual abilities that go beyond the possession of technical skills and subject knowledge. At the most abstract level students should be developing very general abilities and personal qualities, such as being able to think critically and imaginatively, and being able to communicate effectively. As A N Whitehead put it, the:

> 'university imparts information, but it imparts it imaginatively. ... This atmosphere of excitement, arising from imaginative consideration, transforms knowledge. ... Imagination ... is a way of illuminating the facts. It works by eliciting the general principles which apply to facts, as they exist, and then by an

109 See generally Le Brun and Johnstone (1994) ch 1.

110 Thornton (1992) 26.

111 See Duncanson (1994).

112 See Sampford, C J and Wood, D, 'Legal Theory and Legal Education – The Next Step' (1989) 1 *Legal Education Review* 107; Sampford, C J and Wood, D, 'The Place of Legal Theory in the Law School' (1987) 11 *Bulletin of the Australian Society of Legal Philosophy* 98.

113 Cotterrell, R, *The Sociology of Law: An Introduction*, 2nd edn, Butterworths, London, 1993, 3.

114 See Ramsden (1992) ch 3. See also Candy, P, 'A Climate of Intellectual Inquiry: The Ultimate Test of Quality in Higher Education' in Sachs, J, Ramsden, P and Phillips, L, *The Experience of Quality in Higher Education*, Griffith Institute of Higher Education, Brisbane, 1995, 30.

intellectual survey of alternative possibilities which are consistent with these principles ...'[115]

At the second level, our students should be engaging in more specific, and content related, changes in understanding, related to the discipline of law. Law students need to learn how to think like a lawyer or legal theorist in problem solving.

At the third level, we should provide our students with opportunities to develop highly specific skills, such as the ability to develop robust knowledge, technical and manipulative skills, and problem solving skills. We need to facilitate student learning at all these levels.

These different foci of legal education, the development of practical lawyering skills and the location of these skills within a broader reflective and theoretical legal culture, need not be exclusive of each other. We can incorporate all aspects in the learning objectives we establish for our subjects. What are the objectives of legal education, and how can they be achieved within a law school?[116] In brief, they cover four areas, set out in Table 2.

Cognitive objectives	Students learn intellectual skills, including professional and critical modes of thinking.
Skills objectives	Students learn practical legal skills and lifelong learning skills.
Objectives about values	Students have opportunities to explore values and attitudes, and to develop attitudes appropriate to professional practice.
Motivation	Students are motivated to continue learning beyond their law school education.

Table 2: A typology of learning objectives in legal education

These objectives are outlined in greater detail below.

2.3.1 Cognitive objectives

(a) Traditional objectives of legal education

At the basic level, we should teach our students professional modes of thinking. Legal 'experts' approach legal problems with a large amount of 'domain based' knowledge of law and its processes, which includes:

'legal vocabulary; cases; use of analogies; characteristic "patterns" or "moves" in reasoning; relationships between bodies of doctrine, along with an awareness of

115 Whitehead, A N, *The Aims of Education and Other Essays*, Free Press, New York, 1967, 139 quoted in Ramsden (1992) 19.

116 For general discussions on these issues, see Le Brun and Johnstone (1994) 149-176; Pirie, A J, 'Objectives in Legal Education: The Case for Systematic Instructional Design' (1987) 37 *Journal of Legal Education* 576; and Rowles, J P, 'Toward Balancing the Goals of Legal Education' (1981) 31 *Journal of Legal Education* 375. The following discussion of objectives is drawn from Johnstone (1992) 22-28.

general principles and issues that cut across such bodies; the significant questions and historical perspective of each of our areas; procedures for approaching problems, knowledge of the conventions controlling what can or cannot be said. Our "knowledge base", more than any unique cognitive capacities we possess, provides us with an effective framework (ie schema) for approaching and analysing problems. Entering law students ("novices"), however, have no such knowledge base ...'[117]

Students who have acquired basic cognitive skills[118] should:

(i) *Know* and *understand*, and be able to *identify*, the basic rules, principles and concepts of important and basic areas of the substantive law. The emphasis should not be on students needing to know every legal principle, or every case, even within a particular area. Students should be taught a basic framework of principles, and the skills to 'flesh out' the detail of these principles. They should also develop the skills to learn for themselves the basic principles of an area of law, so that they can build up their own required level of detail.

(ii) *Understand the likely future developments* in the substantive law. To do this lawyers need to know from whence the rules, principles and concepts in the substantive law are derived, and the various theories that attempt to systematise them. It requires learning that focuses on the historical, social, political and economic context of the legal principles and institutions, and the internal tensions in the principles and institutions and their operation in society, so that their future development can be anticipated, at least in broad outline. These insights will enable legal practitioners to give advice enabling clients to structure their affairs taking into account future possible developments in the law.

(iii) Be able to *analyse* cases, facts and statutes. Analysis involves breaking down the subject matter into its basic components and examining the relationships between these elements. Our students need to be able to find the law, and then undertake independent analysis of the rules and principles. They should be able to read cases properly, by analysing the basic facts of the case, and extracting the *ratio decidendi*, and important *obiter dicta*. Similarly students should be able to read statutes, so that they can pick up any statute and understand its basic principles and predict the way in which the principles will be interpreted by the courts.

We can teach our students to analyse cases and statutes through problem solving, so that the students practice case and statute reading skills until these skills are internalised and carried out without conscious thought. We should teach these skills intensively early in the law degree, and should then carefully develop and maintain these skills through problem solving in all subjects later in the degree.

We should also teach our students how to elicit, analyse and interpret basic facts from a client. Clients have their own narratives which contain a lot of detail which is irrelevant to the legal solution to the problem, but is very

117 Mitchell (1989) 279.

118 See Le Brun and Johnstone (1994) 161-63.

important to the client. Lawyers need to be able to discern and elicit the important facts in any situation, while being able to listen to and respect the needs of the client.

(iv) Be able to *apply* legal principles, and their likely practical implementation, to the 'facts' of a particular problem. We should give our students every opportunity to acquire the techniques of legal reasoning and argument. Traditional legal education has required students to apply legal principles to facts but has ignored the socio-legal issues relating to the way that the law is implemented or enforced. How do prosecuting authorities enforce the law, and how do legal practitioners resolve civil law disputes? How do courts exercise sentencing discretions?

To achieve these objectives we can provide opportunities for our students to:

- give advice, orally or in writing, to the parties in a specially devised legal problem;
- prepare and present legal argument on behalf of one of the parties;
- place themselves in the position of a judge and to write a judgment which determines the rights and obligations of the parties.
- draft contracts or clauses of contracts based on their knowledge and understanding of a particular area of law; or
- interpret documents and perhaps redraft the document in line with the relevant legal principles, and the client's requirements.[119]

(v) Be able to *synthesise* the legal principles emerging from cases and statutes, and the practice of legal agencies and practitioners. This involves students putting together the component parts of the law into a new form for a particular purpose. We can use the activities discussed in the previous paragraph to provide students with opportunities to develop synthesis skills.

(vi) Be able to *evaluate* the internal logic of an opinion, judgment, statute, empirical study of the law in operation, or any other analysis of the law. Is the analysis consistent within its own terms? Are the arguments internally coherent? Does the evidence presented by the writer support her or his conclusions?

We could require our students to:

- read all material as critically as possible and to support their opinions by evidence and reason; or
- provide a written or oral evaluation of a piece of writing.

(b) Critical and interdisciplinary perspectives

Less traditionally, we should enable our students to develop critical skills. When students learn the cognitive skills to manipulate and evaluate legal rules, we should ensure that they never lose sight of the fact that legal rules are socially constructed, and that legal rules are the product of a process which selects one of the many possible perspectives on an issue, and labels it as the

119 See for example the materials on Agreed Damages Clauses in Part 4.

governing rule. We should remind our students of the manner in which legal rules are turned into 'things' which have a life of their own as a result of the doctrine of precedent and the other principles of rule finding, such as the principles of statutory construction and accepted modes of legal reasoning.

We should link the study of law to other disciplines. Law is a social phenomenon laden with values, ideologies and complex histories. Legal education should equip students to examine the role of law in society by utilising relevant perspectives from the social sciences (particularly feminist analysis, sociology, political science, economics, psychology, and anthropology) and the humanities (particularly history and philosophy). Students will need to familiarise themselves with the basic frameworks and methodologies in these disciplines, and to apply them to legal phenomena. We should ensure that our students are aware of the different cultures or frameworks of these disciplines, which may have conflicting assumptions and values to those embedded in traditional legal scholarship and legal professional practice.

A major benefit of these interdisciplinary perspectives is that our students will learn different types of reasoning. In working towards the different objectives described in the previous section, they will largely develop conditional reasoning skills, or reasoning skills using deductive logic.[120] In their practical work in the social sciences they will develop statistical[121] and methodological[122] reasoning skills.[123]

We should always teach law within the context that it has an impact on society, and its content and practice is shaped by society. We can use interdisciplinary studies to show the impact of law on different groups within society, and the impact of different groups, depending on their power, on the law. We should encourage our students to ask who benefits from different aspects of the law; who is disadvantaged; who has best access to the law; whose rights are ignored by the law; and similar questions.

2.3.2 Skills objectives

In the process of achieving these cognitive objectives, we should encourage our students to develop a raft of important skills: legal research skills; problem solving skills; interviewing, counselling, negotiating, mediating skills; litigation skills; skills in gathering information; and organisational/managerial skills.[124] As Reed has commented, for lawyers to:

> 'apply evolving principles to active conflicts requires considerable skill, usually referred to as interpersonal competence. In the practice of the law recurring conflicts demand that such skills should be used daily and should be used well.'[125]

120 See generally Lehman, D R and Nisbett, R E, 'A Longitudinal Study of the Effects of Undergraduate Training on Reasoning' (1990) 26 *Developmental Psychology* 952, 953.

121 For example, the use of sampling and statistical methods.

122 For example, judgments about results from statistical analysis.

123 Lehman and Nisbett (1990) 952-3.

124 See again American Bar Association Section on Legal Education and Admissions to the Bar (1992); and Le Brun and Johnstone (1994) 170-73.

125 Reed, R M, 'Group Learning in Law School' (1984) 34 *Journal of Legal Education* 674, 676.

Face to face communication skills are important, and encompass interviewing, counselling, negotiation and mediation skills. We can provide students with opportunities to develop these skills in the normal classroom setting, by structuring class discussions, class activities and small group work with these skills in mind.[126] We should ensure that our students learn to communicate with people who are not lawyers, or who have speech, hearing, visual or other impairments. Equally important is the ability to work creatively and constructively with other people, to be open minded, develop points of view and to be willing to have these challenged, to question other viewpoints, and to understand and accept other cultures. We should encourage our students to learn how to listen to others, to work together in a team, and to learn to think creatively.

Lawyers of all types need library research skills, which are integral to the cognitive skills discussed above.[127] Writing skills are also important, particularly the ability to write clearly and concisely in a manner that confers advice, analysis or arguments in a rigorous but easily intelligible way.[128]

2.3.3 Objectives relating to values[129]

I have already argued that law cannot be considered merely as a closed formalistic, logical structure. Certain values and ideologies are built into legal doctrine, procedures, institutions and practice. Our individual responses to law and to the activities of lawyers are shaped by our personal attitudes and values. Accordingly we need to provide students with opportunities to explore these ideologies, attitudes and values, and to develop their own attitudes, values and interests in an environment that is not only supportive of this process, but also challenging and exciting. Students need to engage in activities that expose them to the legal culture they are exploring, so that they can experience for themselves the internal logic of law and of the forces that shape the law. We should ensure that they are able to 'think like lawyers' and at the same time to reflect on 'how lawyers think'.

We should also encourage our students to develop their own system of values pertaining to legal education, legal practice, and the role of law in regulating society's affairs. They should be able to develop and justify their own values about the law in a challenging but supportive learning environment. We should discuss our values openly with the class, so that students see us acting and thinking as 'reflective practitioners', but at the same time clearly understand that they should be developing their own values.

126 See Mack, K, 'Bringing Clinical Learning into a Conventional Classroom' (1993) 4 *Legal Education Review* 89.

127 Library research skills include the use of the array of computerised and non-computerised indices and digests now available to legal researchers.

128 For discussions of the development of legal writing skills, for example, Bean, K S 'Writing Assignments in Law School Classes' (1987) 37 *Legal Education Review* 609; Gordon, J D 'An Integrated First Year Legal Writing Program' (1985) 35 *Legal Education Review* 609; Clanchy (1988).

129 For a detailed discussion, see Le Brun and Johnstone (1994) 164-69.

We do have a role to play in inculcating basic values into our students. In particular we should be developing in students a commitment to promoting justice, and an appreciation of the responsibilities lawyers have to the community, the courts, and the profession.

2.3.4 Objectives relating to motivation for learning

One of our objectives as law teachers should be to motivate our students to learn, to explore all aspects of legal phenomena, and constructively to criticise legal rules, their application in practice, theories about the law, and legal education. We should inculcate in our students a continuing interest in the law, and a love of learning. We should facilitate the development of individual autonomy, and do all we can to enhance the ability of our students to make their own decisions about what they think and do.[130] Adult educators have argued that learning is an internal process, self-initiated and intrinsically motivated, and that the only learning which significantly influences behaviour is self-discovered, self-appropriated learning.[131] Students will be motivated to engage in learning if they perceive a personal goal that learning will help achieve. We should always ensure that our students see the relevance of the subject matter to their lives, concerns and interests.

Legal education should also involve freeing the learner from dependence upon traditional teaching methods, and enabling the learner to learn how to learn. But, as Chene notes, 'to know how to learn, one has to have learned ... [O]ne cannot rely on oneself unless the norms and limits of the learning activity are known'.[132] Before our students can direct their own learning, we have to introduce them to the tradition of knowledge.

The achievement of this motivational objective will require a radical change in law teaching methods. The traditional approach is very much one of teacher control over subject objectives, content, pace of learning, theoretical perspectives, teaching method and assessment. Self-directed learning involves students assuming a lot of the responsibility, control and initiative in relation to these things.[133] We and our students alike will have to liberate ourselves from the traditional model of teaching where we are the source of knowledge. Instead we will need to ensure that students achieve competence in assuming responsibility for their own learning.

2.3.5 Selecting and writing objectives

In this section so far, I have outlined a range of learning objectives in law. We need to express our chosen objectives for student learning clearly, succinctly,

130 See generally Boud (1988).

131 Caffarella, R S and O'Donnell, J M, 'Self-Directed Adult Learning: A Critical Paradigm Revisited' (1987) 37 *Adult Education Quarterly* 199, 206; Oddi, L F, 'Development and Validation of an Instrument to Identify Self-directed Continuing Learners' (1984) 36 *Adult Education Quarterly* 97-107; Tough, A, *The Adult's Learning Projects*, Ontario Institute for Studies in Education, Toronto, 1971, 11.

132 Chene, A, 'The Concept of Autonomy in Adult Education: A Philosophical Discussion' (1983) 34 *Adult Education Quarterly* 38, 42.

133 *Ibid* 40.

unambiguously, and in user-friendly language in our teaching materials, and in the classroom, so that students:

- are clear about the assumptions that underlie our teaching;
- can see that even the most complex tasks can be mastered one step at a time;
- can decide for themselves which part of the material needs the most attention; and
- know what they should be learning so that they can assess their own progress as they proceed through the subject.

We need to ensure that our students clearly understand what their learning objectives are, and how we understand the objectives. Because of the nature of academic learning, objectives for student learning are generally set by us when we design our subjects, and before we meet with our students. But that does not mean that we should not discuss with students in great detail what we understand by the learning objectives. We should seek to clarify student misconceptions of the learning goals, and if necessary and possible, modify the objectives after negotiation with our students to ensure that they understand and are committed to the objectives.

Objectives will be less effective if they are superficial: for example, our students will be none the wiser if we simply rewrite syllabus topics in the language of objectives. Similarly, objectives should not be vague. Superficial or vague objectives will only encourage surface learning. Objectives therefore should indicate specific expectations about the competencies students should be striving to achieve. They should not just concentrate on facts or procedures, but should include the understanding of key concepts and the development of complex skills. They are the framework within which students work, and therefore must be continually reinforced throughout the subject, in the curriculum, teaching methods and assessment regime for the subject.

We will probably need to specify overall subject objectives, and then sub-objectives for each topic within the subject. When specifying learning objectives, it is best not to use words such as 'understand', 'know', 'appreciate', 'be familiar with', 'learn the basics of' because these expressions do not convey to students sufficient detail about what they are expected to do. Rather use words like 'explain how', 'describe', 'discuss', 'show that', 'give examples of', 'evaluate', 'analyse,' 'carry out', 'demonstrate', and 'summarise'.[134]

A well structured law course should enable students to meet a wide range of the objectives that I have outlined in this section, both in and outside class, in teaching materials designed for independent learning, in their choice of essays and other assessment, and in daily interaction with other students. Without an informed, careful and skilled selection and utilisation of teaching methods and media in law classes (including teaching materials) it is unlikely that we or our students will be able to work towards these broader objectives.

We should ensure that the assessment in our subject is closely integrated with the objectives of the subject, and its teaching methods. Our assessment should measure the achievement of the goals of the subject.

---

134 For advice on how to write objectives in printed teaching materials, see Rowntree (1990) 44-47; Rowntree (1994) 49-56; and Race (1992) 47-50.

2.4 THE IMPORTANT ROLE OF ASSESSMENT[135]

As I have already suggested, in the discussion of relational perspectives on student learning in section 2.1, our forms of assessment in our subjects play an extremely significant role in shaping the way in which our students will go about learning our subject. Unless our assessment methods reinforce, and measure the achievement of, our learning objectives, and are integrated with our teaching methods and materials, our students are unlikely to engage in the kind of learning that we envisage for them when we design our subject. This point is cogently expressed by Rowntree:[136]

> 'If we wish to discover the truth about an educational system, we must look to its assessment procedures. What student qualities and achievements are actively valued and rewarded by the system? How are its purposes and intentions realized? To what extent are the hopes and ideals, aims and objectives professed by the system ever truly perceived, valued and striven for by those who make their way within it? The answers to such questions are to be found in what the system requires students to do in order to survive and prosper. The spirit and style of student assessment defines the *de facto* curriculum.'

Rowntree envisages assessment as a process in which formally or informally we find out about our students, in the sense of obtaining and interpreting information about their knowledge and understanding, or their abilities and attitudes. But he notes that students also assess each other, particularly when they work together in team, and that assessment can involve students finding out about themselves (self-assessment).[137] He suggests at least six purposes of assessment:[138]

- As a basis for selecting candidates for educational or employment opportunities. We use high school grades and other criteria to decide which students to admit to law school, and law firms use law school grades and other factors in making employment decisions.
- To maintain standards within an institution. For example, law schools may want to ensure that current students are performing at the same standard or better than students in the past.
- To motivate or encourage students to learn, a 'carrot-stick inducement system'.[139]
- To provide feedback to students. Feedback is the 'lifeblood of learning',[140] and enables each student to identify her or his strengths and weaknesses and to remedy weaknesses and build on strengths.

135 The discussion in this section is drawn principally from Rowntree, D, *Assessing Our Students. How Shall We Know Them?*, Revised edition, Kogan Page, London, 1987; Ramsden (1992) ch 10; Le Brun and Johnstone (1994) 177-226; Boud, D, *Implementing Student Self-Assessment*, HERDSA Green Guide No 5, Kensington, 1986; and Crooks, T J, *Assessing Student Performance*, HERDSA Green Guide No 8, Kensington, 1988.

136 Rowntree (1987) 1.

137 *Ibid* 5.

138 *Ibid* ch 2.

139 *Ibid* 23.

140 *Ibid* 24.

- To provide feedback to us on how well we have taught. We can learn whether we have successfully explained concepts, given students sufficient opportunities to develop and practice skills, and so on. If we know which parts of the subject students find difficult, we can revise our teaching to improve student learning.
- To prepare students for the formal and informal assessment they will encounter later on in life. For example, in their working lives our students will be subjected to continual assessment by their employers in law firms, the public service, universities, or in other forms of employment.

This list of purposes of assessment shows that when we develop teaching materials we need to make sure that we have a flexible and well designed assessment regime which at the bare minimum provides us and our students with good feedback on their progress and motivates students to strive to achieve the learning objectives for the subject. We should devise our assessment regimes so that the forms of assessment encourage our students to take deep approaches to learning the subject matter. We must ensure that our assessment is seen by our students to be an intrinsic part of their learning, and not something which is only done after teaching and learning. Figure 2 provides a very simple model of how we might envisage assessment as an integral part of teaching. It shows how assessment tasks should be integrated into our teaching strategies, so that students: continually get feedback on their learning (formative assessment); we receive information about the effectiveness of our teaching which we can use to modify our teaching strategies to improve student learning; and students can be graded (summative assessment) on a variety of assessment tasks which are central to their learning.

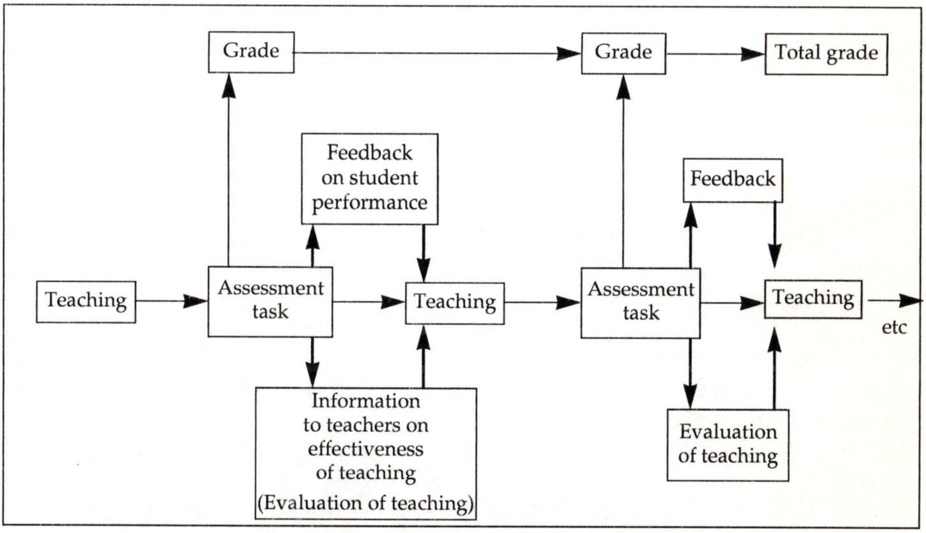

Figure 2: Assessment as an integral part of teaching – based on Rowntree (1987)

If our students see their assessment as an external imposition to be negotiated in order to earn a grade, rather than as a way of learning and of demonstrating understanding, they will be tempted into surface approaches to learning. Assessment is a way of teaching more effectively through expressing clearly to students the goals of the curriculum; through understanding exactly what students know and don't know; and through diagnosing specific misunderstandings in order to help students learn more effectively. Assessment should focus on the significant processes of competence. We need to ensure that our assessment procedures encourage and reward the learning acts and outcomes that we desire. The choice of assessment should ensure that students actively engage in tasks, and have the opportunity to demonstrate how much they understand. We should continually ask ourselves the key question which guides the choice and design of assessment: 'what effect on the outcomes of student learning will this particular form of assessment have'? We should discuss our expectations and criteria for each piece of assessment in detail with our students, and should ensure that our assessment methods minimise student anxiety. It is unlikely that we will find a single method of assessment that satisfies all our educational objectives.[141]

I emphasised earlier in section 2.1 the importance of providing our students with feedback and encouraging them to assess their own performance during our subjects. When students answer questions posed in our teaching materials, or when they undertake activities in the materials, they need feedback which tells them whether they have provided a 'good' answer or performance. If they did not perform at the required level, or had difficulty in understanding the task, they require information to help them work out what they need to do to improve their understanding or performance so that next time they can answer the question or engage in the activity at the required standard. We should design assessment regimes which provide students with continual feedback, and which make use of a variety of formal and informal methods, including problem-based examination questions; short answer examinations; essays; fieldwork reports of, for example, an observation of an aspect of the legal process; student presentations; quizzes in class; simulations; self-assessment; assessments based on group work and so on. The more stimulating and greater the variety in the activities and the feedback, the less chance there is that students will distort or skip the activities and the formative (that is, giving feedback) assessment tasks.[142]

At the outset we should distinguish self-assessment, self-marking, and collaborative assessment.[143] In self-assessment students set the criteria for their performance, and then measure themselves against the criteria. In self-marking, students use criteria set by the teacher to gauge their own progress. Collaborative assessment involves the teacher and student negotiating the final grade on the basis of their different evaluations of the student's work. We should also remember that self-assessment or self-marking can be used principally or solely to ensure that students get good feedback on their work

141 See generally Ramsden (1992) ch 10.

142 Race (1992) 57.

143 See Le Brun and Johnstone (1994) 190.

(formative assessment), rather than for the purposes of grading (summative assessment).

One method we can use to ensure that students get regular feedback is to devise self-assessment or self-diagnostic questions and problems in teaching materials designed to enable students to keep a close check on their own learning. These are not included to provide us with information about students but rather to provide students with information about their own learning so that they can plan further independent study. Students stop to answer carefully drafted self-assessment questions at strategic points in the text, or at the end of the text, and in that way monitor their own learning. The self-assessment questions provide advice through which students actively and reflectively engage with the materials, rather than simply reading passively. Self-assessment questions may require a written response from the student, or may require students to check through a previous section, interpret data, synthesise previous learning, apply previous learning or simply think about the topic. We might also include questions which ask students directly to assess how well they think they understand a topic, or how well they have developed the skills they are learning. For example, we can ask students to indicate three aspects of the subject in which they believe they have performed well, and three aspects in which they believe they can improve. They should then set out a program to guide their efforts towards self-improvement.

We should provide students with more direct feedback to facilitate self-assessment. We can include answers in the text, immediately after the question or at the end of the section. Answers enable students to check that they are on the right track, and can include remedial advice or refer the student to other materials (in the materials or in new sources) where the basis of the answer can be found. Feedback can also be provided in class, through class discussion, small group work, moots, or standardised feedback sheets.

Teaching should involve the teaching of self-assessment. We need to design our teaching strategies to provide our students with coaching and practice in ways which help them to develop self-regulatory skills to reflect on their performance. Students should set incremental standards by which they can judge their own achievement, and develop self-direction to achieve higher performance levels.[144] We might set tasks in the teaching materials and suggest that students perform the tasks until they think they are sufficiently competent to move on to the next task.[145] Students should write about their approach to a problem, the questions that are raised, and the explanations for their solutions.[146]

We should also provide assessment situations in which the student participates in group activity. Performance in a social setting where students contribute to a task and assist others encourages them to develop and question their definitions of competence. The student can observe how others reason, and receive feedback on his or her own efforts. Not only performance, but the way in which students adapt to help and guidance, can be assessed.

144 Glaser (1991).

145 See the discussion of mastery learning in Le Brun and Johnstone (1994) 246-48.

146 Glaser (1991).

We should maximise the opportunities for our students to receive peer feedback, by giving our students opportunities to discuss their different approaches to the tasks, and to determine for themselves which might be the best approaches. We can also use peer-assessment and peer-marking to generate feedback for students. In peer-assessment students develop criteria which they use to assess the work of their peers, and in peer-marking students use criteria established by the teacher to assess a peer's work. Peer-marking and peer-assessment are best used for formative (diagnostic feedback) assessment. To ensure its most effective use, we should discuss openly and honestly with the class the process to be used in peer-assessment or – marking, and should make sure that students are comfortable with the process and participate constructively.

There is not the space in this book to explore all aspects of assessment which influence the way in which students will use teaching materials. In this section I have simply highlighted the key points that we should take into account when we design our materials. In particular we should be aware of the different functions of assessment, and the way in which student learning will be heavily shaped by the summative assessment tasks (that is, assessment for grading purposes) we set students. If we do not integrate the activities in our materials with the assessment tasks we have set for students, students are unlikely to take the kinds of deep approaches to learn that we would like them to take. I have also pointed to the importance of providing opportunities for feedback in the materials. I have stressed the need to involve students in self-assessment activities. I will return to this theme in Part 3 of the book.

2.5 STRUCTURING THE SUBJECT

One point emerging from the discussion of teaching and learning in section 2.1 of this book is that an important factor in the success or failure of a subject is its structure.[147] The design of the syllabus is an important factor in promoting or hindering deep approaches to learning.[148] Students are unlikely to take deep approaches to learning unless they are clear about the structure of the subject, the subject is pitched at the right level for them,[149] they can identify with the subject matter and see its relevance for them, and they have a well developed base of knowledge upon which to build in the new subject. In this section I briefly set out some simple principles to guide us when we structure the syllabus in our subjects.

We need to have a vision of our subject as a whole, with a 'narrative drive'[150] or broad flow of ideas which provides a coherent but flexible framework. We must ensure that we give our students 'the big picture' of our subject, outlining the key issues, questions and problems in the subject, and giving students a structure to negotiate the language of the subject and its

147 See again the discussion of the importance of students' apprehending the structure of a topic in section 2.1 above.

148 See pp 8 to 13 above.

149 Hence the need to know who our students are – see again the beginning of section 2.2.

150 Rowntree (1991) 61.

concepts. We need to display the structure of the subject so that students look for the intended meaning of the subject, and can focus on the central argument and concepts; relate and distinguish evidence and argument; and organise and structure the content into a coherent whole.[151]

A key feature of a well designed syllabus is that it should not be too long. Students should be able to get through the material specified in the syllabus using deep approaches to learning. When we design the content, we should consider what is essential to our subject. If we wish to focus not just on developing student knowledge, but on legal skills and on the exploration of attitudes and values,[152] we will have to reduce the substantive content of the subject. One way of doing this is to imagine what we would include in the subject if it was only half of its actual length – which are core concepts and principles are at the heart of the subject? We will find that 'less is more', because the ideas that remain in the subject are qualitatively different to those that we started with.[153] We should focus on the underlying principles and key concepts in our subject (rather than on too much surplus detail), and on the links between the different principles and concepts in the subject and on the way in which the concepts in our subject relate to the concepts in other subjects.

We must be able to justify on educational grounds (based on the subject aims and objectives) every topic and activity set out in the subject syllabus. There is no fixed and immutable content for any law subject. Even though many subjects have to comply with the requirements of the various professional legal bodies, and even though many subjects traditionally have a certain content, there are many possible ways of putting together a curriculum. In addition to any professional requirements, we should take into account some or all of the following factors:

- workload;
- the broad range of learning objectives outlined in section 2.3 above;
- topics of relevance and interest to students;
- theoretical and social issues that can be explored in the subject;
- topics that lend themselves to exciting new teaching methods or materials;
- possible alternative curricula eschewing male and other forms of dominant cultural biases of most law subjects;[154]

151 See pp 19 to 20, and 28, above.

152 See section 2.3 above.

153 See Le Brun and Johnstone (1994) 268.

154 See Graycar, R and Morgan, J, *The Hidden Gender of Law*, Federation Press, Sydney, 1990, chs 1 and 2; and Graycar, R and Morgan, J, 'Including Gender Issues in the Core Law Curriculum', a paper given at the 'Women, Culture and Universities: A Chilly Climate' Conference, University of Technology, Sydney, 19 and 20 April 1995. In 1995-96 the Federal government's Department of Education, Employment and Training is funding five projects (based at Griffith University/Southern Cross University; the Australian National University/La Trobe University; the University of Western Sydney; the University of Wollongong; and The University of Melbourne) which will produce cross cultural teaching materials in a number of core law subjects, and manuals and other guides to developing such materials.

- the relation of the subject to other subjects that our students have previously studied; and
- simple or complex skills that can be developed in that subject.

When we develop subjects for the law school curriculum we might move away from traditional subjects such as Tort, Contract, Criminal Law and Property, and focus instead on themes or issues: such as work, violence or citizenship.[155] Focusing on issues has the advantage of enabling students to learn how to integrate empirical material, case studies, theoretical themes, and doctrine from different parts of the traditional law curriculum. As Graycar and Morgan point out,[156] such a focus also helps students to understand how violence might be relevant to a legal dispute over, for example, property, rather than simply in relation to the criminal law; or that women's work in the home might need to be valued in a claim against a deceased person's estate in the law of succession rather than simply in a labour law context. More fundamentally, traditional legal categories do not always reflect the way that women, people from non-English backgrounds, lesbians or gay men, or people with disabilities, lead their lives. Legal doctrines and traditional subject categorisations have been built up by heterosexual men, by reference to their own experiences.[157] It is the construction of law and legal categories that we should see as the problem, rather than the place in our legal system of women, people from non-English speaking backgrounds, lesbians and gay men, or people with disabilities. Graycar and Morgan argue that the narrowness of doctrinal categories can serve to exclude a wide range of problems from legal analysis:

> 'Practising lawyers have always known that people's lives do not readily fit into legal categories, yet this has often not been reflected in a legal system which fragments its treatment of people's problems into categories such as tort, crime, family law etc. This fragmentation into narrowly bounded categories is supported by the structure and practice of law, and by textbooks and law school courses which replicate and reinforce those divisions.'[158]

Consequently the definition of legal problems, the categorisation of legal issues, and the development of legal solutions to these problems and issues, may have to cross traditional doctrinal boundaries.[159] We should also be careful not to ignore issues of class and power in our subjects. People may fail to use legal rules or invoke legal processes for reasons which include fear of the repercussions of litigation, lack of resources, lack of education or knowledge, or lack of confidence in the legal system's ability to deal with their perspectives. In seeking the causes of this powerlessness we should not confine our focus to issues of gender, sexual preference, race, ethnicity or disability.

Similarly, the basic principle for sequencing topics is that the sequence has a favourable effect on student learning. We should not simply follow the way in which an expert in the subject matter would sequence the topic (in a textbook

155 See Graycar and Morgan (1995).

156 *Ibid*.

157 *Ibid* Graycar and Morgan (1990) ch 1.

158 Graycar and Morgan (1995) at 4-5.

159 For example, see Dahl, Tove Stang, *Women's Law: An Introduction to Feminist Jurisprudence*, Norwegian University Press, Oslo, 1988; Graycar and Morgan (1990).

for example), but should rather develop a sequence conducive to promoting student learning because the logic of an expert may not facilitate learning by students. The ideas that students encounter early in the subject should help, and not hinder, their later learning.[160]

We should design the opening topics to ease students into the subject and enable them to develop an interest and enthusiasm for the subject. The subject should concentrate on building up understanding from a few basic ideas. We should always consider which concepts or skills are pre-requisites for the understanding of later concepts or the development of later skills, and sequence the subject based on that reasoning. There is also no reason why students should learn concepts first and then apply them to problems. As we have seen in section 2.1, students can start learning by being exposed to a real world problem, and then build up their understanding of the relevant concepts from there. This is simply an application of the principles of situated learning and problem-based learning,[161] and can enable students to avoid artificial divisions between doctrine, theory and practice.[162] For example, we may start building the subject on an interesting and topical case study or problem, or on what students already know, from their common sense or personal experience, or from previous subjects.

Rowntree has identified different ways of sequencing topics within subjects. These include:[163]

- *Topic by topic*, where, after an introduction to the overall purpose of the subject, the subject comprises related themes or topics which can be studied in any order. For example, a subject on advanced issues in tort law may consist of a number of discrete topics which can be tackled in any number of sequences.
- *Chronological sequence*, where happenings or events are presented in the order in which they occurred, because an understanding of any particular stage depends on what happened previously. For instance, a jurisprudence subject may be sequenced to capture the way in which ideas about law developed historically, in the context of broader philosophical, political, cultural, social and technological developments.
- *Structural logic*, where the sequence is dictated by the logical structure of the subject. In most subjects, some topics cannot be learned without prior understanding of some other topic.
- *Problem-centred sequence*, where the subject (or topic) is structured around exploring a problem or issue. This facilitates problem-based learning. Once we have introduced the problem, we can engage our students in developing solutions. For example, in a socio-legal research subject, we can ask our students to think of a research topic, and then facilitate their attempts to learn how to develop a research question, appropriate research methods,

160 Rowntree (1991) 61.

161 See the discussion of these concepts in section 2.1.

162 See pp 13 to 19 and 22 to 24, above.

163 See Rowntree, D, *Developing Courses for Students*, Paul Chapman Publishing Ltd, London, 1981, ch 2; Rowntree (1994) 93-100; and Rowntree (1990) 61-71.

and ways of linking their observations to broader theoretical issues and frameworks.

- *Spiral sequence*, where our students meet a concept again and again as they work through the subject, but each time they consider the concept at a more complex level. For example, in a workplace health and safety and the law subject, we can introduce our students to the basic regulatory model by exploring the weaknesses of the traditional model of regulating workplace health and safety, and then considering the recommendations of the British Robens Report of 1972[164] which outlines the basic model. Students then return to the different aspects of the model as they explore each aspect of standard setting and enforcement. Finally they engage in a critical evaluation of the strengths and weaknesses of the model.
- *Backward chaining*, which is best used whenever objectives involve students learning sequences of activities or decision-making. In an introductory subject which teaches students how to find legal materials in a library, we might start by teaching students the final step in the chain, and then the second last step and so on, until students have worked backwards through the whole process. Rowntree suggests that this sequencing enables students to master the final stage of the task at the beginning of their learning, and motivates them to learn further because they can see the relevance of each new step that they come to learn.[165]

Whatever sequence we choose it should be the most satisfying psychological order for students,[166] which may not be the most logical order. The next step is to identify the main topics and their order. Within each topic we will then develop a sequence of teaching points, or the main statements (definitions, relationships, critical analyses etc) we want to make about each topic. Once we have got this far with the design of our subject, we are in a position to think about what teaching methods we will use to teach each topic. Because this book is about the way in which we can use printed materials as a focus for our teaching, I will return to this discussion of how to structure a topic in Part 3,[167] in the context of structuring teaching materials. But before we can narrow our discussion to teaching materials, we need to see teaching materials in the context of the range of teaching methods available for us to use in and outside the classroom.

2.6 TEACHING METHODS

Once we have considered the characteristics of our students, negotiated the aims and learning objectives for our subject, determined how to assess the subject, and have sequenced the topics within the subject, we are in a position to determine the most appropriate teaching venues and methods for the subject. We have a number of teaching venues and methods to choose from, some more

164 *Report of the Committee on Safety and Health at Work 1970-72*, HMSO, London, 1972.

165 Rowntree (1990) 66.

166 *Ibid*.

167 See table 5 on p 84.

conducive to student participation, to the development of values and attitudes, or oral, interpersonal, writing, research or intellectual skills than others. There are no hard and fast rules as to how we should select the appropriate teaching methods and venues. Our aim should be to consider how best to use the different venues and methods for student learning to achieve the established objectives. The venues are essentially:

- the classroom;
- private study of teaching materials and other sources such as textbooks;
- computer-aided instruction;[168] and
- venues away from the classroom that do not involve the private study of teaching materials or computers. For example, we can require our students to do field work, such as visiting the courts, government departments or a lawyer's office, or engaging in participant observation, interviews, or reading files or official statistics.

We need to integrate the kinds of student learning that our students can undertake in these different venues. We may, for example, want to introduce the topic in a large class. We could give a brief overview of the topic, and then outline the work that our students will need to cover in the teaching materials. Our students will then work through the teaching materials outside class time. They might also engage in some fieldwork (visit a tribunal, interview an enforcement agency, examine contractual documents at a particular venue) or work with a computer-based learning program or simulation. We might structure subsequent classroom activities to allow students to discuss their activities with the materials (or in the field or with the computer), raise difficulties and problems, get feedback on their progress (from their peers and from us) and to develop the knowledge and skills introduced to them by the teaching materials. We can allocate these classroom activities between large classes and smaller seminars or tutorials. We could also require students to do further learning with materials, a computer or in the field.

In this book I will concentrate on two venues for learning, printed teaching materials and classroom teaching methods which do not involve anything more than simple technology (overhead projectors and whiteboards). We can introduce topics in the classroom using any one of the methods outlined below, and then require students to engage in activity-based learning outside class, so that the next class can be devoted to activities which build on this out of class learning. We can integrate our students' work with teaching materials with our classroom activities by indicating in the materials (and in our introductory mini-lecture) just how the activities in the materials will be followed up in class. Our students can then focus their learning on the use that will be made of the material in class. They will understand the basic criteria of performance required of them, and will be able to monitor their out of class learning against the likely use of their learning in class.

In this section I will discuss a range of classroom methods which can be used together with teaching materials to enable students to take deep

168 See generally Laurillard (1993).

approaches to learning about law. In Part 3 I examine ways of developing teaching materials which will promote and facilitate this type of learning. In Part 4 I provide examples of teaching materials that are consistent with the theories and principles discussed in this book, and show how these materials can be integrated with classroom teaching methods.

As we have seen from the discussion in section 2.1 of this book, the best classroom methods are those that enable students to take deep approaches to learning the subject matter. Teaching is too complex an activity for a book like this to provide rules as to what methods should be used in classroom teaching. There are a variety of teaching methods, each with its own advantages and disadvantages, strengths and weaknesses.[169] This section provides some examples of classroom methods that might be used in conjunction with printed teaching materials.

2.6.1 The lecture

A lecture is a period of 'largely uninterrupted discourse from a teacher with no discussion from students and no student activity other than listening and note taking'.[170]

Strengths

Lecturing may be useful for achieving some cognitive objectives, particularly for imparting a small amount of information quickly and concisely. Amongst other things we can use a lecture to

- give students on overview of a topic or an introduction to an activity;
- pull together or summarise the salient points of a class discussion or similar activity;
- model a particular approach to a problem or issue;
- explain (and perhaps simplify) difficult points in a topic;
- convey otherwise unavailable information;
- discuss our own experiences to illustrate the topic; and
- stimulate enthusiasm and interest in a topic.

Limitations

The lecture method may encourage student passivity, and provides little opportunity for students actively to engage with the topic. Its usefulness is limited because it relies wholly on the oral skills of the lecturer and the aural and recording skills of the student. It appears from research that student attention declines after the first few minutes of a lecture, and that after 20 minutes most students lose concentration. When we lecture we get little feedback from students as to how they are learning.

169 For a fuller discussion of these methods, see Le Brun and Johnstone (1994) chs 5 and 6.

170 Gibbs, Habeshaw and Habeshaw (1987) xi.

Tips for use

We should generally only give a 'mini lecture' of no more than 20 minutes before or after some other method is used, and principally use the strengths of the method as outlined above.[171] The characteristics of a good mini lecture are:

- clarity;
- enthusiasm;
- expressiveness;
- good preparation;
- a clear and logical structure;
- the use of visual aids such as overhead slides, whiteboards, videos etc.

Example

We could use a mini lecture to introduce the topic in the materials, and to motivate and inspire our students to work with the materials. In the following class we could pull together the salient points in the teaching materials, and set up an activity or problem solving exercise based on teaching materials which students have studied on their own before coming to class. Alternatively we could model an expert approach to a problem or issue in the materials, so that students can see for themselves how they should tackle the issue or problem.

2.6.2 Class discussion

Class discussion comes in many forms,[172] and can be led by us or by our students. We can:

- ask members of the class to answer specific or general questions, and prompt further discussion with questions or comments;
- engage in a 'Socratic dialogue' where we guide students through an exploration of a question or issue, exposing their lack of knowledge, and helping them construct new knowledge;[173]
- ask students to give a short paper to the class and then lead the ensuing discussion;
- leave students to run the class without our interference, or even without our presence.

Strengths

Amongst other things, class discussion enables students to:

- find out how much they know by contributing their own opinions, and listening to the views of others;
- explore a subject from many angles by hearing the views of others;

171 *Ibid* 101.

172 See generally Dillon, J T, *Using Discussion in Classrooms*, Open University Press, Buckingham and Philadelphia, 1994.

173 See generally Le Brun and Johnstone (1994) 282-86.

- question and probe;
- respond to issues raised in the materials and to clarify difficulties;
- ask for feedback or comments from other students or from us on the work they have done before coming to class;
- develop skills of critical thinking; and
- apply previously learned materials.

Limitations

Most of us are familiar with some of the difficulties with class discussion:

- uncertainty about the objectives of class discussion;
- rambling, directionless and aimless discussions;
- lack of student preparation;
- too much talk from us, and not enough from students;
- a small group of students monopolising the discussion;
- our inability to keep discussion on track; or
- ill-framed, boring or monotonous questions for discussion.

Tips for use

We should:

- prepare our materials keeping in mind their use in class discussion;
- use questions in the materials to focus students' reading on the issues or problems to be discussed or followed up in class;
- ensure that all our students have an opportunity to contribute, and to keep the discussion focused on the topic, and moving at an appropriate pace;
- draw out quieter students and prevent the more aggressive, insensitive or vociferous students from dominating the class;
- use a variety of questions so that students develop different skills during discussion;[174] and
- be prepared to reveal our own values, experiences and interests so that students are encouraged to do the same.

Example

We can use class discussion to individualise general feedback on assignments completed in the teaching materials. We can give a written and/or oral 'solution' to the assignment or problem, and enable students to individualise the feedback by raising particular issues relating to the assignment and the feedback.

We could also ask from one to three students to take particular responsibility for presenting the material to be discussed in a particular class, and to lead and stimulate the ensuing discussion. We must ensure that the

174 See the different types of questions discussed at pp 95 to 96.

presenting students develop the material in some way, so that they do not merely paraphrase what the other students have already read.

2.6.3 Small group work

A most effective teaching method is small group work, where we organise our students into groups of two to six. We then ask each group to engage in an activity, such as solving a problem, answering a question, or devising a research program. We can conclude the activity by asking each group to report to the full class and/or by leading the full class in a discussion of the activity.

Strengths

Small group work enables each member of the class to participate in the activity. The greatest strength of small groups is that they encourage active learning. Quiet students have an opportunity to contribute. As Brown, Collins and Duguid observe,[175] group learning enables:

- collective problem solving in which groups put together the individual knowledge of their members, and can lead to insights and solutions that would not otherwise come about;
- students to understand and play the many different roles needed to carry out a task, and to reflect productively upon their performance;
- the teacher and students to draw out, confront and discuss misconceptions in their learning and ineffective problem solving strategies; and
- students to learn collaborative work skills which may not be developed if students only work on their own.

This suggests that small groups are ideal for problem solving. Our students get a chance to explore a problem and to develop an approach to it. We can ask groups to analyse a certain issue or doctrine, or to put together an argument. We can use small group work to enable our students to prepare for other type of activities – such as moots, debates, and role plays. Above all, small groups develop team work and communication skills.

Limitations

Small group work can be time consuming, particularly if activities are not well planned and organised. We can abuse small groups if we use them without a clear purpose. If students are under-prepared or are not clear about the requirements of the task, they may not be able to engage in the activity. Individual students may dominate the group, impeding the learning opportunities of other members. We might also find that students do not do what we want them to do in small groups, but talk idly amongst themselves about social or other matters.

Tips for use

To ensure that students work well in small groups, we must ensure that:

175 Brown, Collins and Duguid (1989a) 40. For a detailed discussion of group learning, see Jacques (1991).

- the chosen task will enable students to achieve the required learning objectives;
- the task can be achieved within the time allotted;
- we give clear instructions so that students know exactly what they are required to do. We should record our instructions and other details of the task in a handout, in our materials, or on an overhead slide or the board;
- we ask the members of each group to elect a spokesperson before they begin the task;
- we keep an eye on each group so that we can provide assistance to groups in need of help or inspiration; and
- we leave enough time to hear reports from each group, provide feedback, and conclude the activity.

We can use small groups very effectively in large classes. The only compromise may be that not every group gets a chance to report back to the class. We can hear the contributions of a few groups, and then ask the other groups if they raised any points which have not been covered by the previous reporters. Alternatively, groups can report to each other, a variation on pyramiding, which I will discuss later in this section.

We might also establish small groups to operate outside the classroom. We might require, or encourage, our students to establish small self-study groups which work through the materials or meet to review the fruits of each student's work on the materials. The group can then list issues which it does not feel it has fully understood, to provide the basis of full class discussion, or a mini lecture by the teacher. This use of self-study groups gives students an opportunity to take responsibility for, and manage, their own learning.

We can set up permanent small groups in which the same students work together over a long period of time, inside and outside class, to solve a problem or on some other project.

Example

We can use small groups in class to enable students to develop the learning they have gained from self-study materials. We can give each group carefully designed questions to assist students to talk through the issues raised in the materials. For example, our students could:

- discuss their responses to a problem or case study;
- explain to each other diagrams or basic frameworks for the study of the subject, evaluate the material from a critical perspective (for example, feminism, law and economics, Marxist jurisprudence and so on);
- talk about their own values and attitudes in relation to the issues.[176]

The key to the success of such exercises is the careful development and preparation of the teaching materials and the classroom activities. We should prepare our materials with the classroom exercises in mind.

176 See the different types of questions discussed at pp 95 to 96, below.

We might also use small groups to give our students feedback on assignments they have completed or problems they have solved as part of their working through the teaching materials. For example, we can distribute general points for discussion which provide the framework for feedback and a solution to the assignment. Small group discussion, even involving only two students, can focus on a particular assignment and individualise our general feedback. Our students can discuss difficulties they may have had working through the teaching materials, and can crystallise issues of common concern to be discussed with their peers or with us.

2.6.4 Pyramiding (sometimes called 'Snowball groups')

This method involves students in class first working alone, then in pairs, then in fours, and so on.[177] The normal conclusion to the exercise is to ask each final group to report on their deliberations and conclusions. This process is illustrated in Figure 3.

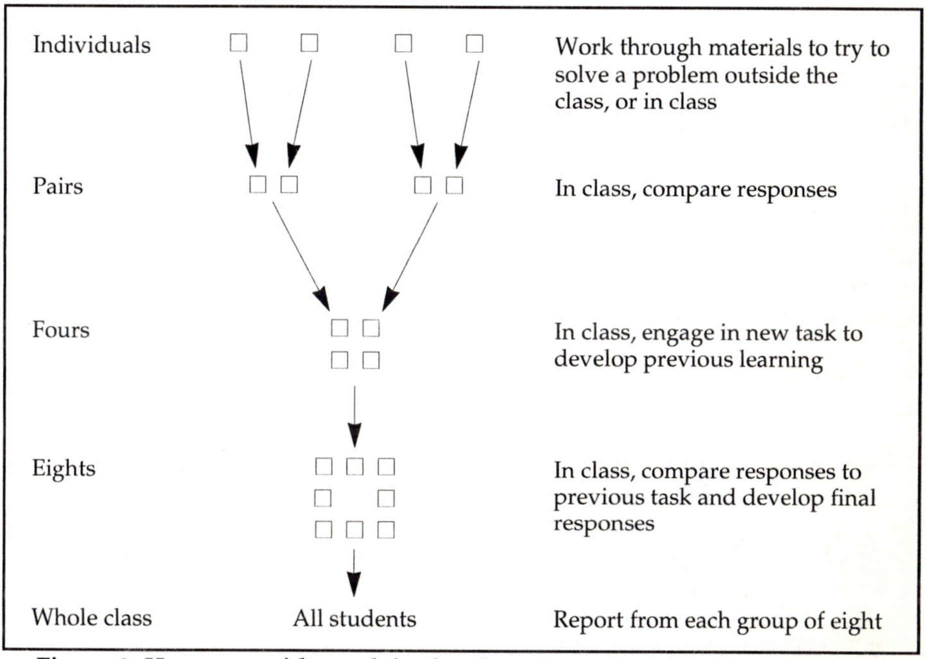

Figure 3: How pyramids work in the classroom – based on Jacques (1991)

Strengths

Pyramids have all the advantages of small groups, and enable a high level of student participation. In addition, they enable us to use class time to explore the nuances, assumptions and issues raised by teaching materials. As students get

177 See generally Northedge, A, 'Learning through Discussion in the Open University' (1975) 2 *Teaching at a Distance* 10.

into larger groups they find that their assumptions and solutions to the problem are challenged by other students who have dealt with the same issue but alone or in a different pair. Students quickly begin to see that there are different approaches, assumptions and value judgments involved in the task they have been set. Students learn how to develop well integrated ideas. Pyramiding enables the group to tackle tasks that are extremely daunting and complex to students if attempted in one go. Pyramiding makes complex tasks more manageable, especially when each stage is accompanied by a progressively more complex and demanding task which builds on the achievement of the previous stage. Students can focus on creative responses to the task, without worrying about avoiding being chosen to report immediately to the whole class, but with enough of a social obligation to produce an outcome so that they can report to their neighbour. The quality of the reporting to the whole class is likely to improve once students have rehearsed the ideas in small groups, have already spoken in a group, and are able to feel that they are not directly responsible for the ideas generated by the group.

Limitations

Pyramids are time consuming, and can break up the cohesive feeling of some classes. We need to plan our use of pyramids very carefully, lest they become directionless, or the questions or activities do not flow on from each other.

Tips for use

Pyramids are most effectively used when there are different instructions to students working on their own, and then in pairs, and then in the larger group of four or more. This enables all the basic steps of problem solving to be worked out by the time the larger group tries to deal with the problem.

Example

We can ask students individually to examine an issue posed in the teaching materials. In class, we can ask pairs of students to compare notes, form a basic agreement about the important points, and begin to resolve the issue without expecting to complete the task. We can ask each pair to team up with another pair, so that each pair explains to the other what they have done thus far, and compares their approaches. The group of four students then sets about resolving the problem. After the time allotted for this task has expired, the whole group comes together in one session, and we ask one group of four to explain their answer to the problem or question. We then ask the other groups whether they took a different approach, and discuss these different approaches in the plenary session.[178]

2.6.5 Peer learning and co-operative learning

Here students learn by teaching their peers. A particularly effective method is the 'Learning Cell' developed by Marcel Goldschmid.[179] It involves co-

178 For an example of this see Gibbs, Habeshaw, and Habeshaw (1987) 123-124.

179 Goldschmid, M L, 'The Learning Cell: An Instructional Innovation' (1971) 2 *Learning and Development* 1-6.

operative learning in pairs in which students alternate in asking and answering questions on materials they have both read. Students prepare by reading assigned materials and while so doing they write out questions dealing with the major points raised in the assigned reading or in other related materials. At the beginning of the class students are randomly assigned to pairs. One of the pair begins by asking the first question. The second student answers the question, and if necessary is corrected or is given additional information. Then the second student puts a question to the first student, and the process continues. While this occurs, we move from pair to pair, giving feedback and asking and answering questions. We can use the method in very large classes.

Strengths

It has been shown that the process of teaching a peer produces significantly better student performances in the peer 'teacher' than learning by seminar, discussion, independent study through the use of essays, straight forward reading, or being taught by a peer with or without reading.[180] The effectiveness of the method is attributed to the fact that in preparing to teach, students involve themselves in deeper study.[181]

Limitations

As with all intensive small group work, the process is time consuming. We need to supervise the process to ensure its success. We may need to train our students to use the method effectively. Not all our students may be good at using this method.

Tips for use

We will need to spend time with our students explaining how the process works, and perhaps modelling the activity with another teacher or with a student. We should develop our teaching materials with this method in mind, and provide appropriate prompts, guides and questions in the materials to make the exercise easier for inexperienced students.

We can vary the procedure, by requiring each of the pair to read different materials. Each then has the task of 'teaching' the other the essentials of her or his readings, and asks the person being taught prepared questions.

Example

In a mini lecture we explain to our students that they will learn the next topic using peer learning. We ask each student to read the same part of the materials, and to ensure that they are able to provide a brief overview of the topic when they come to class, and that they have worked out the key questions and

180 Schirmerhorn, S, Goldschmid, M L and Shore, B S, 'Learning Basic Principles of Probability in Student Dyads: A Cross Age Comparison' (1975) 67 *Journal of Educational Psychology* 551; Annis, L F, 'The Process and Effects of Peer Tutoring' (1983) 2 *Human Learning* 39.

181 Bargh, H A and Schul, Y, 'On the Cognitive Benefits of Teaching' (1980) 72 *Journal of Educational Psychology* 593; Johnson, D W, Maruyama, G, Johnson, R, Nelson, D and Skon, L 'Effects of Cooperative, Competitive, and Individualistic Goal Structures on Achievement: A Meta Analysis' (1981) 89 *Psychological Bulletin* 47.

exercises to ask of a fellow student to develop the other student's learning. In class the pairs teach each other by outlining the overview, and then work through their questions and exercises.

2.6.6 'Brainstorming'

Brainstorming is a technique in creative thinking in which class members generate as many answers as possible to the question or problem raised by the teacher. We, or a student,[182] record the 'answers' on a whiteboard,[183] or overhead projector.

Strengths

We can use brainstorming to:

- generate ideas and new perspectives;
- develop a range of solutions to issues that students may have had difficulty with when they studied the teaching materials;
- generate a number of approaches to consider when studying the teaching materials;
- develop issues, themes or problems raised in teaching materials;
- embed topics within the experience and intuitive responses of students;
- wake up a sleepy group of students.

Limitations

If not properly used brainstorming can be simplistic and unproductive. We should also be aware that some students have difficulty in brainstorming topics.

Tips for use

When we use brainstorming we should ensure that we suspend critical judgments until all ideas are generated. What counts is the quantity of ideas – the more ideas there are, the more likely it is that there will be good ideas. The wilder the idea the better, and if it is possible to develop someone else's idea, so much the better. We must make sure that there is time to go through all the ideas generated, and to use the best ideas as a framework for the rest of the class.

Example

In a class on health and safety at work we can ask the class to generate a list of all the costs (to employers, workers, the community in general) that result from an injury, illness or fatality at work. Once all the suggestions are recorded, we discuss them all and fit them into a framework to launch a discussion of the legal regulation of workplace injury and disease.

---

182 This has the advantage of allowing the teacher to focus on generating answers.

183 Electronic copyboards are most useful in this context, as they enable copies of class contributions to be made and then distributed to the class.

2.6.7 'Simulations', 'role playing' and mooting

As I mentioned in the previous section, with simulations and role plays we provide situations for students to act out problems and issues and make decisions in activities which simulate or are based on the situations lawyers may have to deal with. A simulation is an exercise in which the participants work together within specified rules and within a scenario based on real life to achieve a particular objective. In a role play students explore personal interactions in a defined situation following the implicit rules of everyday life. Moots are a specific form of simulation in which we ask students to argue points of law before a simulated court.

Strengths

We might use simulations, role plays and moots to enable students to engage in an activity which develops their own private study on the internal logic or dynamics of a legal situation. The great advantage of simulations and role plays is that they enable students to experiment with new concepts and behaviour in situations which model the activities of lawyers. Students can 'learn by doing', and can integrate legal doctrine, their values and beliefs, and practical skills such as negotiating, drafting, arguing and investigating. Amongst other things, we can use simulations, role plays and moots to:

- introduce topics by illustrating, for example, how a transaction or process takes place;
- teach the practical implications of legal rules;
- expose students to ethical dilemmas;
- enable students to develop practical legal skills.

Disadvantages

Simulations and role plays are time consuming, and involve considerable preparation. Some students cannot see why they should be involved in these sorts of activities rather than more traditional ways of learning law. Others will be threatened by these activities, and will experience much stress. Students may also be concerned how they will be assessed, if at all, on their work in simulations, role plays and moots.

Tips for use

When we use simulations, moots and role plays we must ensure that:[184]

- our students understand why we are using these methods, and how they will help students to learn better;
- our students understand exactly what is expected of them in the activities;

184 Ingleby, R, 'Translation and the Divorce Lawyer: Simulating the Law and Society Interface' (1989) 1 *Legal Education Review* 237; Bergman, P, Sherr, A, and Burridge, R, 'Learning From Experience: Nonlegally-Specific Role Plays' (1989) 39 *Journal of Legal Education* 535; Brown (1984); Jacques (1991) 101-107; and Burg, E M, 'Clinic in the Classroom: A Step Toward Cooperation' (1987) 37 *Journal of Legal Education* 232.

- we give clear instructions to each student, so that each student fully understands her or his role and objectives in the activity;
- students have sufficient time to prepare for the activity in their private study, or in class (perhaps by discussing their tasks in small groups with other students);
- there is sufficient time to provide students with feedback on their activities, and to enable them to talk about the experience, what they learned from it, and their feelings while participating in the situation; and
- we use our materials to set the scene and provide instructions for the classroom activity.

Examples

We can ask our students, during their private study, to prepare a draft contract to protect the interests of a particular client. In class each student negotiates the final agreement with another student who has been asked to prepare a draft contract protecting the interests of the other contracting party. This can be done in a class of any size. We can ask a few students to read out to the class their final agreement, and to talk about the issues and difficulties raised by the drafting of the contract. We can then check with the other groups that the points raised reflect their own experience.

Alternatively, we can focus our teaching materials on providing students with a 'problem' which forms the structure of their independent learning. In class we ask them to moot a situation based on this learning. We select particular class members, either before or during the class, to present, as best they can, each side of an argument or case. The rest of the class decide which party 'wins' on the facts and on the law. Part 4 of this book includes examples of the use of mooting in teaching materials.

We could also ask class members to debate two sides of a controversial issue. We could convene the class as a legislative body to decide whether to adopt certain legislation. We divide the class into groups, each representing a special interest group, and arguing for or against the proposed legislation. The groups should first convene alone to sort out their position and to prepare their arguments. After hearing from the representatives of all the groups, the legislature convenes. The class members abandon their previous roles and debate the appropriate legislative action.[185]

We could combine the debate and the small group discussion methods by dividing the class into groups of three or six students, with three roles. The first role argues for a certain position, and the second role argues against it. The third role takes notes and makes the decision, and reports to the class about the arguments made, and the decision.[186]

Once again, we must prepare our teaching materials with these exercises in mind. We must give our students the appropriate material (both content and

185 Wildman, S M, 'The Question of Silence: Techniques to Ensure Full Class Participation' (1988) 36 *Journal of Legal Education* 147, 153.

186 *Ibid.*

theoretical framework) as well as guiding questions to help them read and prepare the materials for the classroom exercise.

2.7 EVALUATING OUR TEACHING

However we prepare our teaching materials, and whatever the methods we use in the classroom, as teachers we should continually evaluate our teaching to ensure that everything we do enhances student learning. We should check to see whether we have achieved what we set out to do in designing the curriculum, putting together teaching materials, and choosing classroom teaching methods and methods of assessment.

When we evaluate our teaching, we seek information on our teaching and on our students' learning from as many sources as possible, analyse that information, and develop a plan to improve all aspects of our teaching. Useful sources of information are:[187]

- Student evaluation questionnaires. Wherever possible we should ask open-ended questions seeking qualitative information from our students which indicates which aspects of our teaching have enhanced and hindered their learning. We should ask students to provide examples to support their comments, and suggestions for improvement. Where we are developing new teaching materials, we might include a specific question which asks students to tell us how useful they have found the materials, and whether the materials were properly integrated into classroom teaching.
- Diaries where we make notes of our teaching experiences, our reflections of our teaching, and comments on our teaching which we receive informally from colleagues and students. We should note possible revisions to our teaching materials.
- Structured group discussions with our students in which we ask our students for feedback and suggestions for improvement. Once again, when we are developing new teaching materials we may want to focus part of the discussion on the effectiveness of our materials.
- Comments and feedback from colleagues whom we trust and whom we invite to sit in on our classes to observe our teaching, and who look over our teaching materials.
- Videotapes of our classes which we can examine alone or with a trusted colleague.

We should collate all the gathered information, and come up with a self-evaluation of how our teaching has met our objectives. We may decide then to read more about certain aspects of learning and teaching; to seek advice from

187 See generally Ramsden, P, and Dodds, A, *Improving Teaching and Courses: A Guide to Evaluation*, Centre for the Study of Higher Education, The University of Melbourne, Melbourne, 1989; Johnstone, R, 'Evaluating Law Teaching: Towards the Improvement of Teaching or Performance Assessment' (1990) 2 *Legal Education Review* 101; Le Brun and Johnstone (1994) ch 8; Johnstone, R and Malkin, I, 'Evaluating and Improving Teaching at the University of Melbourne Law School,' in Sachs, J, Ramsden, P and Phillips, L, *The Experience of Quality in Higher Education*, Griffith Institute of Higher Education, Brisbane, 1995.

colleagues about possible improvements; or to attend seminars or workshops on teaching and learning.

In conclusion, when developing subjects and materials for those subjects we should first consider the characteristics of our students, and then determine the aims and objectives of the subject. We should then decide upon the content of the subject, and the sequence of the topics making up the subject matter. We should also decide how we will assess student learning and the teaching methods we will use in the subject. We will then be in a position to develop teaching materials and to choose classroom teaching methods to facilitate our students' efforts to learn the subject matter. Ongoing evaluation of our subject will provide us with information which can help us modify our subject content or structure, or our teaching methods, to improve student learning. This model of teaching and learning is illustrated in Figure 4.

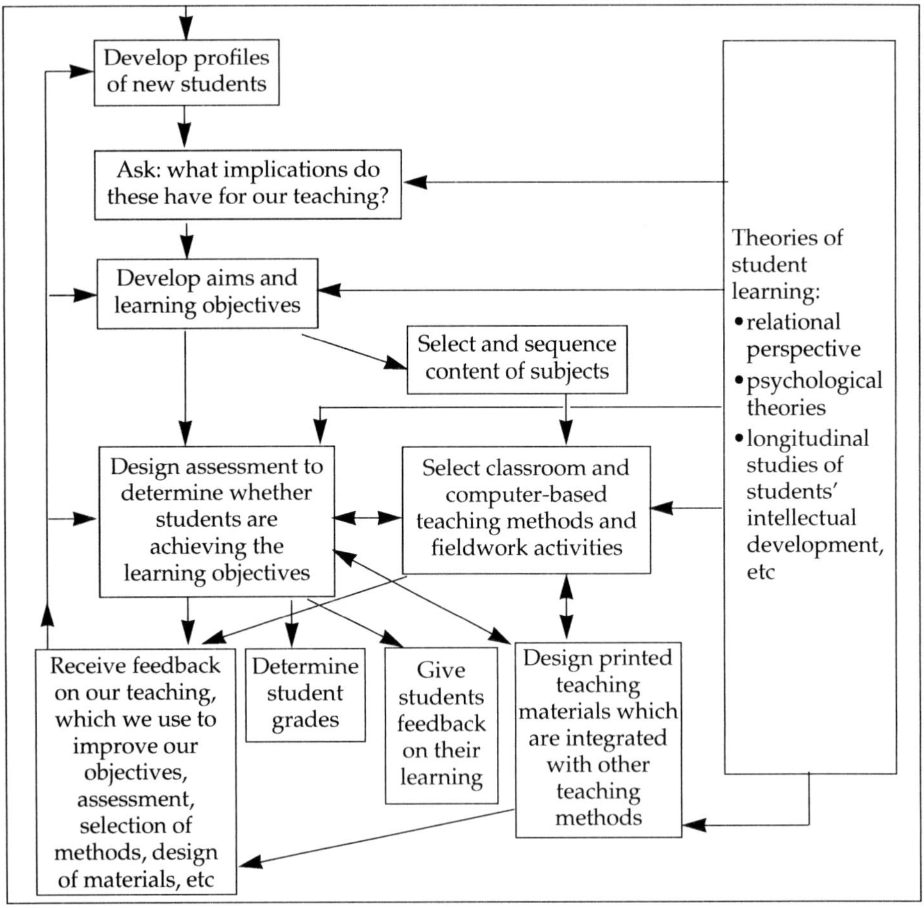

Figure 4: A dynamic model of teaching and learning for developing teaching materials

In Part 3 we will look at basic principles to guide us in putting together printed teaching materials using this model of teaching and learning.

PART 3

PUTTING TOGETHER TEACHING MATERIALS FOR LAW TEACHING

This part of the book is devoted to an exposition of key principles which should govern the development of teaching materials. Ever since the development of the casebook teaching method, law teachers have taken an interest in putting together teaching materials. In recent times, there has been a renewed focus on teaching materials with the development of approaches such as 'Lawteach',[1] 'Mastery Learning',[2] and workbooks.[3] 'Lawteach' relies on teaching materials to provide introductory frameworks and 'advance organisers' to facilitate student reading prior to class. The approach set out in the rest of this book develops many of the principles of 'Lawteach', but attempts to extend the focus to learning objectives beyond learning legal doctrine, and to set up more flexible classroom teaching methods than envisaged by 'Lawteach'.

Written teaching materials are the primary means of communication between the teacher and the student in 'Mastery Learning'. This method, however, does not envisage any classroom teaching, apart from non-compulsory lectures and demonstrations, and again tends to concentrate on doctrinal teaching, rather than on encompassing the breadth of the learning objectives outlined earlier in this book. Nevertheless 'Mastery Learning' provides important insights into the use of teaching materials in teaching.

The framework for developing printed teaching materials set out in this part builds on the principles developed in Part 2, where I suggested that we should develop teaching materials which promote deep approaches to learning, and which draw on the principles of situated, problem-based learning and self-regulated learning. From this discussion we can conclude that our materials should display some, if not all, of the characteristics set out in Table 3 (page 66).

The materials should display a dynamism which enables our students to learn on their own, outside of class, in activities that are meaningful. However well thought out they may be, teaching materials cannot be used in a vacuum. We will need to ensure that our students develop the requisite learning skills as an integral part of the law course. In particular we need to explain to our students the principles of deep approaches to learning, and why we have set up the learning environment the way we have. Students will also need to learn how to:

- assess and monitor their own learning;
- read and summarise teaching materials effectively (so that they focus on the structure and development of the argument); and
- solve problems.

---

1 See Tribe, D M, and Tribe, A J, 'Lawteach: an Interactive Method for Effective Large Group Teaching' (1987) 12 *Studies in Higher Education* 200.

2 See Rawson, S L, and Tyree, A L, 'Fred Keller Goes to Law School' (1991) 2 *Legal Education Review* 253.

3 See Johnson, N, 'Introduction to Law: The Workbook Method' in G Gibbs and A Jenkins (eds),*Teaching Large Classes in Higher Education: How to Maintain Quality with Reduced Resources*, Kogan Page, London, 1992.

Our teaching materials should:

- get our students interested in engaging with the material;
- recap on prior learning which is relevant to new learning;
- relate new ideas to our students' own experience;
- have clearly expressed learning objectives, so that students know what they should be able to do at the end of each topic;
- provide the means for our students to develop well organised and well structured knowledge;
- help our students into and around the subject and the materials, and advise them how to tackle the work;
- have clear explanations of difficult concepts;
- engage students in a dialogue and in authentic activities in a proper context so that they can work over the material they are required to learn, rather than simply read about it;
- provide our students with opportunities to respond to the ideas in the materials;
- be properly integrated with carefully selected assessment and classroom teaching methods;
- enable students to get ongoing and meaningful feedback on their learning, so that they can judge for themselves whether they are learning successfully;
- ensure that our students sum up and reflect on what they have learned; and
- help them build on what they have learned.

Table 3: Characteristics of good teaching materials

We should carefully integrate our students' self-study outside class using teaching materials with our classroom activities.[4] Class activity should complement students' own private study of the basics of the topic, and should provide elaboration, clarification of difficult points and issues, commentary, and an opportunity to develop further skills and explore values. If we do a good job of selecting interesting reading material for students we can spend less time in class on basic knowledge, and can provide the basis for participatory activities aimed at achieving other learning objectives.[5] When students come to class we can ask them to report on their responses to the activities in the materials, and describe the concepts they have learned. This can provide us with information about our students' learning so that we give them appropriate feedback to develop their learning, and so that we can develop class activities which will further engage our students in activity-based learning which will develop their understanding of the concepts they have studied in the materials.

4 See section 2.6 above.

5 See section 2.6.

The importance of using reading materials to promote independent learning outside the classroom becomes apparent when we consider the problems of selecting appropriate teaching methods for large classes.[6] In my experience, law teachers have tended to argue that participatory methods are difficult, or not possible, in large classes because 'it is difficult to get discussion going in a large class' and because the teacher still has 'to get the material across'. If, however, the content of the subject 'gets across' through the use of materials designed to promote and support independent learning in a 'conversational framework', and 'class discussion' is backed up, or even replaced, with participatory teaching methods, particularly the use of pyramiding, debates, moots and syndicate groups, with mini lectures used to reinforce material and to tie topics together,[7] then the dynamics of large group teaching can be radically altered. Our goal should be to motivate students to read well thought out materials before class, so that when they come to class they will have an opportunity to achieve important 'higher level' objectives and to participate in a dialogue with us and with each other. We need to work out what can be done most effectively outside class, and what can best be done in class.

We all know that one of the great problems with requiring students to read and prepare for class is that an inadequate number of students prepare properly for each class. As I have already discussed in section 2.1 in relation to deep learning approaches, we teachers have an important role in motivating our students to learn, and in developing enthusiasm for the subject matter. Well constructed and presented teaching materials can themselves have a motivating effect on students. If students can detect our interest and enthusiasm in the preparation of the materials, and find the materials relevant to their own lives, and interesting and challenging to use, they may be more likely to adopt deep approaches to learning. Yet the design of materials may not be enough to change students' attitudes to pre-class work. Laurillard[8] notes that studies suggest that students will not take deep approaches to learning simply because teaching materials include activities and similar design features:

> 'it is still print, and only print, and therefore open to the same distortions as the original simple text. The students have to imbue an activity with a different status, have to acknowledge that it invites them to stand back from the text and reflect upon it, and then do that.'[9]

Hence the importance of instilling students with an appreciation of the importance of, and an understanding of, the deep approach to learning, and the need for the broader educational environment to encourage deep approaches.[10] Our students will be further motivated to work with our materials if we

---

6 The definition of what is a large class is always fairly arbitrary. It is clear that a class of 300 students is a large class. Depending on the setting, classes of 60 can be a large class. For the purposes of this book 'large classes' are classes with over 100 students. For a discussion of teaching in large classes, see Le Brun and Johnstone (1994) 266-72.

7 For more detailed discussion of these methods, see section 2.6 of this book. See also Le Brun and Johnstone (1994) chs 5 to 7.

8 Laurillard (1993) 111, referring to evaluation studies referred to in Lockwood, F, *Activities in Self-Instructional Texts*, Kogan Page, London, 1992.

9 Laurillard (1993) 111.

10 See again the discussion of deep approaches to learning in section 2.1 above.

integrate classroom activities with their work outside class and if we integrate our learning objectives, materials, classroom teaching methods and assessment. Indeed, unless students see a direct link between their use of materials and their successful negotiation of assessable tasks, other forms of motivation will have a limited impact, if any. There is a danger that if students cannot see any form of connection between studying the materials and their assessment, they will not use the materials. This suggests that we should allocate part of our assessment to examining student responses to the materials and/or to their contributions to class activities based on the materials. Other assessment tasks (for example, essays, assignments and examinations) should replicate or build upon the activities in the materials.

The remainder of this part develops a set of very broad principles and associated techniques for the development of printed teaching materials based on the framework for learning and teaching set out in this part of the book. In brief the principles are that printed teaching materials in law should:

1 include all basic subject information;
2 include as much as possible of the material students will have to work with when engaging in self-study prior to class;
3 be 'user-friendly';
4 be chosen to reflect a variety of learning objectives;
5 be chosen to reflect a variety of voices;
6 use visual aids and signposts; and
7 engage students in activities and in dialogue which:
    - anchor topics within students' own personal experience etc;
    - involve students in different types of activities (simulations, problems, case studies, case preparation, projects, questions etc);
    - give students opportunities to respond to activities; and
    - maximise opportunities for self-assessment and other forms of feedback.

3.1 PRINCIPLE 1: INCLUDE ALL BASIC SUBJECT INFORMATION IN THE TEACHING MATERIALS

The driving force behind all teaching should be a careful consideration of what students are expected to learn, and the clear expression of those requirements to students. Our students should know:

- the basic learning objectives of the subject and of each topic;
- the syllabus;
- the structure of the subject;
- what is expected of them;
- how and why they are going to be exposed to the subject matter; and
- how, and upon what criteria, they are going to be assessed.

We should set out all the information in one place, so that our students can easily find what they are looking for. If we give students a series of handouts, each with a reading guide for a topic in the subject, we might demoralise our students because they have no sense of the basic shape and length of the subject, and may feel that the subject is continually being extended by new reading guides.

The basic information about the subject should include the names of and contact points for teachers, class venues, length of classes, and times. We should set out the aims and objectives[11] of the subject in as much detail as possible, so that students are aware of what exactly is required of them to achieve competence.

We should outline the basic syllabus of the subject in the teaching materials, and make clear the duration of the different topics. At the outset we should explain why the subject is important, and why it is interesting. We should outline the key questions, issues and themes to be examined in the subject, and explain how the topics fit together, their relevance to the overall subject matter and to students personally, and how our subject relates to other subjects in the law degree. We should outline what students need to know when they begin the subject. We also need to explain to students how they should approach our subject. We should give clear details of all forms of assessment – including the types of assessment, how long the assessment is to be, when it is due, what it will cover, what it is worth, the basic criteria we will adopt in marking the assessment, and anything else that will assist students satisfactorily to attempt the assessment. For example, guides to essay writing are useful tools to help students learn to research and write properly. We might also provide examples of problems that students should be able to tackle creatively at the end of the subject, particularly if they promote imaginative approaches to learning about the subject content. We can work over these examples in class so that students can practice the skills required to undertake the assessment. Advice on how to prepare and conduct moots will ensure that students use class time in these activities most beneficially. We should tell our students of arrangements for extensions of due dates for different forms of assessment, and of the process of applying for special consideration in the assessment process.

The teaching materials must provide the means for students to do further reading and exploration around issues that interest them. We should list, and if need be describe, the basic texts in the area, any published bibliographies that may help them follow up points of interest, and any journals that are worth keeping up with.

3.2 PRINCIPLE 2: STUDENTS MUST HAVE EASY ACCESS TO ALL TEACHING MATERIALS

Many Australian law teachers simply give their students a reading guide which indicates to students the cases, statutes, articles and books to be read for each topic. They expect their students to find and read the material in the law library. Their rationale for this approach is that students need to be able to practice library research skills. The problem is that in large classes there are usually too many students chasing too few copies of the relevant materials. Students are

11 See again the discussion of aims and objectives in section 2.3.

frustrated when they find that the material is not available when they want to use it. Often material is difficult to read, very long, or very important, and students wish to make a copy to assist them in their studies. Students sometimes complain that they waste a lot of time waiting to use a photocopier. Not only is this expensive, but it has the long run effect of discouraging students from working constructively for the subject, and is often a cause of resentment against the subject and the teacher. This approach also puts pressure on library resources, and the relevant material can be badly damaged by over-use.[12]

If we expect our students to learn out of class, we should ensure that their working time is spent reading, thinking and engaging in challenging activities, not hunting for materials in libraries. We should therefore ensure that students have in their possession the material to be read. If we wish students to develop library and other research skills, we should set research assignments aimed at these ends, or design special research exercises for class. Alternatively, we should make certain that there are enough copies of material in the library to satisfy demand.

3.3 PRINCIPLE 3: THE MATERIALS SHOULD BE 'USER FRIENDLY'

Our overall strategy should be to ensure that students enjoy reading for class, and that they feel that it is worthwhile. Not only should students have easy access to the required reading, but we should make the reading enjoyable and stimulating to engage in, within the constraints of the chosen learning objectives. We should use our teaching materials to promote as much independent learning as possible outside the classroom, not to provide students with obstacles to test their tenacity and commitment. Students get frustrated and disheartened if they do not know why their reading is relevant, and cannot see how it relates to the subject. They will be tempted to adopt surface approaches to learning.

The materials should set out background and contextual information, instructions, objectives, questions, reading hints, activities and problems to guide, motivate and focus our students' reading and learning activities. We should reinforce these matters orally in the classroom when we foreshadow activities for the following class. Students should know what they are trying to understand, why they are reading the material, how it fits into the rest of the subject and its objectives, what they should be looking for or thinking about in the text, the kinds of issues, questions and activities they should be engaging in when they read the material, and how it will be followed up in class.[13] We might ask them to engage in activities or develop solutions to problems before coming to class. The level of guidance, or scaffolding, provided in the materials will depend on the stage which our students have reached in developing their

12 There may also be instances of students vandalising library materials to prevent other students reading the material.

13 See the discussion of types of questions and the use of questions at pp 93 to 96, below.

ability to monitor their own learning, the way in which we wish to model the activities, and the learning that we wish our students to be engaged in.[14] There is always a difficult balance to be drawn between providing students with a structure and framework, and giving them freedom to manage their own learning and to experiment and think for themselves. If students have advance notice of when reading or other work will be required, they have the opportunity to plan when to do the reading, and can build it into their weekly, or even monthly, routine.

We should, therefore, carefully edit materials that we distribute to students so that only material relevant to our learning objectives is included.[15] Of course, if the objective of the extract is to require the students to determine what is or is not relevant in the extract, then we should include the whole case, statute or article in the materials.

In section 2.1 of this book I argued strongly that learning must not be decontextualised, but rather embedded within genuine activity, and within the cultural tradition being taught. It is important, therefore, that we give students sufficient extracts of a case or article so that the case or article does not lose its context. For example, we might edit judgments to take out parts which are not relevant to our learning objectives, but in decisions with more than one judgment we should have good reasons for excluding whole judgments. We should enable students to assess for themselves which judgments best deal with the issues posed. Editorial decisions often involve strong subjective value judgments and prejudices about judicial styles and philosophical issues. We should not impose these value judgments on our students under the veneer of our 'objective' expertise.

Of course, we may wish our students to read unedited cases, articles or other materials, so that they can develop the ability critically to read, analyse and assimilate new material. If this is the case we should communicate the purpose of the exercise to our students.

This principle of making materials 'user friendly' should not be interpreted as a call for 'spoonfeeding'. I understand 'spoonfeeding' to involve the teacher ladling sanitised and predigested material down their students' throats, without requiring their students to think about the material, or work with it. The approach adopted in this book operates on a completely different basis. It requires us to involve students at all times in activities using the materials, where our students make their own meaning, develop new skills, and transform their understanding of the subject matter by working with the material, with other students, and with us. Our role is not to spoonfeed, but to provide signposts, scaffolding, motivation and inspiration.

14 See again Part 1.

15 For an early discussion of issues relating to the editing of cases for casebooks see Patterson, E W 'The Case Method in American Legal Education: Its Origins and Objectives' (1951) 4 *Journal of Legal Education* 116.

3.4 PRINCIPLE 4: CHOOSE OUR CONTENT TO ACHIEVE A VARIETY OF LEARNING OBJECTIVES

In section 2.1 I stressed that we should use teaching materials to promote deep approaches to learning through activities and problem solving. In section 2.3 I discussed a wide range of learning objectives. In section 2.5 I outlined simple principles to take into account when determining the content of a subject, and when sequencing topics. If we are to develop teaching materials to promote deep approaches to learning, beyond a narrow 'black letter' focus, we should not just include extracts of cases and statutes, but should include other kinds of material to provide insights into the richness and indeterminacy of law as a social phenomenon. Our materials should include examples of legal documents (such as contracts, pleadings, charge sheets), problems faced by practitioners in the relevant legal culture, articles providing multi-disciplinary perspectives on the topic, empirical data on 'the law in action',[16] cross-cultural perspectives and materials reflecting attitudes to the law that are different from those expressed by white, middle class, male, heterosexual lawyers. Law affects all members of society, and lawyers will have to deal with all those affected by law. We should expose our students to these different perspectives, and our teaching materials should utilise different 'voices'.[17]

When selecting cases for teaching materials, some of us include all the 'leading cases' in a particular topic. Of course it is important that students be aware of landmark developments. But there are issues just as important as coverage, or the inclusion of all leading cases in our selection of teaching materials. If we include too many cases we will encourage students to 'skim' and take other surface approaches to learning. There are, however, some more specific principles to consider when selecting cases for inclusion in teaching materials.[18]

(i) The case could be an important means of integrating different principles and doctrines from diverse legal topics, and might therefore be an important vehicle for developing an appropriate conceptual and contextual framework for understanding the subject matter. For example, if we extract a case which covers a number of different issues in full when we first encounter it in the subject, we can return to as it becomes relevant to later topics. Our students will then not have to familiarise themselves with complicated new fact situations when they read a case illustrating the new principle to be discussed, but can simply read a discussion of the application of a different principle to the same facts. Not only is their reading made easier, but they can also begin to see how different principles relate to each other, and how legal problems can be approached from a number of related perspectives. All the better if the case has the kind of facts that we can easily alter to enhance our students' understanding of the particular principles.

16 For example, official statistics on prosecutions, penalties imposed, cases litigated, cases settled etc; data from empirical studies of the law; or data simply collected by the teacher for analysis by students.

17 This point is developed at much greater length at pp 75 to 80, below.

18 Once again, for an early discussion of selection issues, see Patterson (1951) 10-15.

(ii) The case could contain a particularly clear exposition of the relevant legal doctrine, its development or its underlying policy or philosophy. Such cases are extremely important teaching tools because they provide good examples of how judges describe or represent legal concepts,[19] which can be the basis of contextualised learning.

(iii) A case could provide a very good example of 'good' or interesting legal reasoning in the subject under study – a model of good legal practice. It could illustrate just how judges go about developing legal principles, or applying complex facts to the legal principles being learnt. It could illustrate a number of different judicial approaches to decision-making, or could help to develop the kind of 'proceduralised knowledge' so important to experts in law.[20]

(iv) The case could involve interesting facts, which might help our students to understand the basic principles involved, and which allow us to manipulate the facts of the case so that our students can see how the principle under study might be applied in different circumstances. In this way, students can develop abstract principles from multiple factual contexts.[21] Alternatively, by changing the facts we may be able to promote discussion of the policy or philosophical considerations explicitly or tacitly underlying the principle.

(v) We might select cases because they pose conflicting approaches to an issue, and motivate students to learn by providing them with a problem to solve.[22]

(vi) Cases may be excluded because they reinforce certain gender and cultural stereotypes. The value of the case as a 'leading case' may be outweighed by its inappropriateness as a teaching tool.[23]

(vii) There is a good argument that teaching materials should focus on Australian cases and materials. Our teaching materials should play a part in developing a rich Australian jurisprudence. In particular, we should not include English cases as a matter of course, but should treat these cases on the same footing as any other foreign decision. We should include foreign cases in our materials if there are sound educational reasons for including such material. Where an English case is considered to be the leading case, there is no reason why a later Australian case which applies, and perhaps develops the principles in the earlier English case, should not be used instead of the English case.

In sum, we should choose cases because of their usefulness in the teaching of the topic. We may choose to mention the leading cases in a commentary in our materials,[24] and then explain why we have not extracted these cases in the materials, and why we have chosen the extracted cases.

When we extract foreign cases, statutes, articles or empirical studies we should pay proper attention to comparative law methodology. We should

19 See Laurillard's model of a teaching strategy, discussed earlier.

20 See again the characteristics of experts described at pp 19 to 20, above.

21 See again the discussion of situated learning at pp 13 to 19, above.

22 This is a characteristic of 'Lawteach': see Tribe and Tribe (1987).

23 See the discussion at pp 75 to 80, below.

24 With full citations.

provide an appropriate context to the extract, which might include a note explaining its political, legal, cultural and other backgrounds. If we use decontextualised foreign cases, statutes, comments or studies we will teach students sloppy jurisprudential habits.

I stress that the framework for choosing cases for our materials that I am proposing in this book is quite different to the approach adopted by exponents of the 'case method' pioneered by Langdell at the Harvard Law School in the 1870s.[25] The classic casebook contains extracted appellate court cases with little explanatory material. Students are expected to read the cases and work out why the cases are relevant to the topic at hand, what they stand for, how judges reached their decisions in the cases, and how the cases relate to other cases. The approach adopted in this book is different. I argue that we should use materials for different purposes, primarily to provide a framework within which students can construct legal knowledge for themselves by engaging in a dialogue with the materials and in class, and by participating in a wide variety of activities that model the broad range of genuine activities undertaken by lawyers and legal theorists.

We should accordingly be wary of only using appellate court cases in our materials. The appellate courts are merely the 'tip of the iceberg' and so their dominance of the teaching process severely skews the legal knowledge that students are exposed to. A further consideration is that the reports of these cases are confined to the court's decision. Students are not exposed to the whole case, and are generally not aware of what happens in a case before the appellate stage, and what happens if the appellate court refers the matter back to the original court. The meaning of legal concepts is intimately tied to the workings of the legal process. Whatever the appellate court decides has real meaning only if understood in the context of the entire case.[26] We rarely provide our students with access to this material.

We might accordingly include in our teaching materials two variations on the steady diet of appellate court decisions. First, we might insert descriptions of cases heard at lower levels in the court hierarchy, together with statistics on the number of actions initiated in particular subject areas, the number that reach court, and their outcomes. Second, we should try to include in the materials at least one example of a whole case, where students can see a blend of statutory provisions, procedure, evidence, decisions of the lower courts, and scholarly articles as they may have been used by the parties and the court. We could also include transcripts of legal argument, so that students are aware of the advocacy, evidentiary and procedural issues which underpin the appellate decisions.[27]

When we compile our teaching materials we should anticipate the way in which they will be used in the classroom. Section 2.6 of this book describes in some detail the different types of classroom activities that can complement the

25 For a description of this method, see Le Brun and Johnstone (1994) 282-86, and the references cited therein.

26 See Zarr, M, 'Learning Criminal Law Through the Whole Case Method' (1984) 84 *Journal of Legal Education* 697.

27 *Ibid*.

structured knowledge, problems and activities generated in teaching materials. Our teaching materials should clearly indicate to students how their independent learning will be integrated into classroom activities. In this way, our students will be able to monitor their independent study so that their learning is appropriate to the classroom activities that we have in mind.

3.5 PRINCIPLE 5: CHOOSE MATERIALS THAT REFLECT A VARIETY OF DIFFERENT VOICES

We should be wary of assembling teaching materials that suggest to our students that there is only one neutral, 'objective' point of view. Getman, for example, sketches the characteristics of four types of voices used in legal writing and legal education.[28] Most legal education, he argues, is devoted to inculcating the 'professional voice', which addresses questions of justice through the analysis of legal rules. The language of the professional voice is logical, formal and erudite, and:

> 'serves symbolically to remove the lawyer and the law [teacher] from the concerns of everyday people. For this reason, too exclusive a focus on professional voice is dangerous to a lawyer's psyche. There are other reasons why ... legal education ... should [not] be limited to professional voice. Professional voice ... suggests that a lawyer's professional responsibility necessitates responding to complex emotional situations in terms of abstract rules. Pedagogical over-use of the professional voice wearies many students, brings out pedantic qualities in others, and misleads almost everyone about the nature of the enterprise. It suggests that rigorous analysis and careful articulation can somehow compensate for lack of knowledge or understanding.'[29]

Getman argues that exclusive focus on the professional voice fails to equip students for important functions, such as advocacy, negotiation and counselling, which require different, less reserved modes of communication. It is also essentially conservative, in that it hinders critical views of the legal system.

The 'critical voice' borrows the techniques of the professional voice to challenge specific rules and assumptions of the system. It is used to show that rules are applied arbitrarily, motivated as much by political concerns as by logic. Its derivation from the professional voice hinders its adherents from developing an independent vision of how the legal system should be structured.

Getman argues that a third voice, the 'scholarly voice', also challenges the legal system, but utilises language, methods and authorities outside the law, usually philosophy, sociology, political science and economics, to illuminate legal theory by discerning trends, patterns and movements that would escape

28 Getman, J G 'Voices' (1988) 66 *Texas Law Review* 577. See also Yudof, M G 'The Human Voice in Legal Rules'; Hodges, E P 'Writing in a Different Voice', Lawrence, F 'Human Voice and Democratic Political Culture: The Crisis of True Professionalism' and Wald, P M 'Disembodied Voices – An Appellate Judge's Response' all published in the same issue of the *Texas Law Review*.

29 Getman (1988) 578.

attention in traditional legal analysis. It tends to be 'far removed from the emotions, language and understanding of the great majority of human beings',[30] and suggests that legal issues are best analysed through cool detached examination of the operation of the legal system to make it more rational. It 'separates legal educators from lawyers and lawyers from ordinary people even more than the professional voice'.[31] It often fails to display any understanding of the impact of law on human experience.

Getman laments the undervaluing by legal education of a fourth voice, the 'human voice', language that uses ordinary concepts and familiar situations without professional ornamentation in order to analyse legal issues.[32] Legal practice frequently requires human understanding far more than it requires intellectual rigour. A lawyer must comprehend what the case means to her or his clients, and must understand the nuances of communication during negotiations. Often lawyers are required to develop legal solutions that make sense in human terms. Advocates need to convey a client's sense of injury, needs, values and feelings in a way that elicits empathy and understanding. Lawyers have to be able to understand what their clients' lives are like, in order to provide their clients with appropriate legal services. They have to be able to describe legal phenomena in ways accessible to all members of the community, not just professional lawyers or academics.

Getman's analysis suggests that those of us who teach only in the professional, critical or scholarly voices are not properly educating law students in the skills needed for professional practice, nor are we assisting students to explore their values and attitudes to law. To our students justice will appear abstract and alienated from human experience. Getman suggests that teaching which eschews the 'human voice' is likely to alienate students, dampening their humanity and their enthusiasm for learning about the law.

'Point of viewlessness' has also been undermined by feminist critiques of objectivity and the 'maleness' of legal discourse, and the exposure of the value laden nature of teaching materials used in the law class. For example, Mary Joe Frug, in a now classic analysis of a contracts casebook,[33] has shown how readers' 'views about gender affect their understanding of a law casebook' and

30 *Ibid* 580.

31 *Ibid* 581.

32 *Ibid*.

33 'Re-reading Contracts: A Feminist Analysis of the Contracts Casebook' (1985) 34 *The American University Law Review* 1065. Frug's is one of many cogent feminist critiques of the 'maleness' of many casebooks and textbooks: see, for example, Hunter, R, 'Representing Gender in Legal Analysis: A Case/Book Study in Labour Law' (1991) 18 *Melbourne University Law Review* 305; Boyle, C 'Book Review' (1985) 63 *Canadian Bar Review* 427; Graycar and Morgan *op cit*, ch 2; Tobias, C 'Gender Issues and the Prosser, Wade and Schwartz Torts Casebook' (1988) 18 *Golden Gate University Law Review* 495; Coombs, I M, 'Crime in the Stacks, or a Tale of a Text: A Feminist Response to a Criminal Law Textbook' (1988) 38 *Journal of Legal Education* 117; and Becker, M E, 'Obscuring the Struggle: Sex Discrimination, Social Security and Stone, Seidman, Sunstein and Tushnet's *Constitutional Law*' (1989) 89 *Columbia Law Review* 264. See also Naffine, N, *Law and the Sexes*, Allen & Unwin, Sydney, 1990, chs 1 and 2.

'gendered aspects of a casebook affect readers' understanding of the law and of themselves'.[34] She argues that casebooks, and by implication teaching materials in general, can foster and sustain opinions and ideas about gender (and implicitly, ethnicity, disability, and other aspects of social life).[35]

Frug is not just arguing that we should eliminate 'overt sexism' or overt racism from teaching materials.[36] She makes the point that when we compile teaching materials we have a wide range of choice in our case selections, comments, notes, problems and questions. The 'choices [we] make are not inevitable. The editorial choices ... determine how many readers think about the law of a doctrinal area, about lawyering in that field, about clients and about legal reasoning'.[37] Textual facts, 'rather than being the *objects* of interpretation, are its *products*'.[38]

We should take care to ensure that teaching materials do not reinforce any gender, cultural, homophobic, or racial stereotypes. For example, by linking certain social and psychological characteristics to one sex or the other, our ideas about gender shape our beliefs about the kinds of work men and women do, their interests, and the way they can act and feel. Because the traits identified as being male are generally more highly valued than those identified as being female,[39] 'our ideas about gender have a constituting effect on the continuing imbalance of power between men and women'.[40] Teaching materials can, therefore, sustain and further ideas about gender, ethnicity and disability.

Frug gives many examples of gendered aspects of a particular casebook. She focuses, for example, on women as characters in the cases, the extent to which women feature as authors of decisions or legal commentary in the book, and the language of the book.

In this discussion, I do not wish to advocate any form of 'political correctness' (whatever that expression is supposed to mean), but rather wish to remind compilers of teaching materials that these are real issues, about which

34 Frug (1985) 153.

35 While Frug's analysis is directly concerned with a feminist analysis of a casebook, most of her comments about the compilation of instructional materials have some application to issues of race, ethnicity, culture, sexual preference and disability. They are also pertinent to issues of class and political opinion. That is not to say that the issues expounded by Frug in relation to gender issues are the same as those involved in racial and similar issues, but they do highlight points that should be taken into account by the compilers of teaching materials. Compilers of teaching materials should therefore consider Frug's comments in the context of these other issues when making editorial decisions about the compilation of teaching materials.

36 For example, removing instances of pejorative, demeaning treatment of women in teaching materials: Frug (1985) 1068.

37 *Ibid* 1069.

38 *Ibid* 1070, quoting Stanley Fish.

39 For example, men's work is deemed more important than women's, and 'male' analytical skills are more valued than 'female' intuition etc.

40 Frug (1985) 1074.

they have to make choices, explicitly or implicitly.[41] If we wish to avoid the negative educational impact of gender stereotyping, we might try to ensure that as many women as men appear amongst the parties in our teaching materials. We might also try to ensure that when women do appear as characters in the materials they do not assume gender stereotyped roles and are not described in stereotypical or unflattering ways. Not only will this reinforce prejudices about women's roles, but it can also distort our students' understanding of legal doctrine. Our students may believe that a doctrine did not apply simply because, for example, the work sought to be compensated was not important enough for the court to invoke a particular doctrine.[42] If it is not possible to include materials that do not show gender bias (such as women having limited occupations or constricted characterisations), then at the very least our commentary in the materials should draw this to the attention of our students.

Our materials should not just focus on matters traditionally associated with men and ignore matters traditionally more closely linked to women.[43] As Graycar and Morgan point out, women have played no part in defining the traditional legal categories and issues around which traditional law subjects are organised.[44] If approximately half of our law students are women, there are good reasons to situate at least part of our teaching in women's experience of the world, so that our subjects have greater personal relevance to our women students. We should avoid giving the impression that gender (and other issues such as class, race, disability etc) are irrelevant to our subjects.[45] Instead we should ask 'the women question' which involves 'examining how the law fails to take into account the experiences and values that seem more typical of women rather than men ... or how existing legal standards and concepts might disadvantage women'[46] so that we identify the gender implications of otherwise apparently neutral rules and practices. And as I have argued all the way through this section, the 'women question' is not the only question we should ask. There are further questions touching on class, race, disability and sexual preference, to name a few.

We might also try to ensure that women are well represented amongst the judges or authors extracted in the materials, or that some comment is included about their absence.[47] We might also take care to recognise women in the language of the materials, both as characters in questions and problems, and in the use of feminine pronouns when authors or editors write about the generic

41 The accusation that people who raise issues of gender, race, disability and similar issues are proponents of 'political correctness' has become a frequent, and sometimes mindless, technique to stifle discussion about these issues. For a good exposition of the issues of academic freedom and 'political correctness', see (1991/92) 16 *Bulletin of the Australian Society of Legal Philosophy*.

42 Frug (1985) 1081-87.

43 *Ibid* 1088-93.

44 Graycar and Morgan (1990) 3.

45 Hunter (1991) 307.

46 Bartlett, K T, 'Feminist Legal Methods' (1990) 103 *Harvard Law Review* 829, 837. See also Hunter (1991) 307.

47 Frug (1985) 1094-97.

person. If necessary, we might take corrective editorial measures to ensure that women are recognised and addressed in the materials.

Frug notes that what Getman characterises as the professional, critical and scholarly voices are also characteristics that are stereotypically seen as male. 'Point of viewlessness' in reality is usually the male point of view.[48] In compiling our teaching materials we should be wary of using organising frameworks which are not only abstract and analytical in themselves but also encourage abstract analysis in readers. A similar effect can result from a focus primarily on appellate decisions concentrating on doctrinal analysis. Like Getman, Frug argues that readers are not encouraged to nourish what are seen as feminine characteristics, such as their emotional sensibilities or the process of empathising with clients and their problems as part of legal problem solving.[49] The principles of situated learning, particularly the use of problem solving, are a means of avoiding these abstractions. As Frug comments:

> 'Problems require students to personalize casebooks. Problems require students to undertake tasks that involve their interaction with the materials, that allow them to observe contexts which include settings, characters or issues that mirror their lives ...'[50]

Frug also comments that many casebooks are neutral in their style and content and appear to have no editorial presence. The materials avoid controversial material likely to provoke an emotional response from students. Commentary is often dry and technical, and does not offer a larger coherent theoretical perspective. There is no discussion about the way the materials are organised, and questions do not challenge the fairness of, or judicial attitudes underlying, decisions. Casebooks often also do not include changing perspectives in legal thought, or economic or social history, that influenced the decisions and the way that the subject matter was thought about. Frug argues that compilers of materials which take this approach are:

> 'authoritarian about the casebook's neutrality; they offer readers no information about what is left unsaid in their casebook. Because most readers associate detachment and control with men, the authoritarian neutrality ... seems male.'[51]

Such casebooks misleads students as to 'the kinds of questions one can ask about the cases and about the kind of legal history that might be relevant to consider' in studying a particular subject.[52] This:

> 'discourages readers from developing ethical, social, and moral opinions on legal issues ... [and] promotes a narrow concept of professional conduct ...'[53]

Frug's discussion about the 'voice' to be used in the materials has focused on gender, but the points raised also have some application to issues relating to

48 See also MacKinnon, C, 'Feminism, Marxism, Method and the State: Towards a Feminist Jurisprudence' (1983) 8 *Signs* 635, 638-9; Boyle (1985) 432-34; and Graycar and Morgan (1990) 6, 16 and 20.

49 Frug (1985) 1109.

50 *Ibid* 1108.

51 *Ibid* 1109.

52 *Ibid* 1112.

53 *Ibid.*

Aborigines, ethnic minorities, sexual preference and persons with disabilities. We should take care when putting together materials to ensure that the diversity of Australian life is properly reflected in the materials. We should choose cases which do not reinforce stereotypes about women, persons with disabilities, and groups often considered not to be in the mainstream of Australian life.

In summary, issues about the 'voice' used or reflected in teaching materials have been obscured by a common assumption among law teachers that a neutral, 'objective', 'professional' voice should be the basis of legal education. As Getman and Frug, amongst others, have argued, this assumption can no longer be upheld. We need to be concerned about 'voice' in our teaching, and need to reflect a multiplicity of voices to do justice to the complex issues in legal education, and to avoid alienating those students in our classes who are not heterosexual, and white, Anglo-Saxon or Anglo-Celtic males.

We should ensure that when we speak in our materials, our voice is conversational, plain speaking and welcoming. Table 4 (based on Rowntree)[54] provides advice on how to achieve this.

Be conversational

- Refer to ourselves as 'I' or 'we', and to our students as 'you'.
- Use contractions ('you'll', 'that's') where appropriate.
- Use references, analogies and examples which are familiar to our students.
- Use rhetorical questions.

Be welcoming

- Ensure that we don't write as if our students are only of one gender, race, class background, age group, sexual orientation etc.
- Avoid language or examples that might offend any of our students.
- Tell our students who we are and talk about our own experiences of the subject.

Speak plainly

- Remove surplus words – eg replace 'establishing a connection between' with 'link'.
- Use short and more familiar words – eg 'new' rather than 'unprecedented'.
- Use jargon only when necessary, and with an appropriate explanation.
- Keep sentences short, but vary their length.
- Stick to a simple sentence structure – avoid too many sub-clauses.
- Keep paragraphs short.
- Use active rather than passive verb forms – eg 'Use case studies to ... ' rather than 'Case studies can be used to ...'.
- Use headings and sub-headings.

Table 4: How to be reader-friendly

54 Rowntree (1994) 139. For more detail, see Rowntree (1990) 207-32; and Race (1992) 107-20.

3.6 PRINCIPLE 6: USE VISUAL AIDS AND SIGNPOSTS IN THE MATERIALS

3.6.1 Diagrams, tables and other visuals[55]

Most of us rely too much on words in our teaching, and not enough on visuals. We tend to forget that diagrams, flow charts, tables and other visuals are very useful devices for explaining concepts, interrelationships and logical flows in ways that words cannot. We should put lots of visuals in our materials because they are time consuming to draw during class, are time consuming for students to copy down, and can be incorrectly or untidily copied down so that they are useless when referred to at a later date. In teaching materials diagrams, flow diagrams or tables are useful:

- to give students an overview of a topic before they study it;
- to summarise crucial elements in order to reinforce the main points of a topic;
- to relieve the monotony of solid print;
- to amuse our students and increase their interest and motivation;
- to convey emotions and feelings;
- to show things that cannot be portrayed in words; and
- to simplify complex ideas.

We can enhance the usefulness of a diagram by leaving part of it incomplete and requiring students to complete it or label it, or by asking students questions which depend on an understanding or interpretation of the diagram. Alternatively we can require students in class to explain the diagram to each other.[56]

3.6.2 Headings and sub-headings

Headings and sub-headings are important ways of ensuring that students are carried through the activities in the materials and are at all times clear about what they are expected to be thinking about or doing. It is a good idea to ensure that every section of the materials and every discrete activity has a heading or a sub-heading, and that these headings enable students at a glance to see what they should be involved in.

Headings and sub-headings enable students to:

- find parts of the materials they want to consult;
- see where topics begin and end; and
- see how topics fit together.

We can use sub-headings to develop information maps. Where we are setting out similar material which follows a set pattern, we can work out a series

55 See Rowntree (1990) 181-206; Rowntree (1994) 117-122.

56 Gibbs, Habeshaw, and Habeshaw (1987) 53.

of standard sub-headings and then describe each part of the material using these standard sub-headings. For example, we might choose from the following sub-headings:

- Definition
- Problems
- Issues
- Guidelines
- Rationale
- When to apply
- Steps to follow
- Example(s)

I have used an information map in section 2.6 of this book.[57]

3.7 PRINCIPLE 7: TEACHING MATERIALS SHOULD FULLY ENGAGE STUDENTS IN 'DIALOGUE' AND ACTIVITY

In order to be a constructive part of our teaching strategies, our teaching materials need fully to engage our students in their out-of-class reading and activities. At the beginning of this section I outline the important characteristics of teaching materials that will help our students to engage in deep approaches to learning and in situated learning.[58] Above all we must engage our students in active learning and in a dialogue with the materials, with their peers and with us. We should aim to draw *responses* out of our students, and to provide them with opportunities to learn by *doing*. Students should be engaged in trying to 'do something' with their reading, whether it be answering a question, critically analysing a decision or chain of reasoning, solving a problem, or developing an idea or 'project'. These questions, problems, and projects must be genuine activities in the sense of being the kinds of things that lawyers do, or the kinds of activities central to academic learning about law. We want our students to articulate their responses to the materials and the subject content, and to describe their understanding of the concepts they are learning, so that we and their peers can provide feedback to focus and develop their learning.

Rowntree argues that when we devise self-teaching materials 'our aim should be to produce the written equivalent of a one-to-one tutorial'.[59] In putting together our materials we need to imagine that we are tutoring one individual student. We will have to write down everything that we will want to say to this student before he or she comes to our class, so that our materials become a 'tutorial-in-print'. We want to make sure that the student is working *with* us, so we need to present ideas or examples to the student, and then

57 See pp 52 to 62, above.

58 See, for example, Laurillard's model of a teaching strategy in section 2.1.

59 Rowntree (1990) 119. See also 82-83.

encourage the student to respond or to contribute something. For example, we might want to:

- check that the student has understood what we were getting at;
- ask the student for further examples drawn from her or his own experience;
- get the student to apply the ideas being discussed to a new situation;
- invite the student critically to evaluate the ideas put forward; or
- suggest that the student engage in a practical task with the new material.

We should ensure that our materials give our students appropriate scaffolding (prompts, guiding questions, issues to look out for etc) upon which to base their learning and development of skills. As students develop their skills and learning, we can remove the scaffolding so that students can monitor their own learning. We should always give feedback (in the materials, or later in class) to our students, outlining the strengths and weaknesses of their responses, or at least what we found interesting about their efforts. We might also suggest other possible responses to the activity or question.

In section 2.1 of this book I noted that from articulated student responses to our materials, we are able to check on whether students have understood the concepts in the material. If and when we find that student responses to the materials demonstrate misconceptions we can intervene to provide clearer descriptions of concepts, and new activities for students to engage in to develop their learning.

In section 2.5 I discussed ways in which we could schedule topics in our subjects, and deferred until later a discussion of ways of structuring topics. This is an appropriate place to outline some simple ideas to consider when we structure a topic in our teaching materials. In general, our aims in structuring a topic should be to:

- introduce students to the topic in a way that is meaningful to them, and at the most appropriate level to build on their previous learning;
- give students a structure for the topic, and all the essential information (definitions, key concepts, central questions, major issues to look for etc) to understand the topic;
- involve students in activities where they can make their own meaning by working with concepts, questions, problems etc; and where they have opportunities to describe their responses to the material and their understanding of the topic;
- give us opportunities to identify student misconceptions of the subject matter, and to intervene to correct those misconceptions;
- ensure that students have as many opportunities as possible to get feedback on their developing understanding of the topic; and
- provide students with an integrating summary of the topic and a link to the next topic.

Table 5 (page 84) outlines a possible structure to follow when writing a topic in teaching materials.

In the following pages I outline various techniques which enable students to engage in activities and dialogue with the materials.

Introduction	•	Place the topic in context.
	•	Connect the topic to something the student already knows.
	•	Give a very brief outline of the topic.
Objectives	•	Describe what students should be able to do after studying the topic.
	•	Make certain your objectives are clear, achievable and balanced.
Information	•	Present information to students, provide students with a 'big picture' of the topic, explain important concepts, give definitions, and/or direct students to appropriate sources.
	•	Anticipate how students will respond to information and provide assistance with difficult points.
	•	Use headings and sub-headings to provide structure and signposts.
Activities	•	Introduce activities where most appropriate.
	•	See the discussion of activities later in this section.
Feedback	•	Provide feedback or mechanisms for feedback on activities.
Consolidate	•	Summarise the topic or have students generate their own summary.
	•	If necessary, deal with misconceptions that have appeared in students' learning.
	•	Link to the next topic.

Table 5: A pattern for writing a topic
(Thanks to Gordon Joughin for permission to reproduce and modify this table.)

3.7.1 The topic should be anchored within students' own personal experience and problem solving skills

Whenever we begin a topic we must ensure that it is pitched at a level appropriate to our students.[60] As Brown, Collins and Duguid argue[61] 'the task should be embedded in familiar activity', so that our students can draw on their implicit knowledge to develop their learning on the topic, and are able to relate it to their personal experiences. Our aim here is to stimulate interest, and to make the topic personally meaningful to our students. The materials might therefore begin with a realistic example or situation well known to students. Some examples are set out in Table 6 (page 85).

60 Hence the need for us to establish exactly who are students are, and what they already know when they begin our subject: see section 2.2 above.

61 Brown, Collins and Duguid (1989a) 38.

To ensure that our students begin their learning by focusing on situations within their knowledge and experience, at the beginning of a topic we might include in our materials:

- examples of transactions which our students will be studying – for example, clauses of contacts, charge sheets, title deeds etc.
- a scenario which highlights typical situations which students will encounter as they learn the topic;
- a problem typically encountered by a practitioner in the area of law being studied;
- a case study which models the process to be studied or which raises important issues;
- a pre-test to gauge the level of understanding students have at the beginning of the topic, or to enable them to develop certain ideas before the topic commences;
- activities in which we ask our students to think of other examples of the phenomenon they are studying – for example, we can ask them to think of another example of the contractual clause they have just seen in the materials.

Table 6: Beginning learning with examples and well-known situations

Some of these examples are illustrated in the materials for the first class in Part 4 of this book. Our intention is always to ensure that students do not see the topic as irrelevant to them or abstracted from reality, but rather located in a concrete 'real life' situation with which they are reasonably familiar.

In addition, we want our students to articulate their initial conceptions of the subject matter so that we (or other students) can respond, and if necessary, point out possible misconceptions which might hinder future learning. Dialogue should begin early in the learning process, so that we can modify our representation of the subject matter if it appears that we are pitching our teaching at the wrong level for our students, or if it becomes apparent that students lack an understanding of the fundamental concepts upon which learning will be built. The activities designed to introduce the topic of Agreed Damages Clauses in Part 4 give students an opportunity to check whether they understand the basic principles of assessing damages, principles upon which the new topic is built. The activities also enable us to check that students understand what an agreed damages clause is.

From there students can start generating solutions to the problem so that they begin developing some sort of 'logic' or 'intuitive' approach to the problem or issue. Apart from exposing naive conceptions or inappropriate frameworks which we can deal with as the subject unfolds, in the process of generating their own solutions our students have an opportunity to begin to think like practitioners, whether the practitioner be a lawyer, legal theorist, sociologist of law, feminist lawyer or economist. If we follow this up with examples of authentic activities (see below) our students will learn of the way of thinking within the relevant culture, not just its subject matter. Once our students have internalised the appropriate way of thinking, they are well on the way to developing the framework to monitor their own learning.

3.7.2 The materials should involve students in authentic activities

Once we have introduced our students to the topic in a way that is meaningful to them, we can encourage our students to 'learn by doing' by building frequent activities into our materials. These activities will include questions, tasks and exercises.[62] I want to make it clear that this call for the use of activities in our materials is fundamentally different from the way in which questions are generally used in Australian casebooks. Many casebooks currently used in law schools include questions at the *end* of a topic. These questions merely check whether students have learned something from their reading of the text in that topic. The approach advocated in this book is different. Our aim should be to include activities (which may require students to do more than answer questions) *throughout* our materials, so that from the *outset* our students learn through engaging in activities. We want to keep our students purposefully engaged with the material, so that they do more than merely memorise the material. We want them to work with the new material, articulate their responses, and get feedback on their work.

There are no hard and fast rules about how many activities we should include in the materials, but as Rowntree comments:

> '... I would be surprised if you could present more than three pages of reading without mentioning something worth asking learners about before they move on. And if more than four or five pages went by without your requiring the learners to do anything but read, then I'd suggest you'd forgotten about them. And I'd expect them to have dozed off!'[63]

What should activities require students to do?

Activities can demand a variety of responses from our students, based on what they have experienced or learned elsewhere, what we have told them, or what they can find out by reading our materials or from other sources. Amongst other things, we may want our students to:

- stop reading for a few moments and simply think about an issue or reflect on what they have read;
- write a brief response to a question or exercise;
- summarise the key points in the text;
- imagine how a particular legal transaction or rule would affect them in a particular situation;
- simulate or role play a situation;
- provide further examples of a phenomenon;
- engage in some further research for 15 minutes or longer;

62 See generally Rowntree (1990) 119-135; Rowntree (1992) 101-8.

63 Rowntree (1990) 121.

- analyse or evaluate a case or article in the materials;
- re-read a section of the materials (for example a series of cases) in order to apply the principles in the cases to a problem;
- synthesise the principles from a series of cases or articles;
- draft the documentation for a legal transaction, a memorandum or letter of advice, a judgment and so on;
- enter into a discussion with other class members;
- interview a legal practitioner or a member of a government agency to find out more about a topic;
- keep a diary of how their understanding of an issue has changed as they have read and researched the topic; or
- develop a research methodology to investigate a particular issue.

Table 7 provides a useful pattern for writing activities.

Introduction	• Place the activity in the context of the topic. • State the purpose of the activity and the benefits students will derive from it.
Define the activity	• Be as clear and explicit as possible about what the student should do and how, when and where it should be done. Indicate how much time and effort should be required.
Anticipate difficulties	• Note any difficulties students may have and ways of overcoming them.
Feedback	• Feedback or comment is usually appropriate, though this may come in class time. Feedback may take the form of criteria for students to apply to their responses.

Table 7: A pattern for writing activities
(Thanks to Gordon Joughin for permission to reproduce this table.)

Our objective ultimately is to move the student from 'embedded activity' to more abstracted knowledge of the topic. We want our students to examine why their responses are useful or not useful, and to think, behave and reflect as practitioners.[64] We want our students not just to learn to extract legal rules and principles from cases and statutes, but also to understand the transactions or phenomena which the law is operating on, and the way the law is shaped by these phenomena and other social, political and economic forces.

There are many ways of involving students in this type of 'authentic activity'. Some are outlined below. These are merely examples of the general principles discussed in section 2.1 of this book.[65]

64 Once again, the use of the term 'practitioner' does not mean a legal practitioner in its most narrow sense, but rather a practitioner of the discipline concerned.

65 For a discussion of activities using more sophisticated educational technology, see Laurillard (1993) Part II.

Simulations

In simulations[66] we provide our students with an opportunity to 'act out' problems and issues, and enable them to understand for themselves the 'internal logic' of a situation, or to feel for themselves how a situation would have an impact on a particular person, or group of persons. Students might also be given scenarios where they can make legal or tactical decisions, or draft legal documents. In our teaching materials we can require students, for example, to read a description of the contractual requirements of a particular party, and then to draft a contract to achieve the aims of that party. We can require the student to draft a version of the contract that would protect the interests of the other contracting parties, to compare the two draft contracts, and to draw conclusions as to how contracts protect or do not protect the interests of the contracting parties. I have used this technique in the materials in Part 4 of this book.

In the next few paragraphs I discuss activities which involve variations on the basic principles of simulations. In section 2.6 I looked at the use of simulations and role plays in the classroom.

Problems

'Problems' in legal education have come to refer to 'fact situations' in which a situation of conflict between two parties is set out, and our students are then asked to advise a party or both parties as to their legal rights and obligations. To be reasonably authentic these fact situations should be incomplete, so that part of our student's activity is to seek further facts, and justify the enquiry for further facts.

Law teachers have traditionally used 'problems' in tutorials after students have 'learnt' the material in lectures. I have already argued in section 2.1 that this overlooks the basic fact that problem solving is a good way of initially learning the material.[67] The 'lecture followed by tutorial' approach assumes that students favour learning in an abstract, conceptual manner. Students might find it easier to learn by reading about the basic legal principles involved in an area and then *immediately* trying to apply the principles to a fact situation prior to coming to class. We would then use class discussion to give students feedback on their 'solutions', developing the material which was the subject of study, and reflecting on the processes that students have just involved themselves in.

Alternatively we could give our students the 'problem' in teaching materials *before* we expose them to any legal principles or theory. We might provide some guidance as to where they might find the relevant material, and then ask them to learn by solving the problem. Once again we could use class time to provide students with feedback or comments on their work.

We can also use problems to expose students to the situations in which law might have a role to play. For example, we can ask our students to advise clients

66 See Brown, J M 'Simulation Teaching: A Twenty Second Semester Report' (1984) 34 *Journal of Legal Education* 638; and Le Brun and Johnstone (1994) 304-308.

67 See Kurtz, Wylie and Gold (1990) and Ogden (1984).

in relation to a contractual dispute before they are exposed to the law. In this way students are given an idea of the kinds of legal, ethical and theoretical issues which are raised by the situation. This approach is illustrated in the materials in Part 4. It is particularly useful in subjects which are statute based. The following example illustrates how problems can be used to give students the opportunity to use principles of statutory interpretation to tackle a new statutory provision.

An Example of Statutory Interpretation through Problem Solving

The powers and duties of the Occupational Health and Safety Inspectorate

The basic statutory provisions

The powers and duties of the inspectorate under the Occupational Health and Safety Act 1985 (Vic) are set out in Part V (sections 39-46) of the Act. The powers are very similar to those set out in previous Victorian legislation: see section 186 of the Labour and Industry Act 1958 and section 22(1) of the Industrial Safety, Health and Welfare Act 1981. You should refer to Part V of the Occupational Health and Safety Act to answer the following questions in order to build up an understanding of the powers and responsibilities of the inspectorate. Make short notes as a basis for class discussion.

(i) Inspector's powers to enter workplaces are set out in section 39(1)(a) and (b).

What is the essential difference between sections 39(1)(a) and (b)?

Quickly read sections 26 and 31 to 35 of the Act. List the situations in which an inspector may be 'requested or required' to attend a workplace under section 39(1)(b).

(ii) The inspector's investigatory powers and obligations upon attending the workplace are set out in sections 39(1)(c) to (k) of the Act. Note that section 39(1)(f) should be read together with section 40(3), 39(1)(g) together with 40(4) and (5), 39(1)(h) with 40(6). Read also sections 39(2), 40(7), 40(8) and 41.

Applying the provisions

Inspection Problem 1

Your client, Ms Susan Seger, is the production manager of a large chemical company, called Makechem Pty Ltd. She rings you one morning seeking the following advice. An occupational health and safety inspector has just arrived at her premises, together with a Greek interpreter. The inspector has indicated that she has received a complaint from 'the union' about poor ventilation in an area where there are 'toxic' chemicals. The union has alleged that a 'few workers' have 'fainted' due to exposure to chemicals. Ms Seger tells you that the inspector has indicated that she will take air samples, samples of the alleged 'toxic chemical', and has asked for all documentation which might indicate the composition and use of the chemical. The inspector is also photographing the site of the chemicals, and sketching the layout of the area. The inspector has requested that no company employee 'do any work' in the area where the chemicals are situated. She has also asked to see the breathing apparatus that has been provided for employees. The inspector is interviewing all employees in the area (Some of the employees are Greek speaking.) The inspector has also asked to interview Ms Seger. She says that she 'refuses to talk to that ...'

Ms Seger insists that the inspector's activities are 'an unwarranted interference in the running of [her] business.' She wants to know 'what right the inspector has to do all this', and wants to know whether she can take any action to have the investigation stopped or reviewed. She asks for any advice as to how she can 'make life difficult for this ... [inspector].' 'Surely I must be able to appeal to somebody about all this' she says.

Your immediate reaction

You tell Ms Seger that you will need 10 minutes to read the relevant sections of the Act, and that you will ring her back with the appropriate advice once you have done so. Jot down some notes which will form the basis of your telephone advice.

What would your advice be if the inspector had told Ms Seger over the telephone that the workplace should be left undisturbed until the inspector was able to attend the scene?

Read sections 40(1) and (2). Now assume the role of the relevant trade union in the scenario outlined earlier. What should your health and safety representatives at the chemical factory expect from the inspectorate?

Given the inspectors' obligations to health and safety representatives in section 40, how should the union and its representatives organise themselves to make the most of their rights under that section?

The problem method is superior to the case method in that it enables students to generate their own answers, rather than analyse the reasoning of an already decided case. We can also integrate interdisciplinary perspectives into problems, so that our students develop a broad-based approach to problem solving.[68]

One advantage in having problems in a written form, rather than outlining the fact situation in class,[69] is that the problem is more likely to be presented in an unambiguous form. It can be more elaborate, demanding and interesting. At the same time we can supply our students with additional supporting material, including references to text books, cases and other useful sources. We can also give an indication of the procedure which students can follow in solving the problem. We can set out a complex problem in stages or sequences.[70]

68 See generally Le Brun and Johnstone (1994) 303.

69 Gibbs, Habeshaw and Habeshaw (1987) 51.

70 *Ibid.*

In our teaching materials we can use problems to consolidate the learning in a topic or to enable students to assess their own learning. We can require students to grapple with different styles of legal opinions, like judgments and advice of counsel.

Case studies

A case study is a simulation of a complex real-life situation 'in which the experience is second-hand and probably condensed'.[71] In our materials we can give our students a printed description of a specific situation, and ask them to identify specific issues and recommend appropriate strategies to deal with the issues. Case studies can involve elements of individual self-study and group work. Students can study the case on their own or in groups prior to class, and then come to class with notes of their responses.

Case studies can integrate a wide range of subject matter, and encourage a broad view of a subject. We can use them to enable students to develop skills in analysis, application and synthesis. For example, we can provide our students with details of the requirements of a business enterprise and then ask them to recommend the types of labour (employees or independent contractors) that the enterprise should hire. Alternatively, we can require them to read a report describing the gender break down of the workforce in a particular industry, and then asked to devise a strategy to use statutory provisions dealing with, say, occupational health and safety, in such a way as to ensure that the women in the particular workforce obtain the benefit of the legislation. An example of such a case study is set out below. The example is taken from a subject on Occupational Health and Safety Law.

Example of a Case Study in Teaching Materials

Self-regulation Problem 1

The current provisions for designated work groups are set out in section 29 of the Occupational Health and Safety Act 1985 (Vic). Read this section carefully.

You are an industrial officer for the Amalgamated Textile, Clothing and Footwear Workers Union. You have been asked by your union secretary to give her advice as to how the union should go about setting up designated work groups in all workplaces over which the union has coverage. You know that your industry is characterised by the following features.

(i) There is a high proportion of women in the industry (70 per cent of all workers). Fifty five per cent of workers in the industry are women from non-English speaking backgrounds. There are a large number of outworkers in the industry, most of whom are from non-English speaking backgrounds, and most of whom are not members of trade unions.

(ii) At present women workers in the industry tend to be clustered in menial low paid jobs, while men are concentrated in maintenance and technical areas. As a result of recent restructuring this is breaking down to some extent but nevertheless remains a serious problem.

71 Jacques (1991) 94.

(iii) The industry is characterised by workplaces of vastly differing sizes.

(iv) Union coverage includes the Metal Employees Workers Union, the National Union of Workers, the Federated Clerks Union, and, to a lesser extent, the Electrical Trades Union, the Miscellaneous Workers Union, and the Federated Ironworkers Association. In some workplaces, up to fifteen unions may have coverage.

(v) There is a high incidence of illness and injury in the industry. In Victoria, the industry pays the highest accident compensation levies in the State, and levies and penalty levies represent a cost of over 11 per cent of wages and salaries.

(vi) The health and safety risks found in the industry include:

- physical conditions such as temperature, dust, fibres, ventilation, lighting, noise, exposure to chemicals and dangerous machinery;
- lack of adequate job training and health and safety instruction;
- inappropriate work station design such as non-adjustable chairs, benches and equipment which do not take the characteristics of the operator into account;
- manual handling problems, such as continual lifting;
- a 'Taylorist' work system, which divides work into small components to increase productivity. This causes work to be highly repetitive and monotonous. It also results in loss of autonomy and control over speed and the method of work;
- piece rates, bonus pay systems and production quotas supervised oppressively by management result in increased speed of production. This compounds the risks outlined above and results in stress and repetitive strain injuries. You estimate that production linked payment systems are available to about half the workers in the industry;
- shift work is a major risk due to fatigue and disrupted eating and sleeping patterns. It is often undertaken by women with child-care and traditional domestic responsibilities;
- there are other psycho-social factors like monotonous and boring work at high speeds, production enforcement procedures and strict management policies, low level of control over the pace and method of execution of work, lack of communication between workers and management, job insecurity and lack of opportunities for social interaction. These give rise to a high level of stress, and together with the other factors described above can lead to a high incidence of overuse or repetitive strain injuries.

Write a memorandum to your secretary which outlines all relevant points pertaining to the procedure for setting up designated work groups and recommends a strategy for establishing appropriate designated work groups in the industry.

We can ask students to devise a strategy to establish appropriate designated work groups for the workers in the case study. In doing this, students will have to analyse the relevant statutory provisions and manipulate the legal principles to give the requested advice.

Case preparation

A further variation based on the use of problems and simulations in teaching materials is to give our students a fact situation and require them to prepare an argument for one of the parties. We can make the exercise more interesting by:

- giving different sets of students a 'biased version' of the facts based on the kind of story a client is likely to give them. This exercise enables students to learn how to work with facts to prepare arguments to be put in court.
- asking students to jot down a list of questions to be asked of a client in an interview to ascertain further facts and instructions.
- asking our students to make notes of the strengths and weaknesses of their client's case for the purposes of negotiating a settlement or guilty plea.

'Projects'

One problem our students may encounter in learning jurisprudential or sociological material is that it appears to be very abstract and difficult to grasp if read or learnt in a vacuum. Legal philosophy, feminist legal theory, law and social theory, law and economics and other theoretical approaches to law can be very daunting to the uninitiated. We should design materials to enable students to involve themselves in research projects so that they are exposed to the culture of the particular discipline as a scholar or researcher in that discipline. Our students will come to see the relevance and application of these theoretical frameworks, and will develop initiative, creativity and organisation skills. In an introductory subject on legal theory, for example, we might invite our students to work on a 'research project' which will make use of all the materials covered in class. At the beginning of the subject we can ask our students to select an area of law which will be the basis of a research project. They then select a particular issue or research question that interests them: for example, the enforcement of environmental pollution legislation. Then, as they are required to read for each topic in the subject, they design a research methodology to answer their research question. The research methodology should include a discussion of the likely impact of the various debates they are studying in the subject – how will these debates have an impact on their research question, how would they research their question so as to make a contribution to the particular debate and so on. At the end of each week's readings, we can leave a blank page in the materials for our students to jot down notes indicating how the week's topic is relevant to their 'project'.[72]

Questions

Questions are the lifeblood of good teaching materials. We can use questions to engage our students in a running dialogue with us, the materials, and each other. We can use questions in our materials to:[73]

- give our students an opportunity to apply what they have learned;

72 For further discussion of 'projects' see Jacques (1991) 96-101.

73 See Le Brun and Johnstone (1994) 274-280.

- provide students with a challenge to venture beyond their existing knowledge, attitudes and frameworks;
- enable students to make links between different aspects of the subject matter;
- focus students on what they should be reading;
- highlight the key stages of difficult arguments;
- ask students what they understand by certain concepts, to reinforce their learning;
- help students interact with the materials (in-text questions used at frequent intervals in the text);
- include self-assessment questions which enable our students to test themselves at regular intervals, and to check on the progress of their learning; and
- prompt and support deep approaches to learning.

We can use questions to provide 'scaffolding' or frameworks, so that our students learn how to internalise a particular way of thinking and develop their own reasoning processes. For example, the questions can require students to think about a particular issue. Further questions can require students to think about a related issue. A third set of questions can then require students to compare the different arguments or reasoning processes they have just completed. In this way we can show students how to reason their way through issues, and enable them to learn this skill by doing it. We should avoid setting questions the answers to which become an end in themselves, so that students read the material simply to provide superficial answers to the questions. The questions must require students to delve to find real meaning in the material to be read. The use of questions in this way teaches our students how to monitor their own learning. Students eventually internalise the logic of the process, and are able to carry out the process without close guidance. Their familiarity with the problem solving process that they have been practising will enable them to monitor their problem solving when they attempt to deal with different problems.

Similarly, we can use questions to focus student attention on certain issues or phenomena as a means of setting up a particular activity. Once students have thought about and discussed these 'setting up questions', they are in a position to work on a further set of questions which develops their understanding of the phenomenon being explored.

On another level, the question can focus student attention on the relationship between different articles, cases or statutes. We can use questions to prompt students to develop certain points, or to develop responses to points raised, or to apply principles set out in the reading. A question may require students to evaluate an argument from a certain perspective, or demand a student to consider her or his values and attitudes in relation to a particular topic.

We can also use questions to reinforce earlier learning in a topic or subject. We can ask our students to summarise, re-read or revise earlier work, and then to incorporate that earlier learning into a later activity or answer. In that way they can draw connections between different aspects of a topic or subject, and can integrate and reinforce different aspects of their learning.

The key point here is that questions which guide student reading can be distracting or useful depending on how carefully the questions are chosen. If the questions are too narrow, they can actually inhibit student imagination and thinking, rather than stimulating it. We should therefore consider what the point of the question is, using the questions in Table 8.

- Are the questions there to focus attention on important doctrinal issues?
- If so, are the questions too confining?
- Or are the questions there to provoke the reader to consider broader doctrinal, empirical, policy or theoretical issues?
- Do the questions do this?
- Are they liberating and inspiring, or do they inhibit student intuition, thought and reflection?
- Do they promote deep approaches to learning, or do they give a message to students that they are only required to engage in cursory reading to identify particular sections of the text?

Table 8: Questions to ask ourselves about our questions

We can ask many types of questions in our materials. It is counterproductive to set out a comprehensive categorisation of the various types of questions, but the following examples may help us ensure that we ask a variety of questions in our materials.[74] Centra, for example, has divided the kinds of questions that can be asked into four types.[75] I have summarised his typology in Table 9. Each type of question focuses on different areas and levels of the cognitive skills and the objectives relating to values discussed in section 2.3 of this book.

Cognitive memory questions

- These are narrow, closed questions the responses to which can easily be anticipated.
- The intention is to have students recall or recognise information.
- Students are required to recall specific facts, defining, repeating, answering 'yes' or 'no', or quoting.
- Example: ask students to recount the facts of a case, or the elements of a cause of action.

74 See generally Johnstone (1992) 45-47.

75 Centra, J, *Determining Faculty Effectiveness*, Jossey-Bass, San Francisco, 1979.

Convergent questions

- These are also narrow, closed questions. The answers, although generally predictable, are less restricted.
- The questions aim to have students analyse and combine given and remembered information.
- Students interpret, compare, contrast, explain, conclude or summarise information.
- Examples: 'How do the judicial decision-making models of Hart, Dworkin and MacCormick differ?'; or 'How does each judge differ in approach to the issue in dispute?

Divergent questions

- These are broad, open-ended questions which permit a wide variety of thought-provoking, original and unpredictable answers.
- The questions aim to get students independently to develop their own information or view a given topic from a new perspective.
- Students hypothesise, speculate, predict, imply, synthesise, infer, devise plans and solve problems.
- Example: 'Devise a research methodology to determine how legislation might best lower the road toll'.

Evaluative questions

- These are broad open-ended questions, with diverse and unpredictable responses.
- Students project and support their judgments, values and choices. For the most part, these questions involve all of the cognitive operations, and can also involve an exploration of the students' attitudes, values and interests.
- Students judge, value, choose, rate and offer opinions. A student should be challenged to defend her or his opinion by using internal and external standards.
- Example: 'Who is your favourite judge? Why?'

Table 9: Centra's Typology of Questions

We should ask questions at different levels of this spectrum to involve students in the materials they are reading, build up their competence, knowledge and skills, and develop different teaching objectives. We can use lower level questions as a prelude to higher level questions.

Our questions in our materials should be:

- stimulating and interesting;
- brief, direct, and not too general;

- clearly phrased, so our students know exactly what they have to do. Do not ask questions that can be answered with 'yes' or 'no' if the intention is to engage in an activity. Rather ask students to evaluate, analyse and so on.

We should take care not to require our students to deal with too many questions in a particular activity. They may find it difficult to focus on more than two questions during their initial reading of a case or article. We might better assist students by highlighting one or two broad questions to guide the initial reading of the case or article. We can then ask a number of detailed, more focused questions which would require students to re-read parts of the material before providing an answer. In Part 4 I have provided an example of a series of questions before and after extracted superior court decisions.

We might also assist our students with questions which indicate the number of factors that our students should list or consider. This will focus their thoughts, require then to distil the essence of the topic, and provide useful feedback on what they have learnt.[76]

3.7.3 Create opportunities and spaces for students to respond to the materials

If one of our concerns in developing a teaching strategy is to check on our students' conceptions of our subject, when devising our materials we should consider whether and how we want our students to record their responses. Wherever possible, we should require students to respond explicitly to activities, and in writing. To facilitate this we should give students spaces in the materials in which to record their responses. The mere act of recording their responses gives students a form of feedback on their learning. If a student is unable to articulate a response to the materials the student immediately has an indication that she or he needs further work or assistance in developing their understanding of the subject matter.

In order to prompt students to record their responses to the materials, we could:

- leave a space in the materials so that our students can jot down notes, devise a solution to a problem, draft a document and so on;
- require students to compose long answers in a separate notebook or on a separate piece of paper;
- ask students to tick a box to indicate agreement or disagreement or to choose from a number of multiple-choice questions;
- underline key phrases in the text;
- fill in missing words or phrases in blank spaces left in sentences;
- complete a questionnaire;
- draw a flow diagram or chart; or
- write an essay.

76 Gibbs, Habeshaw and Habeshaw (1987) 53.

In our materials we should indicate to students how they will be following up on their responses in class. One option might be to indicate in the materials that we will require students to try out their responses to a problem in the materials by mooting the issues in class, or by participating in a classroom simulation. In Part 4 I provide examples of these links between activities in the materials and in the classroom.

3.7.4 Maximise opportunities for feedback

I emphasised in section 2.4, and earlier in this section, that we should provide our students with as much feedback as possible in our teaching. Feedback enables students to:

- keep actively involved in their learning;
- increase their chances to learn;
- find out how well they are doing;
- overcome problems or correct misconceptions in their learning;
- develop confidence in what they do know; and
- bring their own experience to bear on their studies.

We can provide further feedback by using class time to find out how our students engaged in their private study, and whether they had any difficulties with their learning. We should provide as many opportunities as we can for our students to discuss with us and each other their progress, ideas and solutions to questions we have asked. The best opportunities for students to get feedback from us and from their peers are in group work in class or general class discussion.[77]

Self-assessment questions

We should also maximise the opportunities for self-assessment in our materials. Self-assessment is one of the foundations for active learning.[78] Here are a few examples of the types of self-assessment questions we can include in our materials:[79]

- multiple choice questions – our students choose which of a series of options is correct, and we then provide feedback on their choice;
- true/false questions (limited multiple choice questions);
- questions where our students insert missing words or expressions into spaces left in the materials;
- our students complete unfinished sentences, or complete diagrams or tables;
- we ask our students what is wrong with a statement, diagram or flow chart;
- problems or other exercises where students have to apply what they have learned thus far in the topic.

77 See section 2.6 above, and Le Brun and Johnstone (1994) ch 6.

78 Race (1992) 58.

79 *Ibid* 55-92.

- questions asking students to decide how well they understand a topic; what their strong points are; and the parts of the topic they do not understand. We can also ask them to devise a plan to overcome their weaknesses.

We might also include answers to some of our questions in our teaching materials. The inclusion of an example answer will help students to check that they are on track with their thinking. For example, the materials can specify that before going on to the next questions, our students should check at page x that the answer to the first question was correct. This approach enables modifications in approach can be made where required.

Of course, we need to make ourselves available to be consulted by students who discover weaknesses in their learning as a result of the feedback they receive from us, their peers or through self-assessment.

Summary

This section of the book has set out basic principles for the development of teaching materials for law teaching. The reader will discern in all the basic principles the key underlying concepts set out in sections 2.1 to 2.7 of the book. The principles are summarised in a series of steps in Table 10 below.

Step 1: Determine the characteristics of the students who will be using the materials

For example, we might consider the following questions, and the implications for the design of our teaching materials:

- What is the age group, gender breakdown and background of our students?
- Why are students taking the subject and what are their hopes and fears?
- What are their prior educational experiences, levels of ability etc?
- What knowledge, skills and attitudes do students already have in relation to the subject?
- With all these characteristics in mind, how should we design our subject and at what level should we pitch our materials and classroom teaching?

Step 2: Determine the aims and learning objectives of the subject

- Determine the overall aims of the subject.
- Consider a variety of learning objectives covering cognitive (knowledge, understanding, application, analysis, synthesis and evaluation); affective (the development of interests, attitudes and values) and skills (legal reasoning, legal research, problem solving, interviewing, counselling, mediating, information gathering, litigating and managerial) domains.
- Express chosen objectives clearly, succinctly, unambiguously, and in user-friendly language so that students have sufficient detail about what they are expected to do.

Step 3: Determine the assessment tasks

- Consider the kinds of assessment tasks that focus on the significant processes of competence we want students to develop in the subject and which will enable students to demonstrate that they have achieved the learning objectives established for the subject.

- Ensure the chosen assessment tasks are seen by students as an intrinsic part of their learning, and not just something which occurs after teaching and learning.
- Choose a variety of assessment methods which actively engage students in tasks.
- Explain to students how the teaching materials and classroom activities relate to the assessment tasks.
- Make the expectations and criteria for each piece of assessment clear to students.
- Ensure that students get timely and adequate feedback on each part of their assessment.

Step 4: Determine the structure of the subject

- Take into account the aims and objectives of the subject; student workload; topics of relevance and interest to students; interesting theoretical and social issues that can be explored in the subject and which eschew a white, heterosexual male bias in the subject matter; the relationship between this subject and others in the curriculum; and simple and complex skills that can be developed in the subject.
- In sequencing the topics choose the sequence: that builds an understanding from a few basic ideas; is structured on previous learning; eases students into the subject; and follows a sequence that most facilitates student learning in the subject (this may not be the structure that an expert would use to describe the subject matter).

Step 5: Select appropriate teaching methods

- Choose from a range of classroom methods, printed teaching materials, computer-based learning materials; and fieldwork activities.
- The choice of methods will be governed by the learning objectives chosen in step 2, the assessment tasks outlined in step 3, and the sequence of topics established in step 4.
- Choose methods which promote active learning.
- Choose methods which enable students to demonstrate their level of understanding.
- Provide opportunities for students to receive feedback on their learning.
- Integrate computer-based methods, fieldwork-based methods, printed teaching materials and classroom methods.

Step 6: Design printed teaching materials

- The materials should include all basic subject information.
- They should include as much as possible of the material students will have to work with when engaging in self-study prior to class.
- They should be user-friendly.

- They should be chosen to reflect a variety of learning objectives.
- They should be chosen to reflect a variety of different 'voices'.
- They should include visual aids (flow charts, diagrams etc) and signposts (for example, headings and sub-headings).
- They should clearly express the learning objectives to be achieved through use of the materials.
- They should anchor each topic within students' own personal experiences.
- They should provide examples to illustrate concepts.
- They should involve students in different types of activities (simulations, problems, case studies, case preparation, projects, questions, self-assessment activities) and in dialogue.
- They should provide students with opportunities to respond to activities.
- They should maximise opportunities for self-assessment and other forms of feedback.
- They should be integrated with classroom activities and other teaching methods.
- Students must understand how the relationship between the materials and the assessment tasks in the subject.

Step 7: Evaluate the teaching materials regularly to ensure that they play a role in improving student learning.

Table 10 Summary of steps in developing teaching materials for active learning in law

In Part 4 I provide an example of printed teaching materials which can be used in a subject on the law of contract. The materials have been developed using the model I have outlined in this Part and in Part 2. Part 4 includes a discussion of how the particular materials described in that Part might be integrated with classroom activities.

PART 4

TEACHING MATERIALS IN ACTION: AN EXAMPLE OF THE USE OF TEACHING MATERIALS IN LAW TEACHING

This part of the book provides examples of printed teaching materials which we can use to teach law in situations that encourage our students to deep approaches to learning and which approximate the kind of activities that lawyers and legal theorists engage in. The materials are intended to illustrate the principles and themes set out in Parts 2 and 3 of the book, and to give examples of the ways in which we can prepare our own teaching materials or casebooks. The materials are by no means intended to be the last word on the way that the particular topic could or should be taught. Rather they should simply be seen as examples of the possibilities open to those of us who wish to teach using activity-based printed teaching materials. A lot of work needs to be done to develop good printed teaching materials for law teaching. These examples merely provide a start.

4.1 EXAMPLE: CONTRACT

These materials have been compiled for use in the law of contract, a second year subject taught to approximately 300 students. Let us imagine two scenarios.

First let us assume that we are to teach the subject primarily in two large classes, of about 150 students each. These large classes meet for three hours each week. Our students also meet in smaller seminar groups (15 to 25 students) for an hour each week. In addition, we expect our students to engage in their own private study prior to each class. The materials can be used for these three venues for learning. The materials would be part of a book of teaching materials designed to enable students to study on their own outside class. We will complement and further develop their individual study with activities in class.

The second scenario is that in the subject there are five classes of 60 students, each meeting for two two hour classes each week. Once again we expect students to engage in private study before class.

The materials set out in this part can be used with classes of any size. The larger the class, the greater the argument for using teaching materials to promote deep approaches to learning during students' private study, and the more we will have to rely on teaching methods that break up the class into smaller components. This involves careful planning and preparation. We can use teaching materials in large classes, then, to ensure that our students are stimulated and engaged in active learning from the outset of their class preparation. We should design our classroom activities to develop student learning through stimulating activities, and to provide students with important feedback as to how well they understand the subject matter. The greater the variety of activities, the wider the exposure to, and experience of, the subject, and the more useful the feedback. Our overall objective is to ensure that each student engages actively with the subject matter. In classes where we rely exclusively on lecturing this is unlikely to happen, because our students will tend to operate in passive note-taking mode. They are likely to be involved in the subject matter only as passive recipients of information; they will not have any opportunity to put the subject matter to use; and they will receive no feedback as to misconceptions in their learning.

The topic in this example, **Agreed Damages Clauses**, has been chosen simply because it is relatively self-contained. Generally we would teach it after students have been exposed to the remedy of damages for breach of contract. Normally this topic would be taught in one or two hours in the traditional contracts subject. The materials put together in this section would need at least four hours of class time (large group or seminar) adequately to complement the independent study our students would undertake with the materials. I have divided the materials into four parts. Each part provides a program of independent study to be followed up with class activity.

The materials may be more ambitious than most of us would attempt for a single topic. There are many (probably too many) themes running through the materials. The materials introduce students to drafting skills, interpretation skills, skills of critical evaluation, skills of comprehension and analysis, ideologies of contract and judicial decision-making, law and economics, socio-legal research and law reform. The materials also raise issues of values and of international perspectives. I emphasise that these materials are only examples of how we might approach topics. Each of us will have a different view of what should be included in each stage of our subject. It is up to each of us to tailor our materials and methods to our own objectives, syllabus and assessment. Even for this particular topic, each of us will place a different emphasis on each aspect of the topic, and will probably allocate different amounts of time to each class. In particular, some teachers may find that the second class in the materials is too ambitious to be conducted in an hour long class, and may want to allocate two hours of class time to that part of the topic and less to the other aspects.

Whereas these materials raise all these issues in one topic, we may prefer to spread these issues amongst a number of topics, so that our students come to grips with issues of legal doctrine in each topic and at the same time explore one other theme. Alternatively, this topic could be taught early on in the subject, using four or five class contact hours, as a means of exposing students to a number of themes which can be picked up in later topics as and when appropriate.

Before each 'class' or 'step' in the materials, I have provided a commentary explaining the basis upon which I have compiled the materials. The commentary also indicates the way in which the materials will be integrated with classroom activities.

4.1.1 Overview of the materials and class activities

In the topic covered in these materials students are required to learn the topic Agreed Damages Clauses through a number of activities which are interesting and which will stimulate and encourage students to engage deeply with what could be quite a dry topic. It is very tempting for students simply to extract some of the basic factors that the courts take into account in construing agreed damages clauses, and apply them mechanically to 'problems' that they may encounter in their end of year examination, without ever seriously considering the nature of the issues involved in agreed damages clauses. The objectives of these materials are to draw students into a discussion of these clauses based in their own experience and common sense, and to consider, through being put in particular hypothetical but nevertheless fairly realistic situations, the purpose of agreed damages clauses, and their impact on the contracting parties. They should also have considered the public policy issues surrounding the legal regulation of agreed damages clauses. The materials provide students with opportunities to draft and construe agreed damages clauses before and after learning the law. This should enable them to understand the full impact of the law on agreed damages clauses themselves, while understanding how the law affects the lawyer's functions in relation to the clauses.

The objectives and purposes of activities to be conducted in class and in the materials should be transparent in the sense that students should be able to see very clearly why they are engaging in an activity and how it will be dealt with in class. Students will then know how they should go about the activities, and have a realistic basis upon which to set their own goals and to monitor their own learning.

It is important that students get good feedback at the earliest possible time on their progress in these learning activities. In this way students can check their learning, and thus develop their self-monitoring skills.

The materials give space for students to answer the questions posed in the materials, and to do the exercises set out in the materials. Students are able to use the materials as a workbook. They should come to class having worked through the materials, and should have written 'answers' in the workbook. They should not see these 'answers' as the end product of their work, but as an essential part of the process of learning, in that they are descriptions of how students conceive of the subject and provide the basis for feedback. Once we are aware of how well students understand the topic, we will be able to modify our teaching to cater for difficulties our students encounter with the subject matter.

As I will show, class activity can follow up, develop and give feedback on students self-study in at least four ways.

- We can divide the class, whatever its size, into pairs of students, and ask each pair to participate in a variation of the co-operative learning/learning cell approach set out in Part 3 of this book. We can ask students to teach each other the basic issues raised by the questions in the materials, or to persuade each other of the validity of their responses to the exercises set in the materials. Our role is to move around the class, and to assist pairs in need of guidance. We should ask students to make a note of their difficulties, and we can deal with these in a full class discussion.
- We can give to the class a handout which sets out basic answers or guidelines to the questions and problems found in the materials. We can then divide the class into pairs or slightly larger groups (three or four) to individualise the feedback by discussion. We should encourage our students to write down problems for later discussion when the class regroups.
- We can give feedback by going through each question and exercise with the class. We can call on contributions from the class, or model an expert

approach to the task, so that students can see for themselves how they might have approached the issue.

- Many activities in the materials lead on to specific class activities. For example, the drafting of the agreed damages clause leads on to a simulation exercise in class where the parties have to discuss, question and justify the clause. The construction problem in the third stage also leads directly to a moot in the class, where students are asked to argue the case for one of the parties. In engaging in these tasks students should be able to judge for themselves the extent of their learning.

As I emphasised in section 2.4, the assessment for the contracts subject, of which these materials are part, must be integrated with the learning objectives, the teaching methods and the printed materials selected for the subject. We must provide students with opportunities to assess their own progress in the subject, and to receive as much feedback as possible from their fellow students and from us. It must also be clear to students just how their work with the printed materials and in the classroom will help them tackle the assessment tasks. Better still, student work with the materials or in the classroom might constitute part of the assessment. For example, as part of the summative assessment (that is, for grades) for the subject:

- students might be required to submit their responses to activities in the materials, by submitting the completed workbook or parts of the workbook, when they have worked through the materials;
- we might include written assignments in the materials which cover the issues and skills developed in the material and in class work, so that students submit the assignments when they have completed each topic;
- students might be assessed on their class participation,[1] building on their work with the materials; or
- the end of subject examination, take home examination or written assignment might include the same kinds of activities that students have engaged in when they have worked though the materials.

As I have argued,[2] unless students can see how their work with the materials and in the classroom ties in with their assessment, they are unlikely to engage actively with the materials in the ways we would like them to.

As the following pages show, the materials approach the topic of Agreed Damages Clauses through a number of steps.[3]

1 See Le Brun and Johnstone (1994) 208-215.

2 See above.

3 For a brief discussion of these materials, see Le Brun and Johnstone (1994) 320-26.

4.1.2 Step 1: situating the topic

Commentary

The first step is to situate this topic:

- in students' previous learning;
- in their everyday experience; and
- in a commercial context by considering the reasons for the drafting of the clause.

The fundamental purpose of this step is to get students personally interested in the topic, and motivated to learn. They should be able to see how an agreed damages clause could personally affect them, and should then be able to think about such clauses in terms of broader policy and theoretical issues. It is possible that second year law students have absolutely no idea about the commercial and legal culture surrounding the drafting, use and construction of agreed damages clauses. They may not even see clearly how such clauses fit into the topic of contractual damages. If that is the case, they cannot possibly hope to understand the legal principles that regulate such clauses. At best they will simply engage in surface approaches to learning to get the basics required to answer an examination question. At worst, the topic will by-pass them completely. To encourage students to engage in deep approaches to learning we want them to understand these important contextual issues, to be interested in the subject, and to see the place of the topic within the 'bigger picture'.

(i) We begin by setting out the objectives of the whole topic, so that students know exactly what is expected of them. The objectives are many and varied.[4] Students will be asked to do many things. The objectives give them a good idea of where they are going, why they are doing what they are doing, and what they are expected to achieve in studying the topic. By communicating the objectives at the outset we enable our students immediately to become involved in the learning process and to exercise some control over their own learning.

(ii) The materials then situate the topic in the context of the previous topic, the assessment of damages. The principles for the assessment of damages play an important role in agreed damages clauses, and so the materials ask students to revise the basic principles involved in the assessment of damages. This enables them to check their previous learning, while at the same time integrating that topic into the current topic. Some students may not want to fill in the box set out in the materials. That is their choice. Classroom activity, however, should begin with a few students reporting to the class on their revision exercises, or alternatively by asking students to divide up into pairs to compare their revision summaries. We may then want to give a very short mini lecture introducing Agreed Damages Clauses

4 Once again, the objectives may be too ambitious for some teachers and students. The objectives expressed in the materials set out the objectives which are to be pursued by working with the materials and in the classroom. They should be tailored to meet the objectives of teachers and students actually using the materials.

and ensure that the class is clear about the objectives of the topic, the way in which we will teach it, and how they are to go about learning the topic.

(iii) The topic is then situated in our students' everyday experience by asking them to consider a commonly used Agreed Damages Clause, a 'Cancellation' clause drawn up by a tour operator. Students should examine the clause before they start their study of the law. They should be able to hold it in their hands, read it, and think 'yes, I have come across this type of thing before'. The materials ask them to:

- think about how such clauses have affected them or would affect them; and
- consider why the other party to the transaction, the tour operator, would draft such a clause.

Once again, these activities should be within our students' experience as a party to such a transaction and they should have some idea of the motives of the operator. By the time they encounter this topic, they should have done a bit of contract law, and so should be able to think in commercial terms about these clauses.

The materials reinforce this activity by asking students to think of another agreed damages clause. Once again, this activity draws upon students' own experiences, but this time, the exercise is more difficult, because they have to think of their own clause. If they cannot remember coming across such a clause, they are required to demonstrate their understanding of what agreed damages clauses are by making up one of their own.

When students come to class, we have a number of options to follow up on these activities. We can ask students to discuss their responses in small groups, or in a full class discussion. If responses are sluggish in a full class discussion, we can involve students in a brainstorming exercise, where they are required to generate as many responses as they can, as quickly as possible. Remember, the basic aim is to establish interest, enthusiasm and context.

(iv) The next stage is to situate the topic in relation to the rest of the law of contract, so that students can see contract as a conceptual, schematic whole, and draw links between the various topics. Accordingly, the materials ask students to examine other clauses drafted by the tour operator and to compare them with the cancellation clause. They should consider the difference between the cancellation clause and a deposit, exclusion clause and other clauses. Their learning is integrated, not in an abstract sense by cross referencing to topics they may not yet have covered (if they begin the subject by examining remedies), but by reference to actual clauses in the contract.

Once again, class activity can focus on small or large group discussion. In discussing the relationship between the various clauses, we may find it best to conduct a large group discussion, because that method will enable us to explain, as part of the discussion, some basic principles relating to deposits, exclusion clauses, limitation clauses, and so on. We should take care, in discussions, to add to the enculturation process. That is not to say that we should inculcate students with the 'professional voice', but rather that we should ensure that we are contributing to the engagement of students with a genuine, not an imitation, subject. The teacher should not just talk about the clauses as a lawyer would, but also encourage students to engage in the topic with a 'human voice'.

From our students' responses to this and the previous activity, we are able to determine whether they are in a good position to learn the basic legal principles in the topic.

(v) The next part of the materials requires students to draft an agreed damages clause and to write the client a covering letter explaining why they have drafted the clause in their chosen way. The purpose here is not to draft the perfect agreed damages clause. Rather it is to engage students in an activity in which they have to think through the logic of drafting such clauses. This can best be done by actually drafting. The situation is quite authentic – it is based on a clause in the Conditions of Parking to be found at any premises of a large car parking company.

Class activity to follow up this drafting exercise would be conducted by putting students into pairs, and asking them to discuss the drafting process. They should talk about the issues they considered, the drafting difficulties they experienced, and the policy and ethical issues that occurred to them as they drafted their clauses.

(vi) Students are now in a position to think more broadly about the policy and theoretical issues arising in relation to these clauses. All activities thus far should enable students to see the topic as an important public policy issue, drawing on philosophical and economic perspectives of the functioning of the law of contract and the appropriateness of legal regulation. The final activity for the first class in the materials is to require students to put together all the activities and experiences they have undergone in the first step in order to reflect on a broader theoretical level about the role of law in regulating these clauses.

The classroom activities would end with each pair in the previous exercise pairing with another pair to engage in a discussion of these broader theoretical issues (a pyramid). At the conclusion of the class we should explain to students the activities involved in the following class.

This outline for the first class is summarised in Figure 5 (page 110).[5]

The materials for this first class are set out in the following pages.

5 This figure was first published in Le Brun and Johnstone (1994) 322.

	Private Study Prior to Class Using the Materials	*Classroom Activities*
1	Students read the objectives.	Teacher gives mini lecture in previous class, together with overview of topic.
2	Recap principles of the previous topic.	Students compare summaries in pairs; or Teacher-controlled discussion in which the teacher calls up a few students to report until all principles are before the class; or Teacher clarifies principles causing difficulty to students.
3	Examine a real-life example of an agreed damages clause, and think of other examples.	Small group discussion; or Full class discussion.
4	Examine and compare other clauses in the extracted contract.	Small group discussion; or Full class discussion.
5	Draft an agreed damages clause.	Discuss in pairs.
6	Consider policy and theoretical issues.	Pyramid, pair of pairs from previous activity, and then full class discussion.

Figure 5: Step 1

The materials

Topic X Week Y

Agreed Damages Clauses

In the previous topic, you studied the basic principles of the law relating to damages for breach of contract. In our next topic we will build upon this learning. In particular, we will explore some of the difficult issues that arise when the contracting parties attempt to quantify in advance damages for breach of the contract that they are entering into.

The aim of this section of the subject is to introduce you to agreed damages clauses, the underlying commercial considerations which govern their use, and the legal rules which regulate them. We will be looking at these clauses from a number of angles. The topic should give you a better grasp of the role of the law of contract and of policy issues pertaining to the legal regulation of these clauses. At the end of this topic you should:

(i) be able to describe the legal and commercial functions of agreed damages clauses, and give examples of their impact on the person whose possible breach of contract has given rise to the drafting of the clause;

(ii) be able to describe the basic principles of the law relating to these clauses;

(iii) have further analysed the judicial ideologies and ideologies of contract that have shaped the development of the law by the courts;

(iv) be able to draft and construe these clauses by applying the basic legal principles and your understanding of the commercial functions of these clauses and the underlying policy issues;

(v) be in a position to explain how an economist would analyse these clauses and the law that governs them;

(vi) have developed proposals to reform the law governing these clauses. These proposals should be based on your understanding of the legal principles, and your awareness of the practical, theoretical and policy issues that arise from the use of these clauses;

(vii) have evaluated the Victorian Law Reform Commission and international proposals for reform of the area.

Revision: The Calculation of Contractual Damages

As we have seen, the law relating to agreed damages clauses builds on the last topic, the remedies available to a plaintiff where there has been a breach of the contract by the defendant. We have considered a number of different remedies, including the awarding of damages to the plaintiff.

As basic revision, and as a springboard for the current topic, summarise, in a few lines, the basic principles followed by the courts when awarding damages to the plaintiff. Refer to your class notes or to a textbook if you need to refresh your memory. List the main principles for further revision and reference.

SUMMARY: BASIC PRINCIPLES OF AWARDING DAMAGES TO THE PLAINTIFF

Which aspects of this topic would you like to discuss further in class?

The Functions of Agreed Damages Clauses

In the course of drawing up a contract, the parties may seek to determine in advance the damages that are payable should one party breach the contract. In this part of the topic we want you to explore the commercial function of these clauses, your reaction as a consumer, and the skills and issues involved in drafting contractual clauses and agreed damages clauses in particular. We also want you to begin to develop a critical analysis of the role of the law in regulating these clauses. You will be required to do a lot of work on your own, and then come to class to share your ideas and get some feedback on the issues and skills you have been developing. Please write in the space allotted your responses to the questions, issues and problems posed in the materials. This will give you an opportunity to articulate what you have learnt, so that you can see what you know and what you need to work on. This will also enable you to build on your learning in class so that you can get feedback from other students in the class, and from your teacher.

An Example of an Agreed Damages Clause

Consider, for example, the following conditions of booking drawn up by a tour operator.

General Information and Conditions of Booking

Availability

Miles Tours Limited operates from June until November. As accommodation is at a premium for most of the ski season, we advise that bookings should be made a far ahead as possible.

Deposits/Reservations

Reservations will be accepted for all tours against a deposit of $100 per person payable at the time the booking is confirmed to your Travel Agent and received by Miles Tours within 10 days of that confirmation. Failure to meet the above condition may result in the cancellation of your booking by Miles Tours. The payment indicates acceptance of the terms and conditions of bookings of Miles Tours. Your deposit is accepted as the first instalment of your land content cost.

Final Payment

Full payment for all holidays must be received by Miles Tours 35 days from confirmation. For holidays booked within 35 days of departure full payment is due and payable immediately on confirmation to your Travel Agent. If full payment has not been received 14 days prior to departure, then Miles Tours reserves the right to automatically cancel your booking and deduct any associated cancellation charges and administration fees from deposits held. For payment received within 10 days of departure Miles Tours cannot accept liability or responsibility for delivery of your tour documents but these items will be provided on arrival at your destination.

Cancellations

Should it become necessary to cancel your holiday at any time after it has been confirmed then the following cancellation fees will be levied. A minimum of $50 will be charged on any cancellation. Cancellations made 30 days or more prior to departure may still incur cancellation charges and these will be levied on top of the $50 where applicable. Monies paid will be refunded less applicable cancellation charges.

Notice Given

30 days plus	$50 per person plus cancellation charges where applicable.
14 – 30 days	$50 per person plus 10% of tour cost.
1 – 14 days	$50 per person plus 25% of tour cost.

Refunds

Refunds will not be applicable for clients who amend their itineraries after departure from Australia. No refund will be applicable on any unused arrangements other than in extenuating circumstances at Miles Tours discretion.

Changing Reservation

You will be allowed one set of amendments to your original booking free of charge (unless the cost of that amendment exceeds $25. In this instance $5 per night will be charged). Further alterations will incur a minimum charge of $25 per alteration to cover communication and administration costs.

Alterations

Regrettably tour costs can be subject to fluctuation. Miles Tours reserves the right to amend any tour or cost. All tour prices quoted therefore are subject to amendment prior to departure, should the need arise. Variations in airline, transport accommodation and other services may necessitate alterations to itineraries and hotels. These will be made to best possible advantage with appropriate adjustments to cost. Occasionally it may be necessary to use accommodation other than that listed in the itinerary. Where alternatives are necessary, every endeavour will be made to maintain a similar standard to that used throughout the tour. Accommodation terminates at 10 am on the last day of the tour. Should you require your room longer this may be arranged between yourself and the hotel concerned at an additional cost.

Operator Responsibilities

In arranging and organising the tour Miles Tours is acting as tour organiser. Miles Tours does not itself operate the air, sea or land transport, or conduct the hotel or other accommodation arranged for the tour. Miles Tours, its agents, and/or any company or persons associated with promoting or arranging the tour does not accept responsibility for any act or omission on the part of those actually performing those services or services incidental thereto. Furthermore the responsibilities of the air carriers participating in the tour are limited as specified in their tickets, conditions of contract, conditions of carriage, and tariffs. All tours and quoted tour prices are based on known schedules, exchange rates, fares and tariffs at the time of printing, and the right is hereby specifically reserved to modify the itinerary and tour prices in any way considered necessary or desirable or to change any reservation, hotel, feature and/or means of conveyance without notice and for any reason whatsoever, and the extra cost, if any, to be to the account of the passenger. In the event that any modification to your holiday itinerary prior to the completion of the booking and before your departure causes your itinerary to become materially different from that contemplated prior to the modification being affected, passengers may withdraw from the holiday and any monies already paid will be refunded in full. Alternatively, Miles Tours will re-arrange the holiday by providing alternative arrangements of at least the same standard as that already booked. It is essential that passengers check with their agent whether any modification has occurred in the holiday chosen before completion of the booking. Miles Tours reserves the right to cancel or withdraw any tour or any booking made for a passenger, or to decline to accept or retain any person as a member of a tour. Miles Tours shall be under no obligation or liability to any person as the result of any inaccuracy, misdescription or changes to any tour or its itinerary or for losses or additional expense due to delays or changes in air or any other transport services, sickness, weather, strikes, war, quarantine or other causes.

Client Responsibilities

Baggage and personal effects are the passenger's own risk throughout the tour and it is the responsibility of the passenger to effect insurance if desired. It is your Travel Agent's responsibility to forward deposits and other payments to Miles Tours on your behalf if such payments are made with them but your Travel Agents is not the agent of Miles Tours for the purpose of receipt of monies. Receipt of deposits and subsequent payments by the Travel Agent does not constitute receipt of those monies by Miles Tours and the Travel Agent has no authority expressed or implied to receive monies on our behalf. There is no liability on our behalf in respect of the monies paid to your Travel Agent unless and until we notify you (by way of a Booking Confirmation Advice and Payment Receipt Advice in the case of deposits and by Payment Receipt Advice in the case of other payments) that monies paid have been received by Miles Tours. Such advices will be forwarded by Miles Tours to your Travel Agent for your collection. You should check with your Travel Agent 10 days after paying deposits and other payments to ensure the advices are available for collection by you.

Your Own Reflections on the Conditions of Booking

Now jot down notes on each of these questions and we will discuss them in the next class.

What is the function of the 'cancellation fee'?

Why would the tour operator draw up such a clause? What problem is the operator trying to avoid by including the clause in the contract? In what way might it save the operator time and/or resources in the future?

How would the clause affect you as a consumer?

Your Own Example of an Agreed Damages Clause

Think of an 'agreed damages clause' that you have come into contact with recently. Describe the clause. If you can't think of a clause that you have actually come across, make up your own clause and describe it in the space below.

Why would the drafter of your example of an agreed damages clause have drafted the clause?

Are the reasons you have just given the same as the reasons for the drafting of the 'cancellation' clause?

How did (or how would) your example of an agreed damages clause affect you as an interested party?

The Relationship of the Agreed Damages Clauses to Other Contractual Clauses

Read the other clauses that have been extracted from the conditions of booking example. How is the 'cancellation' clause similar to, or different from:

(i) a 'deposit'?

(ii) provisions under the heading 'Refund'?

(iii) The provisions under the heading 'Alterations'?

(iv) The exclusion, limitation and other clauses under the headings 'Operator Responsibilities' and 'Client Responsibilities'?

Drafting Problem 1[6]

The objective of this drafting problem is to give you an opportunity, as a solicitor, to draft an agreed damages clause on the instructions of a client. At this stage don't worry about the fact that you know nothing about the law relating to these clauses. Use your common sense, imagination and everyday experience of these clauses. Consider carefully the matters that you would take into account in drafting the clause. The clause that you have drafted will give you the basis for further drafting exercises in this topic, so spend some time drafting the best clause you can at this stage. We will discuss your clause

6 This activity was first published in Le Brun and Johnstone (1994) 321.

briefly in the next class, and then you will come back to it once you have studied the legal principles governing the construction of such clauses.

> You are a practising solicitor. A client of yours, Ms Jane De Maggio, is the managing director of a prosperous Melbourne company which owns and operates a whole chain of car parking facilities which offer parking, at a price, to the public. Ms De Maggio indicates to you that the existing terms and conditions of parking offered by the company include terms specifying that customers must display the date and time of issue of tickets whenever requested by a company employee; that customers cannot cause obstructions in the garage; and that customers cannot stand in no parking areas or reserve bays. The company is not sure how to enforce these terms and conditions. How, for example, can it sue customers for contractual damages when these terms and conditions have been breached? The company fears that bringing an action for contractual damages in the courts will be expensive and not worth the time and effort.
>
> Ms De Maggio asks you to draft a clause to insert into the standard parking contract enabling the company to get some compensation for the breach of these conditions without having to initiate litigation each time.

- What do you advise her?

- Indicate the factors you would take into account in drafting your clause. What policy issues and commercial considerations must you take into account?

- What calculations do you need to make?

List, in note form, three or four of the factors to be taken into account in drafting the clause.

-
-
-

Now set out the clause that you have drafted for Ms De Maggio.

Write a brief covering letter to Ms De Maggio explaining why you have drafted the clause in the way that you have.

Policy Issues Arising From Agreed Damages Clauses

Now let us draw the threads together from these activities.

What difficulties or issues did you discover from the points of view of the consumer and of the drafting lawyer during these activities? Give, in note form, three discoveries that you made from each perspective. We will discuss your responses in class.

As a Consumer	**As the Drafting Solicitor**
I discovered	I found
....	....
....	....
....	....

Are there any common issues or difficulties? What are they?

Are there any conflicts between the perspectives of the lawyer and the consumer? What are they?

Now prepare these questions for class discussion. You will work in a small group from your notes.

(i) Should there be legal intervention to regulate these clauses *or* should the parties be free to decide for themselves?

(ii) Is the court, or are the parties, in the best position to assess the damages likely to arise from a breach of the contract?

(iii) Upon what philosophical basis could the courts intervene to strike down these clauses?

(iv) List any existing statutory provisions which may, in certain circumstances, strike down agreed damages clauses?

4.1.3 Step 2: learning the law

Commentary

Students at this point should have a good background to:

- the function of agreed damages clauses;
- the way they will affect the parties;
- the problems of drafting these clauses; and
- broader theoretical issues involved in the use of these clauses.

They should be in a position to learn the basic principles involved in this area of the law. These principles should now have some personal meaning for them.

The second step is for students to read two edited cases which set out the basic legal principles and apply them in a manner that illustrates to students the way that the principles operate. The materials lead students through the cases with carefully worded questions. The questions focus student attention not just on issues of legal doctrine and legal principle, but also on broader issues of legal theory and policy. The questions are broad enough not to confine student thinking, but rather have the aim of encouraging students to think as broadly as possible about the issues, both doctrinal and 'theoretical'. These questions should promote deep approaches to learning in students, because they aim to focus student attention on actually understanding the materials. Students will, however, easily be tempted into surface learning approaches if we do not keep them stimulated, engaged and fully aware of what is expected of them.

The materials include five types of questions in this second step.

(i) The materials require students to read the cases first time through, focusing on two broad questions. Students are unlikely to be able to keep more than about two questions in mind when reading cases for the first time. The two questions raise the two basic themes which govern the legal principles. They are aimed at enabling students to understand the whole topic.

(ii) After each case there are a number of questions which help students analyse each case. Students should re-read the case, or parts of the case, to answer these questions.

(iii) After students have read the first case, the materials both check and reinforce their learning (and thus give students a form of feedback) by asking them to construe the cancellation clause that they looked at in the first class. Students *apply* their learning at the earliest possible moment, so that they do not learn the principles in a vacuum.

(iv) After students have read and analysed both cases, a fourth set of questions asks them to *synthesise* the basic principles emerging from the cases.

(v) A fifth set of questions locates the cases and the principles they set out within broader *theoretical* issues.

This second stage enables students to practise case reading skills, and at the same time helps them to develop a conceptual framework for the topic. Their experience with the issues and the guiding questions should enable them to read and integrate the cases in a meaningful way. Because they have done it themselves, they should develop the ability (and the confidence) to tackle new areas on their own.

The cases have both been edited to remove parts that are not central to the primary objective of their inclusion – to teach students the basic principles in a way that enables them to see how the principles operate; and to raise issues of legal theory and legal policy. Only two cases have been included, but no judgments have been omitted. Students should be able to decide for themselves which judgments are better than others. Note that one of the reasons I chose the second extracted case, the *Esanda* case, was that it includes a discussion by the High Court of another of its important decisions, in the *AMEV* case. Another feature of the *Esanda* extract is that it includes the law reporter's summary of Counsel's arguments before the High Court, which give students an idea of how the case was argued.

Private Study Prior to Class Using the Materials	*Classroom Activities*
1. Read the first case guided by two basic questions which draw out the important themes in the case.	Co-operative learning in which students teach each other or review each others answers to the questions.
2. Re-read the case to answer analytical questions, which 'model' an approach to reading the case, and direct students to particular analytical issues.	List all difficulties for full discussion in class; or Students list their difficulties and discuss in small groups in class. Unresolved difficulties are noted for the teacher who answers them in a mini lecture; or Set up self-study groups outside class to review the answers and list the difficulties arising for discussion in class.
3. Use principles to construe original cancellation clause in class 1.	Students get feedback on their construction through: • discussion in pairs • discussion in buzz groups • teacher modelling an answer in a mini lecture; etc
4. Read second case with two guiding questions and then answer analytical questions.	Similar choices as for first case.
5. Then answer questions which synthesise issues form both cases. These questions ask students to synthesise the relevant principles in response to key questions.	Students discuss and rework their answers in small groups or in pairs, and list difficulties for discussion with the teacher.
6. Answer questions which provide broader context and a theoretical framework.	Full class discussion.

Figure 6: Step 2

We can integrate this private study into classroom activity by using the principles of co-operative learning to enable students to work through the principles that have been drawn out of the cases. Students can work in pairs, and each student can ask the other to answer a question set out in the materials. The first student can then comment upon the answer given, and if need be can ask a supplementary question. The roles can be reversed for the next question. Students can consult the teacher if they are both unable to answer a question.

Another approach would be for the students to discuss the questions in small self-study groups which operate outside the classroom. Students can work through the cases together and list difficulties they experience. A list of such difficulties should be given to the teacher prior to class and should be dealt with in class by full class discussion or mini-lecture. The approach requires students to manage their own learning but in a co-operative environment.

Figure 6 (page 119) summarises the activities before and during the second step.[7]

The materials

The Law Relating to Agreed Damages Clauses

In this part of the topic we will study the law governing agreed damages clauses. These materials will guide you through the cases and enable you to apply the legal principles in the cases to the clause you have already drafted for Ms De Maggio.

The courts have developed rules to distinguish between genuine liquidated damages clauses, and clauses which they regard as penalties. The two cases extracted below set out the basic principles governing the courts' approach to this distinction. Read the two cases.

How to approach the cases

As you first read these cases you should be looking for answers to two basic questions:

- On what basis do the courts decide whether an agreed damages clause is a penalty clause?
- What are the legal consequences of a clause being held to be a penalty?

Two groups of more detailed questions are included to help you come to grips with the important details of the two cases and the principles they are setting out.

- Once you have read each case you will be expected to go back to that case and to write notes to answer detailed questions about the case. These questions are designed to help you comprehend and analyse the case. We will discuss your notes when you come to class.
- Once you have read and analysed both cases, the final set of questions are designed to help you synthesise the principles from the two cases into a basic framework, and to assist you to evaluate the law as it has developed in the cases. Answer the questions by making notes in the spaces provided. When you come to class you will be

7 This figure was first published in Le Brun and Johnstone (1994) 323.

paired with another member of the class and you will be asked to teach each other different aspects of the rule against penalties. While working through the cases and questions, therefore, make sure that you are in a position to teach the basic principles of the rule against penalties to a fellow student.

The cases

But first, the cases. As you would expect, the law reports are filled with many cases dealing with agreed damages clauses. Our current task is not to look at all these cases, but rather to understand the basic principles in the context of the development of the law and the basic problem these principles are trying to regulate. We will therefore concentrate on a couple of recent cases. During the past decade there have been at least three important High Court cases on questions relating to the rule against penalties. Two are extracted below and the third, *AMEV-UDC Finance Ltd v Austin,* is discussed in the *Esanda* case.

The three cases deal with 'acceleration' clauses in contracts of lease or hire purchase. These clauses provide that the periodic payment of rent by the lessee is accelerated if certain events occur. In other words, when the event occurs, the full rent, which was previously only payable in instalments, becomes recoverable at once. There may be present a 'discount rate' which reduces the total sum by a fixed or variable percentage to take account of acceleration. The issue in each case is whether the full amount specified by the contract to be recoverable upon the event is a penalty clause.

Now for the first case. When you first read it, remember to keep in mind the two guiding questions:

- On what basis do the courts decide whether an agreed damages clause is a penalty clause?
- What are the legal consequences of a clause being held to be a penalty?

O'Dea v All States Leasing System (WA) Pty Ltd (1983) 152 CLR 359.

GIBBS CJ

[364] By an agreement in writing made on 13 April 1977 the first respondent, Allstates Leasing System (WA) Pty Ltd (in the agreement called 'the Lessor') leased to Mr and Mrs O'Dea and Mr and Mrs Granich, who, together, traded as cartage contractors under the name of Granich Geraldton (in the agreement called 'the Lessee'), a Mercedes Benz prime mover for a period of thirty-six months. No right was given to the lessee to buy the vehicle and the agreement stated that it was not intended to be a hire purchase agreement (cl 17). Clause I(a) of the agreement stated that the lessor leased to the lessee and the lessee took on lease the vehicle:

> '... upon the terms and conditions hereinafter contained for a period of 36 months at an entire rental of $39,550.32 which shall be due by the LESSEE to the LESSOR upon the signing of this Agreement. PROVIDED THAT if the LESSEE shall duly observe and perform all and singular the covenants and conditions on the part of the LESSEE herein contained or implied and if the LESSEE shall duly and punctually pay on account of such entire rent the following instalments on the days following namely: The sum of $1098.62 per month commencing on the 13TH day of APRIL 1977 up to and including the

> 13TH day of MARCH 1980 ... THEN the LESSOR shall not demand or seek to enforce payment of the entire rent or any balance thereof outstanding otherwise than by the said instalments.'

By cl 6(a) the lessee agreed duly and punctually to pay to the lessor the instalments of rent on the days set forth in cl l(a). Clause 12 provided as follows:

> 'In the event that the LESSEE defaults in the punctual payment of any of the instalments of rent as herein provided or [365] in the payment of the insurance premiums as herein provided or defaults in the performance of any of the terms and conditions of this agreement, the LESSOR may immediately retake possession of the vehicle in respect of which such default has occurred, without notice to the LESSEE, with or without legal process, and the LESSEE hereby authorises and empowers the LESSOR to enter the premises or other places where the said vehicle may be found and take and carry away the said vehicle, and, in such eventuality, the LESSEE'S right to the retention and use of the said vehicle shall terminate. All moneys due for unexpired terms shall become immediately due and payable, plus reasonable costs of repossession. Provided that the LESSOR at its option may lease the leased vehicle for the account of the LESSEE for the remainder of the term and should the rental therefrom be less than that provided herein the LESSEE shall pay the deficiency. Nothing herein shall release the LESSEE from the obligation to pay the rent as herein provided for the unexpired balance of the term of this agreement plus reasonable costs of repossession.'

The agreement contained a number of terms and conditions, varying in importance, which the lessee was bound to observe. Clause 31 provided:

> 'On the goods being received into the LESSOR'S possession consequent upon the expiration of the period of the Lease or any extension thereof or consequent on the LESSOR'S having retaken possession pursuant to cl 12, the LESSOR shall as soon as practicable, sell the goods by Public Auction or to or through traders dealing in goods of a similar description (hereinafter called 'the trade') at the best price the LESSOR can reasonably obtain and the LESSEE agrees to pay the LESSOR on demand additionally to any rentals and other monies payable to the LESSOR and by way of indemnity for the capital loss so suffered the amount (if any) by which the appraisal value stated in the schedule below exceeds the disposal price after allowing for any costs and expenses incidental to such disposal. In the event of any dispute the average of three valuations by 'the trade' shall be accepted by the parties as the value of the said goods.'

The appraisal value was stated in the schedule to be $13,300.

On the same day M G O'Dea Pty Ltd guaranteed the due and punctual observance and performance of all the obligations imposed upon the lessee by the agreement. Nothing turns on the form of the guarantee.

The lessee took possession of the vehicle and made payments of rent which totalled $8,114.28 and which represented the instalments due for the months of April to October 1977 and part of the instalment due for November. After November 1977 no further rent was paid. The first respondent later retook possession of the vehicle and resold it, realizing $20,000 on the sale. To obtain the vehicle it [366] was necessary for the first respondent to pay $7,003.32 to a company which had a lien on the vehicle for repairs.

The first respondent commenced proceedings in the Supreme Court of Western Australia against Mr and Mrs O'Dea, Mr and Mrs Granich and M G O'Dea Pty Ltd, claiming $31,436.04 (the difference between the total rent, $39,550.32, payable under the agreement and the amount of the instalments paid) together with interest, and $7,003.32, the amount paid to discharge the lien. In the alternative, damages of S33,650.39 were claimed. Mr and Mrs Granich did not enter a defence and judgment was given against them by default; they have together been made the second respondent to this appeal, although it is not clear why their joinder was necessary. At the trial of the issues between the first respondent and the remaining defendants, Mr and Mrs O'Dea and M G O'Dea Pty Ltd (who are the present appellants), it was conceded that the amount of $7,003.32 was recoverable and the sole issue fought was whether the amount of $31,436.04 was a penalty. Counsel for the first respondent suggested that if it became necessary to assess damages that could be done in separate proceedings. The learned trial judge (Wallace J) held that the sum was not a penalty and gave judgment for the first respondent against the appellants in the sum of $45,294.95 which included interest. An appeal to the Full Court was dismissed. A further appeal has now been brought to this Court.

The argument on behalf of the first respondent was that the rules which distinguish between a penalty and liquidated damages are simply not relevant to the present case. It was said that the first respondent was suing for the consideration payable under the contract, and was not seeking to recover a sum payable in the event of a breach by the appellants of their contractual obligations, so that the question whether the amount payable was a genuine pre-estimate of damage did not arise. The cases to which counsel for the first respondent referred in support of his argument that there can be no question of penalty in the present case seem to me to fall into two classes. In the first class of case, if a sum of money is payable by instalments, and it is provided that in the event of one instalment not being punctually paid the whole sum shall immediately become payable, the acceleration of payment is not a penalty: *The Protector Loan Co v Crice* [(1880) 5 QBD 592]; *Wallingford v Mutual Society* [(1880) 5 App Cas 685 at pp 696, 702, 705-706, 710]. Similarly there is no penalty where it is agreed to charge a certain rate of interest on [367] condition that if payment is made punctually the rate will be reduced (*Astley v Weldon* [(1801) 2 Bos & Pul 346 at p 353]) or where a creditor agrees to accept payment of part of his debt in full discharge if certain conditions are met but stipulates that if the conditions are not met he will be entitled to recover the original debt: *Thompson v Hudson* [(1869) LR 4 HL 1 at pp15-16, 27-28, 30]; *Ex parte Burden*; *In re Neil* [(1881) 16 Ch D 675] In all the cases of this kind there is a present debt, which, by reason of an indulgence given by the creditor, is payable either in the future, or in a lesser amount, provided that certain conditions are met. The failure of the conditions does not mean that the creditor becomes entitled to damages; the consequence is that the sum which was always owed but which the debtor was allowed to pay by instalments or in a smaller amount, becomes recoverable at once or in full.

The second class of case arises where the parties have stipulated that a sum shall become payable on a certain event which, although brought about by the party required to make the payment, does not involve a breach of contract. It has been held that where there is a contract for the payment of a certain sum in a certain event, and that event has happened, the sum is payable and no question of penalty versus liquidated damages arises: *In re Apex Supply Co* [[1942] 1 Ch 108, at p 119]; *Alder v Moore* [[1961] 12 QB 57, at p 65]. Difficulties have arisen in the application of this principle to contracts of hire purchase which provide that in the event of termination a sum representing all or part of unpaid instalments will be paid by the hirer to the owner. There was some controversy as to the position when the owner's right to terminate the contract and receive payment arose on the happening of any of a number of events, some of which were breaches and some of which were not, but it has now been settled in England that in such a case where the agreement is terminated by reason of a breach committed by the hirer, the sum payable will be a penalty unless it is a genuine pre-estimate of the loss suffered by the owner by reason of the breach: *Cooden Engineering Co Ltd v Stanford* [[1953] 1 QB 86]; *Campbell Discount Co Ltd v Bridge* [[1962] 1 AC 600]; *Financings Ltd v Baldock* [[1963] 2 QB 104]. I respectfully agree with that conclusion. If, however, the agreement is terminated by the hirer himself, eg because he is unable to keep up his payments, it has been held that the question whether the sum payable is liquidated damages or a penalty does not arise, since what has occurred is that the hirer has [368] exercised his option to put an end to the contract on paying a certain sum, and the sum for which he has made himself-liable must be paid: *Associated Distributors Ltd v Hall* [[1938] 2 KB 83]. Conflicting opinions have been expressed as to the correctness of that decision (see *Campbell Discount Co Ltd v Bridge* at [pp 614, 631, and 633] and *United Dominions Trust (Commercial) Ltd v Ennis* [[1968] 1 QB 54, at pp 64, 67] but the question whether it was correct does not fall for consideration in the present case.

In *Dunlop Pneumatic Tyre Co Ltd v New Garage and Motor Co Ltd* [[1915] AC 79, at pp 86-87] Lord Dunedin said:

> 'The question whether a sum stipulated is a penalty or liquidated damages is a question of construction to be decided upon the terms and inherent circumstances of each particular contract, judged as at the time of the making of the contract, not as at the time of the breach.'

Similarly, in my opinion, the question whether the rules which relate to the distinction between penalties and liquidated damages are applicable must be judged as at the time of the making of the contract in question. The question is 'not of words or of forms of speech, but of substance and of things', to use the words cited by Lord Radcliffe in *Campbell Discount Co Ltd v Bridge* [at p 624]. In the present case, the event upon which the outstanding balance of the instalments became payable was a breach by the lessee of its obligations, under cl 6(a), duly and punctually to pay the instalments of rent on the days set forth in cl 1(a). The present case therefore does not fall within the second class of cases on which the first respondent relied – it is not a case in which under the contract money became payable on a certain event which was not a breach of the contract. On the contrary, the reasoning in such cases as *Cooden Engineering Co Ltd v Stanford and Campbell Discount Co Ltd v Bridge* supports the conclusion that the provision requiring payment of the balance of the rent is a penalty, unless of course it can be said to be a genuine pre-estimate of damage.

Nor, in my opinion, is the present case within the first class of cases cited by counsel for the first respondent. The contract did not, in my opinion, merely provide for the acceleration of a presently existing debt. In the argument for the first respondent much reliance was naturally placed on the provisions of cl 1 (a) of the contract, and it was said that the first respondent's claim was based entirely on that clause, and could succeed even if no breach of the contract were proved. If cl 1(a) was read in isolation, it might create a [369] present debt for the entire rental, although it would allow the lessee the indulgence of paying the sum due by instalments, provided the payments were duly and punctually made. In other words, there might then be *debitum in praesenti*, although solvendum in futuro, and, if so, such authorities as *The Protector Loan Co v Crice* [(1880) 5 QBD 592] would apply. But the contract must be viewed as a whole, and not in fragments. When cll 1(a), 6(a) and 12 are read together, it becomes apparent that at the date of the contract there was no presently existing obligation to pay the entire rental. The obligation was to pay the instalments, and if there were a default in payment of the instalments the whole became payable. The clauses, read together, had the effect that the entire rent only became payable in the events specified in cl 12 including default in punctual payment of the instalments. In the circumstances of the present case the obligation to pay the entire rent arose only by reason of a breach, and the amount which the contract makes payable in that event is either a penalty or liquidated damages.

Counsel for the first respondent did not dispute that if the question whether the sum was a penalty or liquidated damages falls for decision the sum must be held to be a penalty. Of course, a lessor is entitled to be compensated for the loss which he is likely to suffer on the premature termination of a hiring. However, the outstanding balance of the entire rental could not in the circumstances possibly represent a genuine pre-estimate of the loss which would be caused to the first respondent by a breach of the contract. In the event of a breach the first respondent was entitled to repossess and resell the vehicle, but it was not bound to account to the lessee for any amount received on a resale, even if it exceeded (as it did) the appraisal value. The first respondent became entitled under the contract to receive the accelerated payments of the rental without any rebate and to receive back the vehicle sooner than would otherwise have been the case without giving credit for its value and in these circumstances the amount receivable by the first respondent was manifestly excessive in comparison with the greatest loss that it could possibly suffer as a result of the default in payment of the instalments. Moreover, the entitlement of the first respondent arose on a number of events, including any default in performance of the terms and conditions of the contract, some of which, by their nature, could lead only to trifling damage.

I have no doubt in principle that the provisions requiring the payment of the entire rent amounted to a penalty. It remains however to consider some Australian decisions, and in particular [370] *Lamson Store Service Co Ltd v Russell Wilkins & Sons Ltd* [(1906) 4 CLR 672] which the Supreme Court felt bound to follow. In that case, the lessors leased to the lessees for a term of ten years a patented apparatus, and the lessees agreed that they would not discontinue the use of the apparatus or use it elsewhere than on specified premises. The agreement by cll 2 and 6 provided for payment of an annual rental in advance and by cl 8 provided that in case of a breach by the lessees of any of the conditions of the lease, or in case the apparatus should be taken from the lessees or attached by process of law by proceedings in bankruptcy or insolvency or otherwise, the whole of the rent for the remainder of the term should immediately become due and the lessors might forthwith take possession of and remove the apparatus. The lessees (a company) – were wound up and it was held by a majority of this Court, reversing the Supreme Court, that the lessors were entitled to prove for the whole of the amount of the ten years' rent. The judgment of the majority was delivered by Griffith CJ. The learned Chief Justice first dealt with the effect of cl 8 in so far as it provided that the whole of the rent should be payable on breach of a condition of the lease, other than a default in payment of an instalment of rent, and held that the sum stipulated for was a genuine pre-estimate of damage [(1906) 4 CLR at pp 68]. In reaching this conclusion he was influenced by the fact that:

> '... it might reasonably have been desired by the lessors, and have been in the contemplation of both parties when fixing the amount of the rent and the conditions of the lease, that a fair opportunity should be given for the public use of the invention in its entirety for a considerable time, on suitable premises, and by persons carrying on a business in which its advantages would commend it to the public, and so be likely to induce future purchases from the patentees' [(1906) 4 CLR at pp 681]:

He then turned to the stipulation for acceleration of the payment of rent in the event of default of payment in any instalment, and said [(1906) 4 CLR at p 683].

> '... Is it a mere agreement of demise for a term of years at a yearly rent, not creating any absolute obligation to pay rent for more than one year, so that the obligation may be terminated by abandoning the demised premises, with a collateral stipulation that an amount equal to 10 years' rent shall be payable on default in payment of that one year's rent? Or is it an agreement creating an absolute obligation to pay 10 years' rent in any event, with a provision that it may be paid in annual [371] instalments? If the first contention is the right one, there is no doubt that the decision appealed from is correct. If the latter is the true construction, there was a debitum in presenti solvendum in futuro.'

He concluded [at p 684] that the agreement expressed a clear intention that a sum equal to the rent for ten years should be paid by the lessees in any event, and that the case was indistinguishable from *The Protector Loan Co v Crice.* He added:

> '... It is true that in that case the consideration was a debt already existing. Here, on the other hand, the only debt is created by agreement of the parties, and is payable in futuro. But for the reasons already given, I do not think that this difference is material.'

The reasons to which he referred appear to have been that there would be nothing unreasonable, in the circumstances, in stipulating for a receipt of the rent for the whole term, and that it would be competent to the parties further to stipulate that in the event of a breach there should be no deduction for acceleration of payment. O'Connor J, who dissented, distinguished *The Protector Loan Co v Crice.* He said:

> '... If in this case the whole amount of rent was actually due on the signing of the contract the provisions of clause 8 might well be

> regarded as providing merely for acceleration of payment within the principle expounded by Lord Hatherley [in *Thompson v Hudson* [[1869] LRHL 1], but, as I have already pointed out, the whole amount of rent was not then due under the agreement. No more than the annual instalment could become due in the first year. Under these circumstances the facts necessary to make the principle of *the Protector Loan Co v Grice* applicable do not exist.'

He added that the stipulation for payment of the rent was in reality one for compensation for breaches of the covenant and, that, not being a genuine estimate of possible damage, it was a penalty ...

[373] The question whether a contractual provision amounts to a penalty depends on all the surrounding circumstances existing at the time of the making of the contract as well as on the terms of the contract itself, and it is therefore not always possible to apply a decision given upon one contract to another case even though that case concerns a contract in identical terms (see *Lombank Ltd v Excell* [l964] 1 QB 415). In *Lamson Store Service Co Ltd v Russell Wilkins & Sons Ltd* there was a particular circumstance on which the majority of the Court relied, namely the commercial importance to the lessor of the continued use of the patented apparatus. That circumstance was regarded as important in relation to the agreement in so far as it [374] provided the consequence of a breach of conditions other than default in payment of an instalment, but I find it difficult to understand how, as a matter of logic, it could be relevant to the question whether there was a present debt for the entire rent. In my opinion the principle of cases such as *The Protector Loan Co v Crice* applies only where there is a present debt, a debt actually due before the breach which accelerated the payment, and with all respect I would prefer the reasoning of O'Connor J to that of Griffith CJ and would hold that in that case there was no present debt for the entire amount. It makes commercial sense that parties may validly agree that payment of a present debt at a reduced rate, or at a future time, or by instalments, will be accepted if, but only if, certain conditions are observed. There is, however, a crucial difference between such an agreement and one under which a sum, originally payable only by instalments, is made payable in full immediately if the instalments are not duly paid. If *Lamson Store Service Co Ltd v Russell Wilkins & Sons Ltd* cannot be confined to its own special facts I would decline to follow it.

For these reasons I consider that the provisions of the contract which required payment of the entire rent amounted to a penalty and that the first respondent's claim to recover $31,436.04 could not succeed. The first respondent is, however, entitled to recover such unpaid instalments as were due before it retook possession of the vehicle and such damages as may be proved to have been occasioned by the breach of the conditions of the lease. Notwithstanding the suggestion of counsel that the damages might be assessed in fresh proceedings, it seems to me that the proper course is to refer the matter back to the Supreme Court to enable an assessment of damages to be made.

I would allow the appeal. For the order made by the Full Court I would substitute an order setting aside the judgment of Wallace J and ordering: (a) that judgment be given in favour of the plaintiff against the third and fourth named first defendants and the second defendant in an amount to be assessed, with no order as to costs; and (b) that the matter be remitted to a single judge of the Supreme Court to enable him to decide such questions as are raised by the parties in relation to the recovery of instalments of rent due before the retaking of possession, the assessment of any damages and the payment of interest and to fix the amount to be assessed (which will include the sum of $7,003.32 and any interest thereon).

[375] MURPHY J

The respondent lessor relies on certain terms of the contract (or lease agreement) which purport to apply on the occurrence of breach by the lessee. For trivial as well as serious breaches, at any time during the lease period, the combined operation of cll 1(a) and 12 is to accelerate instalment payments making the outstanding balance of the entire rental due. Further, the vehicle may then be repossessed without notice, with no provision for rebate of future instalments; and if it is then sold the lessee is not entitled to any surplus received in excess of the appraisal value. These provisions permit the lessor to recover grossly in excess of any genuine pre-estimate of its loss. They are a trap for an unwary or unfortunate lessee. They are unenforceable because, by modern standards, they are unconscionably harsh.

Where a contract provides that failure to comply strictly with conditions on an obligation to pay a certain sum results in an obligation to pay a higher sum, that obligation is treated as an unenforceable penalty unless the increase can be shown to be a genuine pre-estimate of the damage sustained by the non-performance of the conditions. Suppose a second contract states that the obligation is to pay the higher sum, but that it will be satisfied if the lower sum is paid strictly in accordance with the conditions. To describe the contractual right to pay the lower sum as an indulgence is a misdescription; to treat the first contract as penal and the second as non-penal is to elevate form above substance. Similar considerations apply to accelerated payment of a whole sum on occurrence of breach in payment of instalments. In such a case, *Lamson Store Service Co Ltd v Russell Wilkins & Sons Ltd*, a majority of this Court (Griffith CJ and Barton J, O'Connor J dissenting) preferred form to substance. In this case, the Supreme Court of Western Australia felt constrained to follow the *Lamson Case.* The *Lamson Case* should be overruled.

The appeal should be allowed. I agree with the proposed order.

WILSON J

[378] I turn first to a brief description of the case advanced in support of the appeal. In support of their contention, the appellants rely on the effect of cll 12 and 31 as evidenced by their operation in the present circumstances. The contract binds the lessee to the observance of a wide range of terms and conditions which vary greatly in importance. They range from the obligation to pay the instalments of rent punctually to the duty to keep and maintain the vehicle in good order and condition by washing and cleaning as the same may be required. Clause 12 provides for the consequences of any default, no distinction being drawn by reference to the degree of seriousness which the default may exhibit. Upon a default the lessor may immediately retake possession of the vehicle without notice to the lessee, with or without legal process; in that event, the lessee's right to the retention and use of the vehicle shall terminate. All moneys due for unexpired terms shall become immediately due and payable, plus reasonable costs of repossession. The clause also provides the lessor with the option of leasing the vehicle for the account of the lessee for the remainder of the term, whereupon the lessee shall pay the

amount of any deficiency that may result. The clause does not advert to the possibility of a surplus by reason of the vehicle being leased at a higher rental; in that event, presumably, the lessor is intended to benefit.

Three points of significance to the construction of the agreement arise from cl 12. The first is that the lessor, if it is going to exercise [379] its rights under that clause, must repossess the vehicle. This is an essential condition precedent to the accelerated liability of the lessee to pay the moneys due for unexpired terms. The second is that no discount is allowed for the acceleration in payment of those moneys. The third is that the lessor is not obliged to attempt a leasing for the unexpired term of the original lease in order to mitigate the loss otherwise accruing to the lessee by reason of the default.

Clause 31, as may be seen, provides that the lessor, having retaken possession pursuant to cl 12, shall sell the vehicle as soon as practicable at the best price it can reasonably obtain. Should that price, less any costs and expenses incidental to the sale, fail to reach the appraisal value of the vehicle stated in the schedule, the lessee will pay to the lessor on demand the amount of the deficiency 'by way of indemnity for the capital loss so suffered'. In the present case, the appraisal value is stated in the schedule as $13,300.00. The clause makes no provision for the consequences of a capital gain arising on the sale of the vehicle by reason of the net sale price exceeding the appraisal value; the lessee can derive no benefit from such an eventuality. It is common ground that, following its repossession of the vehicle in May 1978, Allstates sold the vehicle at a price of $20,000.00.

It requires little argument to demonstrate that this agreement could operate to the extreme disadvantage of the lessee. One can suppose circumstances in which the default occurs very early in the term of the lease. The vehicle can then be repossessed at a time when little depreciation would have occurred. The lessor would receive both the entire rental and possession of the vehicle. In direct contrast to the agreement which was under consideration in *IAC (Leasing) Ltd* [(1972) 126 CLR 131] the amount of the rental is not subject to any adjustment to allow for the accelerated payment, nor is the lessee entitled to any credit for the amount by which the value of the vehicle when repossessed exceeds its appraisal value. Subject, therefore, to any merit which the argument advanced on behalf of Allstates may be found to possess, these features of the agreement afford strong support to the appellants' defence to the claim. It is to Allstates' argument that I now turn.

Mr Pullin, counsel for Allstates, submits that the question whether the sum claimed is or is not a penalty does not arise. That question would arise, in his submission, only if the claim was one for liquidated damages. Here, however, the lessor has sued to enforce the principal obligation imposed on the lessee under the lease. It relies on cl 1(a), which provides that the entire rental of $39,550.32 [380] 'shall be due by the LESSEE to the LESSOR upon the signing of this Agreement'. The provision permitting the lessee to discharge that obligation by the payment of instalments spread over the term of the lease is an indulgence which is liable to be withdrawn upon any default. The obligation to pay the entire rental lies at the heart of the agreement between the parties. Mr Pullin argues that, unless the Court is to assume a general responsibility to review bargains which might be thought to be oppressive, there is no basis on which it should intervene ...

[Wilson J then discussed a number of cases expounding the principles relied upon by Allstates Leasing.]

[382] It seems to me that *Lamson Store* is an authority applicable to this case only if Allstates' claim proceeds on the basis that cl 1(a) established a present liability in the lessee for the entire rent subject to an indulgence in the form of a proviso permitting payment by instalments and that default in the payment of those instalments entitled the lessor to withdraw that indulgence and sue immediately for the entire rental. Such a cause of action might well be established by reference solely to cl 1(a) of the agreement. The question of penalty or liquidated damages would not then arise. But it is quite clear that Allstates' claim did not proceed on this basis. If it had done so, there would have been no question of repossession of the vehicle. The obligation to pay an entire rent supplies the consideration for a lease of that vehicle for a period of three years. The only clause which entitles Allstates to repossess the vehicle at an earlier time is cl 12. Given a repossession pursuant to cl 12, the respective rights of the parties are wholly governed by that clause and cl 31 [383] The lease is terminated, the lessee no longer having any right to the retention and use of the vehicle. The clause does not purport to operate to withdraw the indulgence of deferred payment of rent which is the subject of the proviso to cl 1(a). Significantly, it makes no reference to rent. On the contrary, it says, 'All moneys due for unexpired terms shall become immediately due and payable.' In my opinion, it is this provision which supplies the basis to Allstates' claim.

It follows from this conclusion that the decision in *Lamson Store* does not govern the present case. It is therefore unnecessary to consider the alternative submission advanced by Mr Malcolm on behalf of the appellants that its correctness should be re-examined.

It remains, then, to consider whether the acceleration provision in cl 12 can be considered to be a 'genuine pre-estimate of the creditor's [Allstates'] probable or possible interest in the due performance of the principal obligation': *Public Works Commissioner v Hills* [[1906] 1 AC, at pp 375-376] or whether it is a penalty inserted 'merely to secure the enjoyment of a collateral object': *Sloman v Walter* [[1783] 1 Bro CC 418] per Lord Thurlow LC Bearing in mind that the possible defaults that may activate the powers of the lessor under cl 12 encompass both trivial and serious breaches without distinction in the remedy and that the clause may operate at any time during the currency of the lease with no provision for rebate of future instalments or for crediting the lessee with any capital gain represented by the amount by which the value of the vehicle on repossession exceeds its appraisal value, it is in my opinion quite impossible to conclude that the clause reflects on the part of the parties a genuine pre-estimate of damage. It is a penalty against which the lessee is entitled to relief. Such a conclusion finds support in the reasoning of O'Connor J in *Lamson Store*, and by reference to the contrasting provisions which led Walsh J to a different conclusion in *IAC (Leasing) Ltd.* Indeed, I understood Mr Pullin to acknowledge, very frankly and fairly, that such a conclusion was inevitable if his consideration argument were to fail.

Of course, this conclusion does not mean that the lessee cannot be liable to Allstates, in addition to the amount of $7,003.32 which the latter paid to release the repairer's lien on the vehicle, for the arrears of rent payable in respect of the period prior to repossession and perhaps for damages. At no stage in the proceedings has Allstates made a specific claim for arrears of rent. A claim for damages was [384] made but was abandoned at the hearing for reasons which it is unnecessary to mention. Mr Pullin has indicated his readiness should the claim for accelerated rental fail, to institute fresh proceedings and it is acknowledged by Mr Malcolm that there is no estoppel operative in that regard. However, in my opinion the preferable course is for the Court to remit the matter to the Supreme Court, leaving Allstates to take such action as it wishes by way of amendment of the claim or otherwise. There should of course be judgment in any event for Allstates in the sum of $7,003.32. For these reasons, I would allow the appeal in part, set aside the decision of the Full Court and remit the matter to the Supreme Court. The appellants should have their costs in the two appeals.

BRENNAN J

[386] If the contract in the present case were construed as imposing an absolute obligation to pay three years' rent on the signing of the contract with a provision that that debt might be paid in monthly instalments, the rule stated by Brett LJ would govern the present case, as it was held to govern *Lamson Store Service*. But the debt created by cl 1(a) is not a debt to be paid on the signing of the contract; it is a debt payable by instalments over thirty-six months; it does not otherwise become payable in full unless there be a default. [387] In *Lamson Store Service*, Griffith CJ did not think it material that the debt created by the agreement of the parties was payable in futuro. If the result in the present case depended upon the acceptance of that opinion, I should wish to consider whether it should now be followed.

There seems to be an air of commercial unreality in a time of high interest rates to hold that a debt which a creditor is not entitled to recover except by instalments over a period is to be equated with a debt which the creditor is entitled to recover immediately but which he agrees to receive by instalments over such a period. In the latter case, the value of the debt is greater than the value of the instalments payable over the period (cf *McCain v Federal Commissioner of Taxation* [(1965) 12 CLR 523] in the former case the value of the debt is the value of the instalments by which it is payable ...

[389] Neither cl 1(a) nor cl12 is drawn as a provision for liquidated damages; or, for that matter, as a [390] provision relating to damages at all. Neither clause purports to create or impose a new pecuniary liability, but only to accelerate the time for payment of moneys already 'due' ... If, after a default which enlivened cl 12, the lessor sued to recover the unpaid balance of the entire rental, leaving the lessees in possession of the vehicle, the lessees could not point to the right to repossess to transform their debt payable under the contract into damages for its breach. The balance of opinion in this Court has favoured the view that no question of penalty arises unless the obligation to pay arises upon breach of contract. In *IAC (Leasing)*, Walsh J said [at p 143]:

> '... there has been a preponderance of opinion in favour of the view that it is only when a provision operates so that the event upon which an obligation is placed upon a party to pay a sum of money to another party to a contract is the breach by the former party of a term of the contract, that the question arises whether an obligation arising upon that event is a penal provision.'

The mere obligation to pay the entire rental cannot be characterized as penal. What gives to that obligation the flavour of a penalty is the lessor's right, in the event of a default by the lessees, to repossess the vehicle. If the lessor was to repossess the vehicle and recover the entire rental, he would have both the price of the hiring and possession of the vehicle which was to be hired. That would be inconsistent with the respective rights of the parties under the agreement if the agreement should be duly performed. The contract was to be performed by the lessees' paying the entire rental to the lessor and by the lessor allowing the lessees possession and use of the vehicle for thirty-six months. Clause 12 confers upon the lessor in the event of and by reason of a default by the lessees a right to recover both the moneys due for unexpired terms and possession of the vehicle, so that the lessor becomes entitled to more than it would be entitled to if no default occurs. However, cl 12 leaves the lessees [391] with the right to retain and use the vehicle until the lessor actually takes the vehicle and carries it away. The lessor is not bound upon a default by the lessees to repossess the vehicle before the expiry of the hiring period; it may choose not to do so. Unless the lessor repossesses the vehicle, there is no ground for denying it the right to payment of the entire rental to which it is entitled under the agreement.

By conferring on the lessor the right in the event of the lessees' default to recover both possession of the vehicle hired and the entire price of the hiring before the hiring period expires, cl 12 provides an incentive for the due and punctual performance of the lessees' obligations – pecuniary and other – by imposing a liability to forfeiture. The lessees may lose both possession and use of the vehicle for the remaining period of thirty-six months and that proportion of the entire rental which is attributable to the hiring period remaining after repossession. Although a stipulation as to the price payable for the sale of hiring of goods is not itself-in the nature of a penalty, a stipulation which provides for the forfeiture on breach by the buyer or hirer of both the price and the consideration for which it is payable is in the nature of a penalty and equity will relieve against it. The foundation of the jurisdiction to relieve against forfeiture is that the stipulation for the forfeiture is really in the nature of a penalty: *Pitt v Curotta* [(1931) 31 SR (NSW) 477, at pp 480-481]. In *The Protector Loan Co v Grice* [at p 595] Baggallay LJ said:

> 'The doctrine in equity is stated by Lord Macclesfield LC, in *Peachy v Duke of Somerset* [2 W & TLC (5d) 1100, at p 1108]. "The true ground of relief against penalties is from the original intent of the case, where the penalty is designed only to secure money, and the Court gives him all that he expected or desired;" but it has been long established that relief in equity is also given where the penalty is intended to secure the performance of a collateral object: *Sloman v Walter*. Familiar instances of the relief afforded in equity, may be found in those cases where a default has occurred in repayment of a loan secured by a mortgage ...'

Clause 12 is in the nature of a penalty, for the lessor who exacts the full measure of his entitlement under that clause receives more than the damages he would suffer by reason of many of the defaults which enliven that clause ... [392] agreement in *IAC (Leasing)* with an agreement exhibiting the features of the present agreement, saying:

> 'The fact that those provisions could operate upon breaches varying greatly in their seriousness and in their likely consequences might suggest a conclusion that the imposition of such a liability as a consequence of a breach, followed by a termination of the contract,

> could not be a genuine pre-estimate of damage. Such a conclusion might be warranted if the lessor might regain the possession and the right of disposal of the equipment when only a small part of the term of the lease had gone by and might do this in consequence of a minor breach, which would really have little damaging effect upon the value of the equipment, and if the lessor might thus receive in those events a large profit not related to any damage which had actually been suffered.'

In this branch of its jurisdiction equity relieves against forfeiture of the purchase money (other than the deposit) paid by a defaulting purchaser under a contract of sale of land when the vendor rescinds for breach (*McDonald v Dennys Lascelles Ltd* [(1933) 48 CLR 457]; *Mayson v Clouet* [[1924] AC 980]) and relief has been granted in like circumstances in the case of a contract for the sale of chattels (*Stockloser v Johnson* [[1954] 1 QB 476]). In those cases, however, the consideration for which the price was payable – title to the land or chattels – failed totally; in the present case, part of the consideration – the possession and use of the vehicle for part of the hiring period – has been enjoyed. That circumstance does not preclude the grant of equitable relief, whatever be its significance for a common law action to recover money or property which has been forfeited under a stipulation in the nature of a penalty.

[394] It follows that the appeal by both the lessees and the guarantor should be allowed. The judgment of the Full Court should be set aside and in lieu thereof it should be ordered that the appeal to the [395] Full Court be allowed. The judgment of Wallace J should be set aside. The lessor is entitled to judgment for the $7,003.32 paid to Diesel Motors Ltd, for the unpaid instalments which became due prior to the date of repossession, for any damages for the lessees' breach of contract which the lessor may be able to establish and for interest. These issues should be remitted for decision by a single judge who should assess the whole amount due by the lessees and the guarantor. There should be no order for the costs of the trial, but the appellants should have the costs of both appeals.

DEANE J

[399] Subject to what is said hereunder, the principles applicable in deciding whether a sum stipulated to be payable by one party to a contract to another party upon breach is recoverable as liquidated damages or irrecoverable as representing a penalty are, in my view, set out in convenient form in the speech of Lord Dunedin in *Dunlop Pneumatic Tyre Co Ltd v New Carriage and Motor Co Ltd* [[1915] AC 79, at pp 86-88]. They need not be repeated in detail. As Lord Radcliffe commented in *Campbell Discount Co Ltd v Bridge* [at pp 621-622] 'the line of demarcation is drawn in its simplest form ... if one says that a sum cannot be legally exacted as liquidated damages unless it is found to amount to "a genuine pre-estimate of loss" ... if it does not amount to such a pre-estimate, then it is to be regarded as a penalty, and I do not myself-think that it helps to identify a penalty, to describe it as in the nature of a threat "to be enforced in terrorem"' (see, also, *Public Works Commissioner v Hills* [[1901] AC 368, at pp 375-376]). The question is one 'not of words or of forms of speech, but of substance and of things' (per Lord Davey, *Clydebank Engineering and Shipbuilding Co v Don Jose Ramos Yzquierdo y Castaneda* [(l905) 1 AC 6, at p 15]. 'The Court must find out whether the payment stipulated is in truth a penalty or liquidated damages' by reference to 'the

terms and inherent circumstances of each particular contract, judged of as at the time of the making of the contract, not as at the time of the breach' (per Lord Dunedin, *Dunlop Pneumatic Tyre Case* [[l915] I AC, at pp 86-87]). There is a presumption (but nothing more) that it is a penalty when 'a single lump sum is made payable by way of compensation, on the occurrence of one or more or all of several events, some of which may occasion serious and others but trifling damage' (per Lord Dunedin [(1915) 1 AC at p 87], quoting Lord Watson in *Lord Elphinstone v Monkland Iron and Coal Co* [(1886) 11 App Cas 332 at p 342]). It will be a penalty 'if the sum stipulated for is extravagant and unconscionable in amount in comparison with the greatest loss that could conceivably be proved to have followed from the breach' (per Lord Dunedin [(1915) 1 AC at p 87]). In that regard, a pre-estimate of damages will not, for the purposes of determining whether a stipulated sum is a penalty, be regarded as 'genuine' if it be unreasonable (see the *Dunlop Pneumatic Tyre Case*, and the *Cooden Engineering Case*).

[400] In what is written above, I have omitted the statement to be found in many cases, including Lord Dunedin's judgment in the *Dunlop Pneumatic Tyre Case*, to the effect that 'the question whether a sum stipulated is penalty or liquidated damages is a question of construction'. Properly understood, that statement is unobjectionable: whether or not a provision of a contract imposes a penalty must be determined with reference to the true operation of that provision. That question must however be determined as a question of substance which cannot be foreclosed by statements of the parties in their agreement, no matter how genuine they may be, as to their intention in stipulating the sum. The parties to an agreement may have subjectively intended to make a pre-estimate of damages in the event of breach. If, however, that pre-estimate is either extravagant or unconscionable in amount in comparison with the greatest loss that could conceivably be proved to have followed from the breach or, judged as at the time of making the contract, is unreasonable in the burden that it imposes in the circumstances which have arisen, it is a penalty regardless of the intention of the parties in making it.

The application of the above principles to the present case leads to the conclusion that the provisions of cl 12 impose a penalty. There is nothing at all in the contract to suggest that those provisions represent a genuine or reasonable pre-estimate of damages which Allstates would sustain in the event of breach by the lessees. They are applicable on the occurrence of any default in the punctual payment of an instalment of rent or of an insurance premium or in the performance of any one of a large number of terms and conditions ranging from the trivial to the serious. They could result in an unreasonable windfall to Allstates and an unconscionable burden upon the lessees in the event of breach of the most trivial condition. Thus, if breach occurred immediately after commencement of the agreement, Allstates would be entitled to retake possession of the prime mover and to recover, pursuant to cl 12, the amount necessary to bring its total receipts from the lessees to $39,550.32 for a hiring period that might be measured in hours or days. It follows that, if the matter be approached in accordance with what I consider to be established principle, it is apparent that the provision of cl 12 requiring that the lessee pay to Allstates all 'moneys due for unexpired terms' are unenforceable for the reason that they impose a penalty. As I have said, I consider that, upon the proper construction of the agreement as a whole, the obligation under cl 1 (a) to pay rent attributable to future periods did not survive the election of Allstates to invoke the provisions of cl 12 and terminate the hiring. If I be mistaken in that regard however and the provisions of cl 1(a), upon their proper construction, requires the payment of 'rent' attributable to future periods notwithstanding that Allstates had terminated the hiring pursuant to cl 12, I am of the view that cl 1(a), in those circumstances, required payment of a sum on breach which as a matter of substance was neither rent nor liquidated damages but a penalty.

I turn to a consideration of the *Lamson Store Case* ...

[403] To the extent to which either the *Protector Loan Co Case* or the *Lamson Store Case* is an authority for any general principle precluding a finding that a payment under cl 12 in the present case was a penalty, they accord neither with the principle that the question whether a sum is a penalty is a question of substance and not of mere form nor with the [404] approach adopted in subsequent cases (see eg *Campbell Discount Co Ltd v Bridge*; *Anglo Auto Finance Co Ltd v James* [[1963] 1 WLR 1042]; *United Dominions Trust Commercial Ltd v Ennis*; *Charterhouse Leasing Corp Ltd v Sanmac Holdings Ltd* [[1966] 58 DLR (2nd) 656] and should not be followed ...

In the result, I would uphold the appeal and set aside the judgment in the amount of $45,294.95 in Allstates' favour against the appellants. It is common ground that Allstates is entitled to retain judgment in the amount of $7,003.32 against the appellants on account of the amount it had to pay a third party in order to effect a discharge of a lien held by that third party over the prime mover. *Prima facie*, Allstates is also entitled to claim the sum of $1,773.30 representing that balance of the November 1977 instalment, any further instalments due before the retaking of possession and any additional amount of damage which it has actually sustained (see *Public Works Commissioner v Hills*). While the approach was taken by the parties that the question of actual damage should be left to be determined in separate proceedings, I consider that, in all the circumstances, the preferable course is that suggested by Wilson J and I agree with the orders which he proposes.

Analysis of O'Dea

Once you have read *O'Dea*, answer the following questions in note form.

(i) Trace the steps followed by each judge in *O'Dea*. If you prefer, draw a diagram showing the logic in each judge's reasoning.

- Gibbs CJ

- Murphy J

- Wilson J

- Brennan J

- Deane J

(ii) How do the approaches of the judges differ? Can you discern any differences in their philosophies about contract or judicial decision-making?

(iii) Is there any suggestion in the judgments that the rule against penalties could be subsumed by the development of principles of unconscionability? Explain.

(iv) Does Deane J's restatement of the principles modify the principles set out in the *Dunlop* case? If your answer is yes, describe the way in which the principles are modified.

(v) What general principles for the construction of contracts emerge from the judgments?

Construction Problem 1

Before you read the next case, apply Lord Dunedin's tests in the *Dunlop* case to the 'cancellation' clause considered earlier in these materials. Is the clause a penalty? Give reasons, in note form, for your conclusion. We will discuss your reasons in class.

Construction Problem 2

Is the clause you have drafted for Ms De Maggio a penalty? Give reasons for your opinion. Once again, we will discuss your opinion in class.

The second case

Now let us look at a second High Court case on agreed damages clauses. When you read the case, follow the same procedure as for *O'Dea* – that is on first reading, bear in mind the two overriding questions, and then go back and look at the questions guiding you through an analysis of the case.

Esanda Finance Corporation Ltd v Plessnig (1988) 166 CLR 131 is the most recent High Court case on the rule against penalties. In four separate judgments the court displays a wide range of reasoning.

[132] *BJ Shaw QC (*with him *IJ Hardingham* and *L Ferdinandy*), for the appellant. Clauses regulating the amount payable on breach of contract need not be genuine pre-estimates of damage to be enforceable. For example they may validly exempt the guilty party from all liability or may fix that party's liability at an agreed amount (so long as it is not penal) or limit it to actual loss not exceeding an agreed maximum amount, neither of which amounts may represent a pre-estimate: *Davis v Pearce Parking Station Pty Ltd* [(1954) 91 CLR 642 at 649]; *Suisse Atlantique Societe d'Armements Maritime SA v Rotterdamsche Kolen Centrale* [[1967] 1 AC 361, at 395]; *Ailsa Craig Fishing Co Ltd v Malvern Fishing Co Ltd* [[1983] 1 WLR 964]. The mere fact that a power exercisable by the innocent party upon breach of contract by the other party may be predicted to benefit the innocent party does not invalidate the power although it may in some circumstances enliven equity's power to relieve against forfeiture. [He referred to *Howe v Smith* [[1884] 27 Ch D 89]; *Transfer of Land Act* 1958 (Vict), Seventh Sched, Table A, Condition 6; *Voumard on the Sale of Land*, 4th ed (1986), p 455; *Sale of Goods Act* 1985 (SA), s 47; and *Ward v Bignall* [[1967] 1 QB 534 at 543. Early hire-purchase legislation was directed to denying to owners benefits available to them by way of having both the goods and the money: 'The Victorian Hire Purchase Act 1936', *Australian Law Journal*, vol 10 (1937), p 432; Else-Mitchell, 'The Hire Purchase Agreements Act 1941 (NSW)', *Australian Law Journal*, vol 15 (1941), p 228; 'Hire Purchase Legislation in Queensland 1956-1959', *University of Queensland Law Journal*, vol 3 (1956), 56, p 61. The rule that renders provision for recovery of a [133] penalty unenforceable or void is derived historically from equity's power to relieve against penalties. It would therefore be surprising if a provision is a penalty where there are no circumstances in which such relief could be given against its operation. Here there could never be relief against payment of the recoverable amount because when anything at all is recoverable it is calculated by reference to a formula which in these circumstances produces an acceptable (non-penal) outcome. If the formula has in the particular circumstances a negative outcome, there is nothing to be recovered or relieved against under the provision. Relief might theoretically be given against the determination of the

hiring and the forfeiture of the hirer's rights under the agreement, but that is a different matter. The provision for recovery of the recoverable amount is therefore not such a provision as equity would originally have operated upon. In ordinary English usage the word 'penalty' refers to a punishment imposed for breach of contract. It refers to the sum exacted rather than the provision imposing it. Thus the jurisdiction to declare a penalty void or unenforceable ought logically to be exercisable only where it is contended that a sum is due to the claimant. A penalty is said to arise here not because something is exacted from the hirer but because a benefit is not conferred on him. The rule rendering penalties void or unenforceable is thus being extended beyond penalties in the ordinary meaning of the word. In any case, to provide that the estimated loss suffered by the owner may be recovered from the hirer is not to punish the latter but only to preserve the position of the former. The defect in the contract discerned by the Full Court is that it does not enable the hirer to sue the owner for the recovery of any 'surplus' or 'profit' that might result to the owner. The absence of such a provision cannot be a penalty in any ordinary meaning of the word. If circumstances were to occur giving rise to equity's power to relieve against forfeiture, the contract would not attempt to regulate its exercise of that power. A provision is unenforceable or void as providing for the recovery of a penalty only if it provides for recovery of a sum manifestly intended to be, in some circumstances at least, in excess of the loss suffered by the innocent party. This clause does not have that character. For this purpose 'loss' includes, where the contract so provides, loss resulting from termination of the contract pursuant to its terms consequent upon breach of a term otherwise non-essential or non-fundamental. [He referred to *Dunlop Pneumatic Tyre Co Ltd v New Garage and Motor Co Ltd*; *Legione v Hateley*; *Robophone Facilities Ltd v Blank*; *Export Credit Guarantee Department v Universal Oil Products Co*; *Photo Production Ltd v Securicor Ltd*; and *Stockloser v Johnson*.] *AMEV-UDC Finance Ltd v Austin* [(1986) 164 CLR at 194, 197, 205-206, 210]. The fact that the contract is a hire-purchase contract and not a simple contract of hire is immaterial. It is a hiring contract until the option is exercised. In any case, by the termination of the contract, if the hirer had any interest in the goods, it too is terminated. The benefit which might be obtained in some circumstances by the owner is thus not at the expense of the hirer. [He also referred to *AMEV UDC Finance Ltd v Austin*; *Helby v Matthews*; *Ward v Bignall*; and *IAC (Leasing) v Humphrey*.]

D N Angel QC (with him *N Niarchos*), for the respondents. Because cl 6 operates in the event of a breach of contract it is subject to the law against penalties. This is so even if cl 5 enables recovery of the same recoverable sum on a voluntary return of goods by the hirer: *O'Dea v Allstates Leasing System (WA) Pty Ltd*; *Financings Ltd v Baldock*. Whether cl 6 is a penalty depends, *inter alia*, upon whether the recoverable sum under cl 5 is a genuine pre-estimate of the owner's loss caused by the hirers' breach: *O'Dea v Allstates Leasing System (WA) Pty Ltd*; *Financings Ltd v Baldock*; *AMEV-UDC Finance Ltd v Austin*; *Malouf (WT) Pty Ltd v Brinds Ltd*; *Campbell Discount Co Ltd v Bridge*. Clauses 5 and 6 seek to enable the owner to indemnify itself against its loss of bargain in the event of any breach of contract by the hirers: *O'Dea v Allstates Leasing System (WA) Pty Ltd*. Clauses 5 and 6 apart, the owner is entitled to claim damages for loss of bargain only following a termination of the contract which is justified by a repudiatory breach, a fundamental breach, or a breach of an essential term: *AMEV-UDC Finance Ltd v Austin*; *Financings Ltd v Baldock*; *Shevill v Builders*

Licensing Board; *Citicorp Australia Ltd v Hendry*; *Lombard North Central Plc v Butterworth*. [He also referred to Goode, 'Penalties in Finance Leases', *Law Quarterly Review*, vol 104 (1988), p 25]. Even if cl 6 makes every term essential, it is penal. Clauses 5 and 6 can result in an unconscionable burden upon the hirers in the event of a breach of a trivial term and result in the forfeiture of the hirers' interest in the transaction: *O'Dea v Allstates Leasing System (WA) Pty Ltd*; *AMEV UDC Finance Ltd v Austin*. If cl 6 makes every term fundamental, the recoverable sum in cl 5 is not a genuine pre-estimate of the owner's loss of bargain because it allows credit only for the wholesale value of the vehicle and not the best price reasonably obtainable therefor: *Universal Guarantee Pty Ltd v Carlile*; *O'Dea v Allstates Leasing System (WA) Pty Ltd* Further, it takes no account of the owner's duty to mitigate its loss: *O'Dea v Allstates Leasing System (WA) Pty Ltd*. It also allows the owner to retain a surplus at the expense of the hirers: *O'Dea v Allstates Leasing System (WA) Pty Ltd*.

WILSON AND TOOHEY JJ

In April 1982 the appellant advanced the finance necessary to enable the respondents to acquire possession of a secondhand Scania prime mover which was for sale for a cash price of $44,000. Initially, the respondents sought finance over a four year period but were told by an officer of the appellant that because of the age of the vehicle the money would only be available over a three year term. The transaction was completed by the execution of a hire-purchase agreement between the appellant as [136] owner and the respondents as hirers. The total rent, payable by 36 monthly instalments each of $1,878.78, amounted to $67,636.08. The last-mentioned figure was reached by taking the cash price of $44,000 and adding $792.00 stamp duty and terms charges of $22,844.08. The respondents acquired the vehicle with a view to engaging in the transport industry. Unfortunately, they encountered difficulties in the conduct of their business, including the cost of repairing and maintaining the vehicle and recovering moneys owing to them by consignors. They failed to pay the monthly instalments of rent due in June, July and August 1983. On 16 September 1983 the respondents delivered the prime mover to a location nominated by the appellant. In the courts below the parties were at issue over the question whether the vehicle was voluntarily returned by the respondents (as contended for by the appellant) or repossessed by the appellant (as contended for by the respondents). That issue was resolved against the appellant and is not in contest in this appeal. On termination, the appellant called for tenders for the purchase of the vehicle and it was sold for $27,000. Thereafter the appellant made a claim against the respondents for moneys due under the agreement. Failing satisfaction, the claim proceeded in the District Court of Adelaide.

The particulars of the claim, as amended at the trial, were as follows:

Total amount of rent payable under the agreement		67,636.08
Plus expenses incurred in consequence of termination –		
cost of storage	38.00	
repossession costs and valuation	35.00	73.00
		67,709.08
Less – instalments and other amounts paid	24,891.58	
sale proceeds	27,000.00	

rebate calculated in accordance with cl 13 of agreement	6,517.08	54,408.66
	Balance	9,300.42
Plus interest		3,676.85
TOTAL		$12,977.27

[137] The learned trial judge found the appellant's claim proved and entered judgment for $12,977.27.

The respondents appealed to the Full Court of the Supreme Court of South Australia. By majority (King CJ and Mohr J, von Doussa J dissenting), the appeal was allowed, their Honours holding that the agreed method of calculating the sum payable by the respondents in the event of termination of the agreement for breach was unenforceable by reason of it being a penalty. Consequent on that conclusion, the Court entered judgment for the appellant in the sum of $9,835.01, this being the arrears of hire at the date of the termination of the contract plus interest.

Special leave to appeal to this Court was limited to the question whether in all the circumstances the Full Court was correct in characterizing the 'recoverable amount' prescribed by cl 5 of the agreement as a penalty. Special leave was refused in relation to a proposed ground of appeal that the respondents' failure to pay several instalments of rent amounted to a repudiation of the agreement; we therefore proceed on the basis that the respondents did not repudiate the agreement.

The material provisions of the agreement are the following:

'TERMS AND CONDITIONS by which I the within Hirer by my signature on the face hereof agree to be bound: –

> 2. The deposit stated in the Schedule shall constitute the consideration for the option to purchase contained in Clause 10 ... I further agree to pay until the hiring is determined the rent stated in the Schedule.
>
> 5. I may at any time terminate the hiring by returning the goods freight and charges prepaid. I agree in that event to pay forthwith and you shall be entitled to recover from me the recoverable amount being the total rent as set out in the Schedule overleaf and all other moneys payable for the full period of hire (including your costs of repossession storage maintenance and selling expenses) less:
>
> (a) all moneys paid by me to you by way of deposit and rentals for the goods; and
>
> (b) the value of the goods (being the best wholesale price reasonably obtainable for them in their then condition as at the time of your taking possession of them); and
>
> (c) a rebate of charges calculated in accordance with Clause 13 hereof.
>
> [T]he amount calculated in accordance with this Clause is hereinafter called 'the recoverable amount'.
>
> 6. If during the hiring I commit any indictable offence or default in any payment or commit any breach of this agreement or if an order be

made or a resolution passed [138] for winding me up or if distress or execution for an amount exceeding $200.00 and be not withdrawn or satisfied within seven (7) days or if (I being a company) a receiver or receiver and manager be appointed of my undertaking assets or income then and in any such event you shall become entitled to immediate possession of the goods and you may without notice to me retake possession thereof and upon such repossession the hiring of those goods shall terminate and you may recover from me as liquidated damages the recoverable amount as defined in the preceding Clause, and I shall pay you the recoverable amount forthwith.

10. I may elect to become the owner of the goods by paying the total rent and fulfilling my other obligations to you and I understand that when I pay these moneys to you before the expiration of the full period of hire I shall be entitled to a rebate of charges calculated in accordance with Clause 13 hereof. Until I so become the owner I shall have no property in the goods and shall be only a bailee.

13. The rebate of charges herein referred to shall be an amount equal to:

(a) [not applicable]

(b) ... the amount stated in the Schedule overleaf as terms charges when multiplied by the sum of all the whole numbers from one (1) to the number which is the number of complete months in the period of the hiring still to go (after the early return repossession or early completion as the case may be) and divided by the sum of all the whole numbers from one (1) to the number which is the total number of complete months in the period of hiring.'

It is common ground that the resolution of the dispute between the parties is to be found in the common law. The *Hire-Purchase Agreements Act* 1960 (SA) was repealed by the *Consumer Transactions Act* 1972 (SA) and that Act does not relevantly apply to a hire-purchase transaction the value of which (excluding credit charges) exceeds $10,000.

The question for decision in this case is a narrow one. It is whether cl 6 of the agreement, in authorizing in the event of a termination of the contract in consequence of the hirer's default the recovery by the owner of an amount determined in accordance with cl 5, is penal rather than compensatory in character. We are not concerned with the characterization of a clause which provides for the payment of a sum of money on the happening of a specified event other than a breach of contractual duty...

[139] The Court has considered the doctrine of penalties on a number of occasions in recent years: *IAC (Leasing) Ltd v Humphrey*; *O'Dea v Allstates Leasing System (WA) Pty Ltd*; *AMEV-UDC Finance Ltd v Austin.* In considering whether a term of a contract is penal in character rather than a genuine pre-estimate of damage, Mason and Wilson JJ observed in *AMEV-UDC* [at p 193] that the test:

> 'is one of degree and will depend on a number of circumstances, including (1) the degree of disproportion between the stipulated sum and the loss likely to be suffered by the plaintiff, a factor relevant to the oppressiveness of the term to the defendant, and (2) the nature of the relationship between the contracting parties, a factor relevant to

the unconscionability of the plaintiffs conduct in seeking to enforce the term.'

Earlier in their reasons their Honours had discussed the first of these circumstances. After referring to the decisions of the House of Lords in *Clydebank Engineering and Shipbuilding Co v Don Jose Ramos Yzquierdo y Castaneda* and *Dunlop Pneumatic Tyre Co Ltd v New Garage and Motor Co Ltd*, they said [at p 190]:

'In both these decisions, in conformity with the doctrine's historic antecedents, the concept is that an agreed sum is a penalty if it is 'extravagant, exorbitant or unconscionable': *Clydebank*; *Dunlop*. This concept has been eroded by more recent decisions which, in the interests of greater certainty, have struck down provisions for the payment of an agreed sum merely because it may be greater than the amount of damages which could possibly be awarded for the breach of contract in respect of which the agreed sum is to be paid: see *Cooden Engineering Co Ltd v Stanford.* These decisions are more consistent with an underlying policy of restricting the parties, in case of breach of contract, to the recovery of an amount of damages no greater than that for which the law provides. However, there is much to be said for the view that the courts should return to the *Clydebank* and *Dunlop* concept, thereby allowing parties to a contract greater latitude in determining what their rights and liabilities will be, so that an agreed sum is only characterized as a penalty if it is out of all proportion to damage likely to be suffered as a result of breach: [140] see *Robophone Facilities Ltd v Blank* [at pp 1447-1448]; UK Law Commission, paras 33, 42-44.'

A similar view was expressed in *Elsley v J G Collins Insurance Agencies Ltd* [[1978] 83 DLR (3d) 1, at p 15], where Dickson J, in delivering the judgment of the Supreme Court of Canada, said:

'It is now evident that the power to strike down a penalty clause is a blatant interference with freedom of contract and is designed for the sole purpose of providing relief against oppression for the party having to pay the stipulated sum. It has no place where there is no oppression.'

As *O'Dea* and *AMEV-UDC* show, the fact that the 'recoverable amount' payable by the respondents under cl 6 is payable upon termination of the agreement consequent upon breach, rather than in respect of the breach alone, does not mean that the clause escapes the scrutiny of the law relating to penalties. But it does mean that in determining whether the 'recoverable amount' is a genuine pre-estimate of loss or a penalty, 'relevant loss is not restricted to the loss flowing immediately and merely from the actual breach of contract: it includes the loss of the benefit of the contract resulting from the election to terminate for breach ...': *AMEV-UDC* [at p 197] per Deane J; see also pp 181, 194, 205-206, 210. The respondents' submission to the contrary must be rejected.

In the Full Court the Chief Justice, with whose judgment Mohr J agreed, noted that, upon superficial examination, the formula prescribed in cl 5 for determining the 'recoverable amount' corresponded generally to the criteria sanctioned by Walsh J in *IAC (Leasing)* [at p 141] and by Mason and Wilson JJ in *AMEV-UDC* [at p 194]. However, his Honour distanced himself-from a close adherence to those criteria by observing that they were set in the context of cases dealing with leases of chattels containing no element of purchase whereas the present case involved a hire-purchase agreement. With all respect to his Honour, it may be doubted whether, at least in the present case, any real significance attaches to the distinction between a contract of hire and one of hire-purchase, although it is a distinction upon which counsel for the respondents relied in the appeal to this Court. Clause 10 of the agreement contains an option to purchase, providing that the hirer may elect to become the owner of the goods by paying the total rent and fulfilling his other obligations to the owner, but that until then [141] he shall have no property in the goods and shall be only a bailee. It is clear from that clause that until the exercise of the option the respondents had no proprietary interest in the prime mover. Nor were they bound to make the 36 instalments; they were free to terminate the agreement at any time. It may be noted that in *AMEV-UDC* [at p 194] Mason and Wilson JJ did not draw any distinction between a leasing contract and a hire-purchase agreement. In any event, if one leaves aside for the moment the reference to wholesale rather than retail value, the loss of any potential proprietary interest in the vehicle held by the respondents would seem to be compensated for in the formula defining the 'recoverable amount'. It will be remembered that the formula provided for the total rent (inclusive of repossession, storage, maintenance and selling costs) to be offset not only by all moneys paid as rent and an appropriate rebate of the terms charges but also by the value of the goods, being the best wholesale price reasonably obtainable for them in their then condition at the time of repossession. The respondents by their default forfeited any right to an option to purchase the vehicle.

The Chief Justice rightly drew from the character of the agreement as one of hire-purchase the conclusion that the maximum loss which the appellant could sustain in consequence of the termination of the hiring was the amount of any payments of rent in arrears, together with the total of unpaid future payments appropriately rebated for acceleration of payments and the expenses associated with termination. His Honour acknowledged that the formula in cl 5 could well be regarded as a genuine pre-estimate of such a loss in all cases save where the aggregate of rent already paid together with the value of the vehicle, less expenses of termination, exceeded the maximum loss capable of being sustained by the owner. After stressing the imbalance in bargaining power between the parties with consequent potential advantage to the appellant, the Chief Justice concluded that the failure of the formula to ensure that any excess resulting from the calculation of the recoverable amount be refunded to the respondents conferred a penal character upon cl 6. As we have said, Mohr J agreed with the Chief Justice.

We are unable to accept their Honours' process of reasoning. It overlooks the principle that the payment of an agreed sum is a penalty only if it is 'out of all proportion' or 'extravagant, exorbitant or unconscionable': *AMEV-UDC* [at p 196]; see also *O'Dea* [at p 400]; per Deane J. The reasoning of the majority places too much emphasis upon the superior bargaining position of a finance company, resulting in a conclusion that the mere possibility of unfairness lurking in the formula [142] contained in cl 5 is sufficient to characterize cl 6 as a penalty. The adoption of such a criterion fails to allow for the latitude that necessarily attends the conception of a genuine pre-estimate of damage. The clause is to be construed from the point of view of the parties at the time of entering into the transaction. The character of a clause as penal or compensatory is then to be perceived as a matter of degree depending on all the circumstances, including the nature of the subject matter of the agreement. The vehicle in the present case was a secondhand prime mover, such that the appellant would not grant to the respondents the requested term of four years and therefore limited the term of the hiring to a period of three years. The possibility that in the event of a termination upon default the moneys paid by the respondents, together with the value of the vehicle on repossession (less costs of repossession), would exceed the total rent appropriately rebated would seem to us to be unlikely. If the hiring were terminated early in the term the payments of rent would be likely to be matched by the diminution in value of the vehicle engaged in heavy haulage in the transport industry. It could only happen, if at all, later in the term when a substantial amount of rent had been paid and the vehicle retained a saleable value of some significance. The mere possibility in these circumstances of an excess is not sufficient, in our opinion, to render cl 6 unenforceable as a penalty.

It was argued for the respondents that the formula was not a genuine pre-estimate of the appellant's loss of bargain because it allowed credit only for the best wholesale value of the vehicle and not the best price reasonably obtainable. Von Doussa J addressed this issue at some length in his reasons for judgment and we are in general agreement with those reasons. We find it sufficient to observe that the appellant was not in the business of selling secondhand vehicles by retail and it was not unreasonable to anticipate the loss it would be likely to suffer in the event of breach by assuming a sale of the repossessed vehicle to a dealer. ... We would allow the appeal, set aside the decision of the Full Court and restore the decision of the trial Judge. Special leave to appeal was granted on condition that the appellant pay the respondents' costs of the appeal to this Court in any event.

BRENNAN J

One of the tests stated by Lord Dunedin in *Dunlop Pneumatic Tyre Co Ltd v New Garage and Motor Co Ltd* to assist in ascertaining whether a stipulated sum is a penalty is whether the sum 'is extravagant and unconscionable in amount in comparison with the greatest loss that could conceivably be proved to have followed from the breach'. To apply this test, it is necessary to identify the breach prescribed by the clause which imposes the supposed penalty and to ascertain the measure of loss which might follow from that breach. If the stipulated sum is payable on the occurrence of any breach of the contract, whether serious or trifling in its consequences, there is a presumption that the sum is a penalty.

By cl 6 of the parties' hire-purchase contract, the owner (the appellant) is authorized in the event of any breach by the hirer (the respondents) to retake possession of the goods hired, and thereby to terminate the hiring and to recover 'as liquidated damages' a sum calculated by the formula prescribed by cl 5 and described as 'the recoverable amount'. The recoverable amount includes an amount which compensates the owner for his loss of instalments of rental which would have become payable if the hiring had not been terminated. Rental instalments are expressed to be 'payable during the hiring' and the hirer agrees to pay the rent until the hiring is determined: cl 2. The right to be paid those instalments is therefore lost on the termination of the hiring. But is the owner's right to be paid future rental instalments lost because of the hirer's breach, which may be a trifling breach, or because of the owner's election to terminate the hiring? Under the general law a party who breaches a condition in a contract or who commits a fundamental breach of or repudiates a contract – a party who commits what I shall call a repudiatory breach – is exposed to the loss of all his future contractual rights and to liability to compensate an innocent party for loss of his bargain; but a non-repudiatory breach does not expose the party in default to that liability in the absence of a stipulation in [144] that behalf. If a hire-purchase contract confers on the owner a contractual right to terminate the hiring for any breach, that right is distinct from and cumulative upon the owner's general law right to terminate the contract for a repudiatory breach. In such a case the source of the right to terminate the hiring is the contract ...

In this Court, no clear opinion has emerged as to the effect for the purpose of the law of penalties of a loss suffered by an innocent party in consequence of his exercise of a contractual power to terminate for breach of a non-essential term. In *AMEV-UDC Finance Ltd v Austin*, a hirer of equipment defaulted in paying an instalment of rent on the due date whereupon the owner, in exercise of a contractual power, terminated the hiring and demanded payment of a sum calculated in accordance with a contractual formula: the whole unpaid balance of the total rent payable under the hiring agreement subject to certain adjustments representing the difference between the residual value of the equipment specified in the agreement and the sale price of the equipment. The hirer was found not to have repudiated the agreement. As the clause entitling the owner on termination of the hiring to the whole unpaid balance of the total rent without discount was held to impose a penalty (see *O'Dea v Allstates Leasing System (WA) Pty Ltd*), the issue for determination was whether the owner was entitled to no more than the instalments unpaid at the date of termination together with interest as damages for the hirer's breach or whether the owner was entitled to enforce the hirer's contractual obligation to pay up to the amount of any loss sustained by the owner in consequence of the termination of the hiring. A sharp division of opinion appeared in the answers given by the majority (Gibbs CJ, Mason and Wilson JJ) and by the minority (Deane and Dawson JJ). The majority held that the owner was entitled only to the former relief: the minority held that the owner was entitled to the latter relief. Gibbs CJ, agreeing with the decision of the English Court of Appeal in *Financings Ltd v Baldock*, which had held the [145] owner's damages for non-repudiatory breach to be limited to instalments in arrears at the date of termination with interest, said:

> 'The ratio of that part of the decision was that where there has been no repudiation by the hirer, and the owner has exercised his power to determine the hiring because the hirer was in arrears with his payments, any loss occurring after the determination will have resulted, not from the hirer's breach of contract in being late in his payments, but from the owner's election to determine the hiring [[1963] 12 QB at pp 111, 112, 115 and 122-123] ... Very similar reasoning was accepted by this Court in *Shevill v Builders Licensing Board* [(1982) 149 CLR 620], a case in which a lessor exercised a power of re-entry when the lessee fell into arrears in the payment of rent.'

Mason and Wilson JJ said [at 186]:

> 'The point is that when the lessor terminates pursuant to the contractual right given to him for breach by the lessee, the loss which

> he can recover for non-fundamental breach is limited to the loss which flows from the lessee's breach. The lessor cannot recover the loss which he sustains as a result of his termination because that loss is attributable to his act, not to the conduct of the Lessee. It is otherwise in the case of fundamental breach, breach of an essential term or repudiation: see *Progressive Mailing House Pty Ltd v Tabali Pty Ltd* [(1985) 157 CLR I7, at p 31].'

In rejecting a submission that equity would condition the granting of relief against a penalty by requiring the guilty party to compensate the innocent party for loss incurred consequent on termination for non-fundamental breach, their Honours said (at p 191):

> 'it would now be inconsistent with modern authority for equity to condition its relief by imposing on the obligor a liability to pay damage which flows, not from the obligor's breach of contract, but from the obligee's act in exercising his contractual right to terminate for non-fundamental breach.'

If, for the purpose of applying the Dunlop test, regard is had solely to the damages which the majority in *AMEV-UDC* held to flow from the hirer's breach, a stipulation for liquidated damages to be paid by a hirer on termination of the hiring for non-repudiatory breach which imposes a liability to pay for losses flowing from the termination should be treated as imposing a penalty. However, a further examination of *AMEV-UDC* shows that a majority of the Court said that that is not the law. Deane J, in dissent, held that the loss against which the supposed penalty was [146] to be measured to determine whether it was in truth a penalty, included the loss sustained upon termination. His Honour, accepting the explanation for this proposition advanced by the majority in *Cooden Engineering Co Ltd v Stanford*, said [at p 204]:

> 'In essence, that explanation is that, at least for the purposes of the rules relating to penalties, the loss sustained by reason of the exercise of a contractual right to terminate upon breach in a case such as the present is to be seen as flowing from the breach. The point was clearly made by Hodson LJ in *Cooden* [at 116] when he expressed his difficulty in seeing 'the validity of the distinction between a claim to receive payment of a sum of money because of a right to determine arising from breach of contract and a claim to receive payment of the same sum by reason of breach of contract giving a right to determine': see also Somervell LJ [at 96-97]. In that context and notwithstanding the support for the contrary view which can be found in some cases, I am unable to accept that the common law would found upon that very distinction between breach and termination to reduce the extent to which a penalty clause can be enforced below the actual amount of the loss sustained upon termination for breach.'

Dawson J, also in dissent, perceived a logical but not a legal distinction between loss flowing from non-repudiatory breach and loss flowing from termination pursuant to a contractual power, observing [at p 213]:

> 'Moreover, if, as is logical but is not done, the provision for loss upon termination of the agreement were to be compared in amount with the loss flowing from a breach not amounting to a repudiation, it would almost certainly be markedly more and for that reason a penalty even though a genuine pre estimate of the lessor's damage upon the

> exercise of his contractual right to terminate the agreement. It is not done because the result is obviously unsatisfactory, but I shall return to that point shortly.'

And [at p 215]:

> '... if a provision stipulating a payment by way of accelerated rent or the like upon repossession is to be regarded as payable upon breach rather than upon termination of the agreement for the purpose of characterizing it as a penalty and if upon the provision being characterized as a penalty the only recovery permitted is for the breach and not for the loss of the bargain (assuming no repudiation), there can be no justification for having regard to the loss arising from termination in determining whether the provision is a genuine pre-estimate of damage or a penalty.'

[147] Yet, his Honour said, 'that is what is done'. If that is so, losses flowing not from the breach alone but from the termination as well are taken into account in determining whether a pecuniary liability is a penalty. Mason and Wilson J expressed, albeit obiter, a view which bears out Dawson J's observation. First, their Honours did not regard termination as an event supervening on an antecedent breach and, on that account, to place post-termination loss outside the purview of the law relating to penalties. Their Honours said [[1986] 162 CLR, at pp 184-194]:

> 'If the option (to terminate) is exercised on the occasion of the hirer's breach of contract, it accords with principle and authority to say that the sum is payable in respect of the breach of contract and is a penalty, unless it is a genuine pre-estimate of the damage.'

Although their Honours held that losses caused by the termination of the contract were not to be included in the owner's damages, they thought it right to take them into account in determining whether a pecuniary liability imposed by the contract is a penalty. Their Honours said [at 194]:

> 'Our rejection of the appellant's arguments should not be taken as throwing any doubt on the right of the owner or the lessor to recover his actual loss on his early termination of a hire-purchase agreement or chattel lease, pursuant to a contractual right, for the hirer's non-fundamental breach, under a correctly drawn indemnity provision.'

In the light of these observations, I take the law to accept an incongruity in holding that an owner's damages at law for a non-repudiatory breach are limited to losses caused by the breach alone while holding that a clause which imposes a liability on the hirer to pay the losses caused by exercise of a power to terminate a hiring upon breach is not a penalty. It may be appropriate to reconsider this incongruity in some later case and, if that is done, it may well be necessary to canvass the correctness of some earlier decisions of this Court. For the moment I adopt, in common with the other members of the Court, the view that the owner's loss consequent upon the termination of the hiring for non-repudiatory breach is to be taken into account in determining whether the recoverable amount prescribed by cl 5 is a penalty. It is implicit in this view that a contractual power to terminate a hiring is not itself-a penalty though the fact of termination is relevant to the determination whether a pecuniary liability then imposed on the hirer is a penalty: *O'Dea v Allstates*. Depending on the circumstances, the [148] exercise of such a contractual power might be oppressive to the hirer and productive of a windfall profit for the owner. This consideration draws attention to equity's jurisdiction to grant relief against the unconscionable exercise of legal rights to which reference will presently be made. For the moment, assuming that the power to terminate the hiring for a non-repudiatory breach is effectively exercised, the question is whether the amount of the hirer's liability imposed pursuant to cl 6 is extravagant or unconscionable in comparison with the greatest losses that could conceivably be proved to have followed the breach and the termination.

The 'recoverable amount' prescribed by cl 5 is a balance struck by debiting the hirer with certain items and crediting him with others. The items debited consist in 'the total rent ... and all other moneys payable for the full period of hire (including ... costs of repossession storage maintenance and selling expenses), from which are deducted all moneys paid by the hirer, the wholesale value of the goods repossessed and 'a rebate of charges calculated in accordance with Clause 13 hereof': cl 5. The cl 13 rebate represents the interest or terms charges attributable to the portion of the original hiring period which is still to go at the time of termination. On termination of the hiring, the owner loses the right to receive future rental instalments and may incur costs in repossessing, storing, maintaining and selling the goods the subject of the contract, but he acquires possession of the goods and a discharge of the hirer's option to purchase them. The owner's loss on termination is the balance of the 'cash price' which it has outlaid to acquire the hired goods (see cl 1 and 2 and the 'Hirer's Declaration' embodied in the 'Offer to Hire') to the extent to which it has not been recouped, unrecouped interest earned and administration charges incurred up to the time of termination and the costs associated with repossessing and selling the hired goods less the value of the repossessed goods. If the loss is recovered on termination, the owner's capital is available for alternative investment and its outgoings are covered. Clauses 5 and 13 contain a formula which so quantifies the recoverable amount as to equate it with the net loss suffered by the owner, assuming that the value of the goods which the owner repossesses and sells to a third party is properly set at 'the best wholesale price reasonably obtainable for them in their then condition as at the time of ... taking possession of them': cl 5(b). As the owner is a finance company which outlays money to acquire goods selected by the hirer and is not a retailer of goods, the best wholesale price obtainable on repossession cannot be said to be an extravagant and unconscionable under-estimate of [149] what the owner is likely to obtain if it sells the goods after termination of the hiring.

In the Full Court of the Supreme Court of South Australia, King CJ with the concurrence of Mohr J (von Doussa J dissenting) nevertheless held that the formula prescribed by cl 5 resulted in the imposition of a penalty. His Honour would have accepted the formula as being a genuine pre-estimate of the owner's loss on termination, but only:

> 'if its operation were limited to situations in which the aggregate of amounts already paid and the value of the vehicle, less expenses of termination did not exceed the maximum loss ... which could result from termination and if it were supplemented by provision for reimbursement to the hirer of the amount of any such excess.'

His Honour held that the formula resulted in the imposition of a penalty because:

> 'The contract under consideration does not so limit the operation of the formula and makes no provision for reimbursement of excess.'

In my respectful opinion, there are flaws in each of the grounds on which his Honour held the recoverable amount to be a penalty. First, the formula has no operation except where the value of the repossessed goods is insufficient to meet what are otherwise the net losses of the owner. Where the formula produces no debit balance, the contract imposes no liability on the hirer: no penalty is imposed. Secondly, if one leaves aside any question of relief against an unconscionable exercise of the power to terminate, an owner who terminates the hiring in exercise of its contractual power to do so is entitled to all the rights of an owner freed from the hirer's right to possess the goods and the hirer's right under cl 10 to acquire ownership of them 'by paying the total rent and fulfilling my other obligations'. The owner is under no obligation to account for the value, or proceeds of sale, of his goods to another who had but no longer has an interest in them. If the owner, having extinguished the rights of the hirer, makes a profit by selling or rehiring the goods, the absence of a stipulation requiring it to account for the profit does not convert a stipulation which requires the hirer to compensate the owner for any loss into a stipulation imposing a penalty.

However, the assumption which underlies the notion of 'profit' or 'loss' in this context is that the owner's loss is not recouped unless the amount put back in its pocket equals the outlays it has made in acquiring the goods – the 'cash price' mentioned in the present contract – together with interest and other charges up to [150] the time of repossession and the costs associated with repossession and sale. That assumption is correct if the contract is treated, in substance if not in form, as a money lending transaction; but it is not correct if the contract is treated, in substance as well as in form, as a hiring contract conferring an option to purchase. A non-repudiatory breach of a hire-purchase contract does not give rise to those losses which would not arise but for the owner's election to terminate the hiring under a contractual power ...

If a clause which requires the hirer to pay the owner for losses occasioned by termination for breach under a contractual power is not a penalty provision, the reason must be that the court regards that clause and the clause authorizing the owner to terminate the hiring, to repossess and sell the goods and to recover the net losses then outstanding as provisions to secure the owner's interests as a moneylender, as well as to secure the due performance of the hirer's obligations. The right to recover post-termination losses is needed to secure the owner's return of the money lent with interest and the recoupment of the owner's costs and expenses. The owner's rights to terminate the hiring, to repossess and sell the goods and to recover the recoverable amount can hardly be supported as a stipulation for the payment of a genuine pre-estimate of damage caused by any non-repudiatory breach of the hirer's obligations, but they can be seen to be security for the due performance of the hirer's obligations *and* the protection of the owner's interests as a [151] moneylender. In other words, if it be right to uphold a stipulation for the payment of post-termination losses as a stipulation for the payment of liquidated damages, the corollary is that the transaction be treated in much the same way as a chattel mortgage and the contractual power to terminate, repossess and sell be treated merely as security for the repayment of the moneys lent with interest and recoupment of the owner's costs and expenses.

If a hire-purchase contract is so regarded, equity may grant the hirer relief against an exercise by an owner of its contractual right to terminate, repossess and sell the hired goods in the event of a non-repudiatory breach of the contract because the contractual right may be seen as a penalty designed to secure money and a court of equity can give the owner all that he is entitled to as a moneylender. The jurisdiction was asserted in *Peachy v Duke of Somerset* [[1721] 1 Str 447, at p 453] and was discussed in *Shiloh Spinners Ltd v Harding* [[1973] AC 691, at pp 722-723]; *Legione v Hateley* [(1983) 152 CLR 406]; and *Stern v McArthur* [(1988) 165 CLR 489]; and see *Stockloser v Johnson* [[1954] 1 QB 476]; and *Starside Properties Ltd v Mustapha* [[1974] 1 WLR 816, at pp 822-824]. In *BICC Plc v Burndy Corporation* [[1985] Ch 232], it was held that there is jurisdiction in equity to grant relief against forfeiture of a possessory or proprietary interest in personal property (see per Dillon LJ [at pp 251-252]) and those are the kinds of interests held by a hirer who has committed no repudiatory breach. Under the general law, the hirer is entitled to continued possession of the goods and, if payment of rental instalments entitles him to purchase the goods, he acquires a proprietary interest in the property which is susceptible of protection in equity. Though he has no legal title to the goods until he has fulfilled the conditions prescribed by the contract (but cf *Wickham Holdings Ltd v Brooke House Motors Ltd* [[1967] 1 WLR 295] his contractual right to acquire the title by fulfilling those conditions may be protected. It is neither necessary nor possible to state exhaustively the circumstances in which equity will intervene to protect a hirer's possessory or proprietary interests against an exercise of the owner's contractual rights. The circumstances will be identified more clearly as the jurisdiction to grant relief is argued and exercised in particular cases. This is not one of them. For the moment, it is sufficient to note that there are two factors which are of general relevance. First, the deliberation and seriousness of the hirer's [152] breach and, secondly, the likelihood of the owner, by exercise of its contractual rights, making a windfall profit which the owner is not contractually required to account for to the hirer.

In the present case, the hirers did not seek relief against the exercise by the owner of its contractual rights. Had they done so, it is unlikely that they would have succeeded. The hirers had defaulted in the payment of four successive monthly rental instalments and, at the time of repossession, $7,048.46 of a total sum of $31,939.26 which had become payable was outstanding. The owner gave the hirers a reasonable opportunity to make good their default but they did not take that opportunity. The goods – a prime mover – were sold for $27,000 which was insufficient to meet the unpaid balance of the owner's outlays, interest, charges and expenses. A recoverable amount of $9,300.42 became due. This amount, together with interest at 15 per cent per annum under cl 4(c), was the basis of the owner's claim in the action.

In the Full Court of the Supreme Court of South Australia the owner's award was reduced to the instalments in arrears, $7,048.46 together with interest, solely on the ground that cl 6 imposed a penalty. Once it is accepted that it is right to have regard to the owner's losses on termination in determining whether the recoverable amount is 'extravagant and unconscionable', the hirer's attack on cl 6 is limited to two points: the adoption of the best wholesale price rather than the retail price as the amount to be credited to the hirer in calculating the recoverable amount and the absence of any liability on the part of the owner to account to the hirer for any surplus over the amount due under cl 5 resulting from the sale of the goods repossessed. For the reasons given, neither of these points stamps the recoverable amount with the character of a penalty. Having failed to sustain their attack on cl 6, the hirers must be held liable to pay the recoverable amount. The appeal must be allowed.

DEANE J

[153] The question whether particular provisions of an agreement defining the rights and liabilities of the parties upon termination for breach purport to impose a penalty must be determined as a matter of substance. If such provisions do no more than impose upon the defaulting party an obligation to pay an amount (whether specified or to be calculated in accordance with a nominated formula) which represents a genuine pre-estimate of the damage (including loss of bargain) which the innocent party will sustain by reason of the breach and consequent termination, the provisions will not impose a penalty. Nor will they impose a penalty merely because they operate to withdraw an incentive for observance by the defaulting party of the terms of the agreement. Such provisions will not be penal unless their operation is, as a matter of substance, to impose some additional or different financial obligation or burden upon the defaulting party in the nature of a disincentive or punishment for breach: cf *Acron Pacific Ltd v Offshore Oil NL* [(1985) 157 CLR 514, at p 520].

There are two particular aspects of the agreement upon which Mr and Mrs Plessnig base their claim that the provisions of cl 6 are penal in nature and therefore void. The first is the absence of any provision which would require Esanda to make some refund to Mr and Mrs Plessnig in circumstances where (unlike the present) the value of the repossessed goods exceeded the total of unpaid past and rebated future instalments of 'rent' and the expenses of [154] repossession and realization. The second is that cl 6, by adopting the recoverable amount as defined by cl 5, allows credit only for the wholesale, as distinct from the retail, value of the repossessed goods. Apart from those two particular aspects, it was not suggested that the provisions of cl 6 constitute a penalty. Indeed, it is difficult to see how they could since, in a case of termination by the owner (Esanda) for breach by the hirers (Mr and Mrs Plessnig), the formula for calculating the recoverable amount represents, apart from those two particular aspects, an obviously fair method of estimating in advance the owner's likely damages including loss of bargain: it rebates future rental charges by, in effect, reducing them to present value and it provides for a deduction of the present value of the repossessed goods: cf Ziegel, 'Measuring Damages for Breach of a Chattel Lease' [1988] *Lloyd's Maritime and Commercial Law Quarterly*, 276, at pp 280-282. I turn to consider the two particular aspects of the agreement upon which the argument that cl 6 imposes a penalty is founded.

There is nothing in the actual provisions of cl 6 which would cause the clause to operate as a penalty in the circumstances postulated as the basis of the respondents' primary argument (ie where the agreement is terminated by the owner for breach by the hirers at a time when the wholesale value of the repossessed goods after the expenses of repossession and realization exceeds unpaid past and rebated future instalments of 'rent'). As has been mentioned, the provisions of cl 6 would not, in those circumstances, entitle Esanda to recover any amount on account of future rent or in respect of the costs of repossession or resale. The operation of the clause would be that Esanda was entitled to terminate the hiring of its vehicle and, as owner, take possession of it. It could scarcely be, and has not been, suggested that such an operation of the provisions of the clause, upon breach by the hirers of the terms of the agreement for hire, was penal in nature. Yet that is effectively all that cl 6 would authorize or effect. It is true that the overall agreement could, on one conceivable construction of its terms, have led to a windfall profit for Esanda in those hypothetical circumstances. The reason for that is not, however, to be found in the provisions of cl 6. It lies in the combination of the failure of the agreement to require Esanda to account for any excess upon realization and the fact that the right to 'elect to become the' owner of the vehicle conferred by cl 10 was exercisable by Mr and Mrs Plessnig by payment of outstanding past and rebated future rent *and* fulfilment of their 'other obligations to' Esanda. If the requirement of fulfilment of 'other obligations' were construed as referring not only to the outstanding obligation but as requiring [155] that there had been no past breach of the agreement, the practical effect of the requirement would be that the right to 'elect to become the owner of' the vehicle was lost upon any breach. On that construction, the operation of the overall agreement could be harsh and unfair in the hypothetical circumstances. For example, the right to become the owner of the vehicle could be lost at a time when the vehicle remained of very substantial value and but one instalment of 'rent' remained unpaid. If such circumstances had occurred and that somewhat unlikely construction of cl 10 had prevailed, questions might have arisen about what, if any, relief was available to Mr and Mrs Plessnig against any such harsh and unfair operation of the agreement. It may have been argued that the provision to the effect that Mr and Mrs Plessnig could only exercise the right to become the owner of the vehicle if they had performed all their 'other obligations to' Esanda was itself-void as a penalty notwithstanding that it did not impose any obligation to make a payment in cash or in kind. Alternatively, it might have been argued on behalf of Mr and Mrs Plessnig that they were entitled, under principles of unjust enrichment operating in all the circumstances of the case, to recover from Esanda the amount of any excess received by it upon sale of the vehicle or that they were entitled to relief against the loss of the right to become the owner upon payment of the appropriate amount under cl 10. It is, however, unnecessary to pursue those questions. The postulated circumstances did not arise. At the time of repossession, the vehicle was worth substantially less than the total of the unpaid past and rebated future instalments of 'rent'. Mr and Mrs Plessnig neither sought nor desired to exercise the right to become its owner by payment of the appropriate amount under cl 10. More important for present purposes, the possibly harsh and unfair operation of the agreement in those postulated hypothetical circumstances would not be the result of the provisions of cl 6.

The second basis for the argument that cl 6 constituted a penalty was, as has been said, that the credit allowed for the repossessed vehicle in calculating the recoverable amount defined in cl 5 is determined by reference to wholesale, rather than retail, value. There is, in my view, no substance in that argument. Esanda was not in the business of retailing vehicles. It has not been suggested that it should be seen as able or required to mitigate damages by a re-letting of the equipment: cf *Keneric Tractor Sales Ltd v Langille* [(1987) 43 DLR (4th) 171]. An appropriate measure of the amount to be credited in respect of the value of the repossessed vehicle for the purpose of [156] estimating the loss Esanda would be likely to sustain in the event of breach was the amount it could expect to recover upon sale of the repossessed vehicle to a dealer. I would allow the appeal and substitute, for the orders of the Full Court, orders dismissing the appeal to that Court with costs. In accordance with the condition upon which special leave to appeal to this Court was granted, Esanda should pay Mr and Mrs Plessnig's costs of the appeal to this Court.

GAUDRON J

The matters which are said to constitute the clause a penalty are four in number: 1. The clause makes no provision for refund to the respondents of any surplus arising on resale of the goods the subject of the agreement; 2. The clause allows for the crediting of the wholesale rather than the retail value of the goods the subject of the agreement; 3. A clause providing for payment of loss of bargain damages in relation to a hire-purchase agreement (other than in consequence of a repudiatory or fundamental breach) is a penalty; and 4. A clause providing for payment by the hirer to the owner in the event of early termination of a hire-purchase agreement is not a genuine pre-estimate of loss of bargain damages unless it takes account of the duty to mitigate loss.

I agree with Deane J, for the reasons that his Honour gives, that the first two matters do not constitute cl 6 a penalty. In my view, by reason of the manner in which cl 6 operates, neither the third nor the fourth matter serves to constitute cl 6 a penalty. The agreement is in familiar form, reflecting the nature of a hire-purchase agreement as an agreement for the provision of finance taking the form of an agreement for the hire of goods with an option for the hirer to become owner of the goods. The bargain constituted by the present agreement involves a promise by the respondents to pay instalments 'during the hiring' and, in some circumstances, to pay a further amount in the event of early termination of the hiring. The agreement contemplates that there may be early termination by early completion, early termination at the election of the respondents and early termination at the election of the appellant on specified grounds, including upon default by the [157] respondents in payment of instalments. In each case the total of the agreed rental payments is rebated in accordance with cl 13 of the agreement. In the case of termination by election the amount payable is the same whether the agreement is terminated at the election of the appellant or the respondents. Breach and damage flowing from breach are irrelevant to its calculation. None the less, the clause operates in an area in which the rules relating to contractual penalties have been seen to have application: see *O'Dea v Allstates Leasing System (W A) Pty Ltd*; *AMEV-UDC Finance Ltd v Austin*; especially per Deane J [at pp 197-200].

In *AMEV-UDC* this Court considered a contractual provision obliging a lessee to pay certain amounts in the event of early termination of a chattel lease. In that case termination was effected at the election of the lessor upon the lessee's breach. Mason and Wilson JJ [at p 194] expressed the view that an owner could 'recover his actual loss on his early termination of a hire-purchase agreement or chattel lease, pursuant to a contractual right, for the hirer's non-fundamental breach, under a correctly drawn indemnity provision. Deane J [at p 197] noted that 'in determining whether the amounts payable by (a) lessee upon such termination are properly to be seen as a genuine pre-estimate of loss or as a penalty, relevant loss is not restricted to the loss flowing immediately and merely from the actual breach of contract; it includes the loss of the benefit of the contract resulting from the election to terminate for breach'. I agree with these observations but prefer to express the relevant consideration (whether in relation to a chattel lease or a hire-purchase agreement) in terms of an assessment or calculation of the value to the owner or the hirer of the performance of the primary obligation according to its terms: see *Public Works Commissioner v Hills* [(l906) AC 368, at pp 375-376]; O'Dea [at p 383], per Wilson J.

Where the parties to a hire-purchase agreement stipulate events within the general responsibility of the hirer (see *AMEV-UDC* [at p 199-200] which will give rise to a right to early termination the further stipulation of an ensuing indebtedness on the part of the hirer in an amount which is a genuine pre-estimate or an amount calculated by a method giving a substantially accurate assessment of the difference between the value of the benefit which would accrue to the owner from the complete performance of the hiring and the [158] value of the benefit (if any) accruing from early termination cannot, in my view, be characterized as a penalty: see, in relation to assessment of damages generally, *Buchanan v Byrnes* [(1906) 3 CLR 704, at p 715], per Griffith CJ.

Ordinarily, in the case of a hire-purchase agreement, the major component of the difference in relevant values will be the difference between the outstanding component of the purchase price outlaid for the goods the subject of the agreement (which component would be recouped from instalments payable during the remainder of the agreed period of hire) and the value of those goods at the date of early termination. Leaving aside charges payable by reason of repossession (as to which there is no present issue), cl 6 operates to disclose an indebtedness which is neither more nor less than this difference.

The instalments payable under the agreement are calculated by reference to the purchase price paid for the goods and the terms charges referable to the agreed period of hire. In order to ascertain the outstanding component of the purchase price as at the date of early termination it is necessary that there be some formula for the apportionment of instalments already paid as between terms charges and purchase price. For the latter purpose it is necessary that there also be a formula for the ascertainment of that proportion of the total terms charges referable to the actual period of hire. So long as the formulae involve no imposition of additional terms charges or terms charges for a period extending beyond the time at which the outstanding component of the purchase price is reasonably to be regarded as available to the finance company there can be no question of their operating in a manner penalizing the hirer.

The rebate formula in cl 13 of the agreement allows for the ascertainment of the terms charges referable to the period from termination until the hiring would have terminated if the agreement had run its course. When that amount is deducted from the total charges (ie purchase price plus total terms charges) there is ascertained an amount which is the sum of the purchase price and the terms charges referable to the actual period of hire. The amount which is disclosed by the deduction of the instalments paid is the outstanding component of the purchase price.

The benefit which accrues to an owner upon early termination of a hire-purchase agreement is possession of the goods the subject of the agreement freed from the hiring obligation and the option for the hirer to become owner. As a hire-purchase agreement is in substance an agreement for the provision of finance (to which the [159] hiring is merely the formal or legal incident) the value of that benefit is taken into account by the deduction of that value from the outstanding component of the purchase price.

> There is only one other matter which might be regarded as a benefit accruing to the owner by reason of early termination. Assuming prompt payment of the moneys payable by the hirer in consequence of the operation of cl 6 of the agreement there is an accelerated availability of moneys representing the outstanding component of the purchase price: see *Yeoman Credit Ltd v McLean.* See also *O'Dea* [at pp 386-387] where Brennan J noted a number of matters pertinent to the accelerated payment of a debt due in futuro. If the sum payable upon early termination included an amount for terms charges referable to the remainder of the hire period (or any part period after the moneys are reasonably to be regarded as available to the owner) then, in my view, a contractual provision which allowed no account for that accelerated availability would not represent a substantially accurate assessment of the difference in value between performance of the primary obligation according to its terms and early termination. However, where, as here, the sum payable on early termination is the difference between the outstanding component of the purchase price and the value of the goods, the accelerated availability of that money is not properly characterized as a benefit. Its payment merely puts the owner in a position to earn income which would otherwise have been received if the hiring agreement had been performed according to its terms.
>
> Because of the manner in which cl 6 operates (ie by reference to the difference in value between performance of the primary obligation according to its terms and early termination) the question of mitigating loss is irrelevant to its characterization as a penalty. On the analysis that I prefer those matters usually comprehended in the duty to mitigate loss are more appropriately analysed in terms of benefit accruing to an owner by reason of early termination.
>
> The appeal should be allowed.

Analysis of Esanda

Once you have read *Esanda,* answer, in note form, the following questions. It may be useful to refer in your notes to key passages in the judgments.

(i) What were the salient facts in *Esanda*?

(ii) What issues did counsel raise in their arguments?

Are these issues properly dealt with by the judgments of the court?

(iii) Does each judgment state the basic principles to be applied in the rule against penalties in the same way? Explain any differences.

(iv) Briefly trace the reasoning in each of the four judgments. What differences are there in the application of the rule against penalties to the facts of the case?

- Wilson and Toohey JJ

- Brennan J

- Deane J

- Gaudron J

(v) Can the judgments in *Esanda* be summed up by a basic proposition?

If so, what is it?

(vi) What, according to the court in *Esanda*, was the basic principle emerging from the *AMEV* case?

What inconsistencies in the rule against penalties arise from the *AMEV* case?

Synthesis of the Legal Principles

Now that you have read and analysed the two cases, you should be in a position to synthesise the basic principles governing the drafting and construction of agreed damages clauses. Once again, write short notes to consolidate your learning.

(i) Upon what basis do the courts enforce or strike down agreed damages clauses?

(ii) In what circumstances have the courts decided that the distinction between genuine pre-estimates of damages and penalty clauses is not to be applied?

(iii) As at what point in time do the courts examine clauses to see whether they are genuine pre-estimates of damages or penalty clauses?

(iv) What general rules of construction do the courts apply in construing such clauses?

What criteria and factors do they take into account in deciding whether a clause is a penalty clause?

How does the court calculate the innocent party's loss to determine whether the agreed damages clause is a penalty?

(v) What are the consequences of the clause being a penalty? In particular, is a penalty clause enforced by the courts?

(vi) Can the plaintiff claim damages under the general law? If so, how does the court calculate the quantum of damages? Is the amount fixed by the penalty in any way relevant to the assessment of the claim?

(vii) List any issues arising in either case that you would like to clarify when you come to class.

Evaluation of the Rule Against Penalties

Now that you have drafted a few agreed damages clauses and read two leading cases on the rule against penalties you are in a good position to evaluate the principles in this area as developed by the courts. Jot down brief notes to answer the following questions. We will discuss these issues in class.

(i) What is the proper role of the law of contract in relation to business relations and the negotiation and enforcement of agreements?

(ii) Are the rules set out in the cases still appropriate for distinguishing between penalties and genuine pre-estimates of damages?

(iii) Do these cases give clear guidance as to how to draft agreed damages clauses without infringing the rule against penalties? Give reasons for your answer.

If you decide that the rules are not as clear as they could be, consider whether this lack of clarity will have any consequences for the level of litigation arising out of the use of agreed damages clauses.

(iv) How much change can you trace in the way the courts have construed these clauses? Read again Adams and Brownsword's article on 'The Ideologies of Contract' (1987) 7 *Legal Studies* 205. Describe any changes in the courts' underlying philosophy of contract or of judicial decision-making which may have an impact on the way these clauses have been construed by the courts over time?

4.1.4 Step 3: developing the principles through use and application, and checking on learning

Commentary

The third step requires students to apply their learning to interpreting and drafting agreed damages clauses. In this way they can integrate their understanding of the area, while at the same time learn through doing. These activities will provide them with a form of feedback, so that they should also be able to monitor for themselves their understanding of the legal principles by their ability to solve the problems.

This third step consists essentially of two activities – a drafting problem and a construction problem. In each problem students are required to work out solutions outside class, and then to use their work in a new activity in class. The drafting problem builds on the previous drafting problems by requiring students to redraft their clauses in the light of their reading of the cases in step 2. This will enable them to see for themselves how much they have learned. Once they have redrafted the clause, the materials require them to assess for themselves how well they have drafted the clause.

The drafting problem is to be developed in the classroom by requiring students to simulate or role play a negotiation in which the clause is examined by the client and the solicitor. The solicitor has to justify the draft clause to the client. Alternatively, the simulation can involve one student playing an articled clerk who has drafted the clause. She or he has to justify the drafted clause to the client and/or her or his principal.

The second problem is a construction problem. The clause is drawn from a leading High Court case decided before the cases extracted in the materials. The extract in the materials gives students details of the contract and the surrounding facts. This construction task then forms the basis of a moot in class, where we can ask students to either defend or attack the clause. A third student gives a decision. This approach is outlined in Figure 7.[8]

8 This figure was first published in Le Brun and Johnstone (1994) 324.

	Private Study Prior to Class Using the Materials	*Classroom Activities*
1	Students are required to redraft their agreed damages clause in the light of their learning in Step 2. Self-assessment in which the student is asked to assess the clause and comment on its strengths and weaknesses.	Simulation/role play involving solicitor and client; or Junior solicitor and supervising solicitor. The solicitor/junior solicitor has to explain and justify the clause to the client/supervising solicitor.
2	Construction problem in which students construe a new clause.	Moot in groups of three students. In each group there are two barristers and a judge. The
3	Self-assessment in which the students evaluate the strengths and weaknesses of their opinions.	barristers argue that the clause is or is not a penalty clause, and the judge reports to the class, setting out the arguments and her or his decision.
		Full class discussion of the issues arising from the two activities.
		Clarification of issues still unclear to students.
		Feedback and summary from the teacher.

Figure 7 Step 3

The Materials

In this part of the materials you an opportunity to develop your learning by using the legal principles you have learned by doing what legal practitioners do with the legal principles governing agreed damages clauses. You should complete the following activities during your private study. These activities:

(i) provide you with an opportunity to practise your *drafting skills* and your ability to *construe* contractual clauses.

(ii) enable you to *assess for yourself* how well you have *integrated* the principles from the cases, and the extent to which you are able to *apply* these principles to situations that will arise in legal practice.

(iii) will *reinforce* and *deepen* your understanding of those principles.

(iv) will enable you to *identify issues for reform* that will form the basis of the fourth step in this topic.

Drafting Problem 2

Now that you have considered the basic principles developed by the courts concerning the rule against penalties, **redraft** your clause for Ms De Maggio.

Set out your revised clause in this space.

How confident are you that you have drafted a good clause now?

No Confidence Very Confident

1...........2.............3.............4.............5.............6.............7 ....8.............9 10

What weaknesses do you think there may be in your clause as it is now drafted?

Explain, in a covering letter to Ms De Maggio, the changes (if any) that you have made to the clause.

When you come to class you will be involved in a role play in which you will be assigned a role in which you will either be critical of a clause drafted for Ms De Maggio, or will defend the drafted clause. The notes you have made during your study of this topic will assist you in this task.

Construction Exercise 3

Using all the principles you have learnt in the previous classes, construe the following clause in the context of the facts set out below (taken verbatim from the facts in *Pigram v Attorney General for New South Wales* (1975) 132 CLR 216).

[217] The deed recites that the appellant, then employed as a teacher of the Department of Education of the State of New South Wales, had applied for leave of absence from his employment to enable him to accept a scholarship tenable at the University of New England and that the Department had agreed that the appellant should have such leave without pay but with financial assistance equivalent to half the salary to which he would be entitled as a teacher in the service of the Department, such leave to be treated as service with the Department for incremental and extended leave purposes.

The deed in its first clause bound the appellant to resume duty as a teacher on a stated day and for a period of three years (subsequently extended by deed to five years) 'to be calculated from the date of his resuming duty as aforesaid faithfully diligently and thoroughly and in whatever locality or localities in the said State as may be directed by the Minister or the Director General or other proper authority of [218] the said State and in all respects in accordance with and subject to the provisions of the *Public Service Act*, 1902, as amended, and the *Public Instruction Act* of 1880, as amended, and the Regulations from time to time in force under those Acts serve Her Majesty Her Heirs and Successors as a Teacher in the said Department and perform the duties required of or allotted to the Officer by the Minister or the Director General or other proper authority of the said State ...'

The appellant took his leave during which he studied pursuant to the scholarship to the University of New England: but upon the successful conclusion of his course he decided to resign from the service of the Department of Education. Consequently, he did not resume his duties as promised on the stated day or at all. Thereafter, the Attorney-General of the State in this action successfully sued the appellant on cl 2 (b) of the deed. It is appropriate to set out in full the terms of cl 2 of the deed as amended and operative at the relevant time:

'2. The Officer DOTH HEREBY further covenant and agree with Her Majesty Her Heirs and Successors that if either of the following events shall happen namely –

(a) if the Officer shall at any time before the expiration of the period of service required of the Officer under paragraph (a) of cl 1 of this Deed by reason of the acceptance of a resignation tendered by the Officer or for any other cause whatsoever and of whatever kind (except his death or his dismissal from the Public Service of New South Wales otherwise than–

(i) for misconduct, or

(ii) under any of the provisions contained in ss 44, 51 56, 58, 61 and 65 of the *Public Service Act*, 1902, as amended)

cease to be employed in the service of the said Department, or if the Officer shall cease to carry out duties pursuant to the tender of a resignation; or

(b) if the Officer shall by reason of the acceptance of a resignation tendered by the Officer or for any other cause whatsoever and of whatever kind (other than his death or his dismissal from the Public Service of the State of New South Wales otherwise than –

(i) for misconduct, or

(ii) under any of the provisions contained in ss 44, 51, 56, 58, 61 or 65 of the *Public Service Act*, 1902, as amended)

fail to resume as provided by para (a) of cl 1 of this Deed the actual and full discharge of his duties in the said Department as aforesaid and faithfully diligently and thoroughly to serve Her Majesty Her Heirs and Successors as a Teacher in the said Department for the period of service required of the Officer under the said para (a) of cl 1 of this Deed then the Officer will on demand made by the Secretary to the Board [219] or the Director General forthwith pay to Her Majesty Her Heirs or Successors as and for liquidated damages and not by way of penalty a sum being the cost incurred by the State for or in respect of the period commencing on the date of commencement of the said leave of absence and ending on whichever of the following dates shall first occur namely the date on which the Officer is required by para (a) of cl 1 hereof to resume the actual and full discharge of his duties in the Department as aforesaid or the date on which the Officer shall for any reason whatsoever cease to be employed in the service of the said Department PROVIDED ALWAYS that if after the commencement and before the expiration of the period of service required of the Officer under para (a) of cl 1 of this Deed the following event shall happen namely the Officer shall by reason of the acceptance of a resignation tendered by the Officer or for any other cause whatsoever and of whatever kind (except his death or his dismissal from the Public Service of the said State of New South Wales otherwise than –

(i) for misconduct, or

(ii) under any of the provisions contained in ss. 44, 51, 56, 58, 61 or 65 of the *Public Service Act*, 1902, as amended)

cease to be employed as a Teacher in the service of the said Department the said sum so payable to Her Majesty Her Heirs or Successors shall be reduced to the sum that bears the same proportion to the cost incurred by the State as the part of the period of service required of the Officer under para (a) of cl 1 of this Deed which is unexpired at the date of the happening of such event bears to the whole of such period of service.

PROVIDED ALWAYS AND IT IS HEREBY AGREED AND DECLARED that –

(a) without in any way limiting the meaning thereof the expression 'the cost incurred by the State' shall include:

(i) all amounts paid to the Officer during the period of leave by or on behalf of Her Majesty Her Heirs and Successors or the Government of the State of New South Wales by way of salary financial assistance and allowances;

(ii) all amounts paid by or on behalf of Her Majesty Her Heirs and Successors or the said Government in respect of the Officer as employer contributions to the State Superannuation Fund established under the *Superannuation Act*, 1912, as amended;

(iii) an amount calculated at the rate of Two hundred dollars ($200) per annum (it being agreed that an amount so calculated represents a fair and genuine pre-estimate of the value of the leave and incremental advantages preserved to the Officer);

AND a certificate or Statement as to the amount of the cost incurred by the State signed by the Secretary to the Board or the Director General shall be conclusive [220] evidence of such cost and absolutely final and binding on the Officer:

(b) A certificate or statement signed by the Secretary to the Board or the Director General as to the date upon which the Officer shall have resumed duty as provided in paragraph (a) of cl 1 of this Deed and/or as to the date on which the Officer for any reason whatsoever ceased to be employed in the service of the said Department shall be conclusive evidence of all matters therein set out and absolutely final and binding upon the Officer:

(c) The acceptance of any resignation from the Public Service or from office duty or employment as Teacher in the service of the said Department tendered by the Officer at any time before the expiration of the period of service required of the Officer under para (a) of cl 1 of this Deed shall not release discharge or in any manner prejudice or affect any claim or demand which Her Majesty Her Heirs or Successors has or shall have against the Officer under the provisions of cl 2 of this Deed or otherwise release discharge or affect the liabilities of the Officer under this Deed:

(d) Nothing in this Deed contained shall be construed as prejudicing or affecting in any way the power of Her Majesty Her Heirs or Successors or of the Board or of any other proper authority of the State of New South Wales to terminate at any time at pleasure or for any cause whatsoever the Officer's employment in the Public Service of the said State and whether before or after him resuming duty as aforesaid:

(e) Any notice direction demand or communication required to be or that may be given or made to the Officer by or on behalf of Her Majesty Her Heirs or Successors or the Minister or the Board shall be sufficiently given or made if signed by the Secretary to the Board or by the Director General and either delivered personally to the Officer or sent by post addressed to the Officer at his last-known place of abode or business in or out of New South Wales and in any case where the same is so sent by post it shall be deemed to be given or made to the Officer at the time when it would in the ordinary course of post be delivered:

(f) In this Deed unless the context otherwise requires the expression 'the Board' means the Public Service Board constituted by the *Public Service Act*, 1902, as amended the expression 'the Minister' means the Minister for Education of the said State and includes his successors in office the expression 'the Director General' means the Director General Of Education of the said State and includes the person for the time being acting as such and all references to the Secretary to the Board include the person for the time being acting as such Secretary and 'year' means calendar year and 'month' means calendar month and the singular includes the plural.'

Once you have read this clause carefully:

(a) Make notes of the arguments suggesting that the clause is a penalty?

(b) Note the arguments for the clause being construed as a *genuine agreed damages clause.*

(c) Which argument do you find most persuasive?

(d) If it is a penalty, what should the order of the court be? Give reasons for your opinion.

When you come to class you will required to participate in a **moot** involving two other people. One of you will be briefed to argue that the clause is a penalty. A second person will be briefed to argue that the clause is a genuine pre-estimate of damages. The third will make a decision as to whether or not the clause is a genuine pre-estimate, or a penalty. The third person will also be required to make an order of the court based on the arguments heard and the order sought by the two counsel.

4.1.5 Step 4: law reform, socio-legal research and economic analysis

Commentary

By now we should have a good idea of whether our students:

- understand the basic commercial issues involved in agreed damages clauses;
- are conversant with the basic legal principles; and
- have used the principles in drafting and construing clauses.

The fourth step deepens the theoretical perspectives on the topic. It requires students to consider whether there should be reform of the area. The materials enable students to design a program of law reform research, based on socio-legal research methods that they learnt earlier in their studies of law.

The materials also require students to evaluate:

- the tentative reforms proposed by a writer in the law and economics school;
- reforms proposed by the Victorian Law Reform Commission's 1988 discussion paper; and
- some internationally-based solutions to the problem.

In this way legal theory is anchored in concrete situations. Students will begin to see how every-day legal problems have a deeper theoretical dimension. Hopefully they will not see legal theory as an abstract body of knowledge, but rather as intensely useful in the solution of every-day legal problems. For example, the materials ask students to redraft their agreed damages clause in the light of an economist's analysis of agreed damages clauses. This analysis will raise new issues about how the parties and the courts should be dealing with the risks associated with breach of contract. Note that the extract on law and economics has not been heavily edited to preserve the coherence of the argument put by the author. One objective of this extract is to enable students to see the assumptions and reasoning involved in this perspective on law.

Class activity would comprise small group discussion or full class discussion.

Figure 8 (page 166) illustrates the processes involved in the fourth step.[9]

9 This figure was first published in Le Brun and Johnstone (1994) 325.

	Private Study Prior to Class Using the Materials	*Classroom Activities*
1	Recap criticisms of the legal principles and their application.	Teacher deals with any miscon ceptions in students' learning which have emerged in previous classes.
2	Develop a socio-legal research program as a basis of law reform.	Small group discussion
3	Read and critically evaluate an economic analysis of agreed damages clauses.	Small group discussion or Full class discussion.
4	Evaluation of Law Reform Proposals.	Small group discussion.
5	Redraft clause.	Discuss in pairs.
6	Evaluate international solutions.	Full class discussion.

Figure 8: Step 4

The Materials

By now you should:

- have examined the basic commercial issues involved in agreed damages clauses;
- be able to state the basic legal principles governing agreed damages clauses; and
- have used the principles in drafting and construing clauses.

This part of the topic will focus on three issues:

- the reform of the rules against penalties;
- the economic analysis of the rule against penalties; and
- an international perspective on the issue.

Law Reform Problem

Generate Issues for Reform

In previous classes you have considered the basic policy issues behind the rule against penalties, looked at the basic principles governing the interpretation of the agreed damages clauses, and drafted and construed such clauses.

Now make brief notes of your criticisms of the rule against penalties as currently enunciated by the courts?

What issues for reform arise from your consideration of the cases?

In History and Philosophy of Law you learnt about basic socio-legal research methods that can be used develop good proposals for Law Reform. You also had an opportunity to develop research programs which would provide a basis for law reform. You were required in that subject to develop such proposals for topics about which you were not well acquainted. Now that you have a good grasp of the rule against penalties and its problems, develop a research program which would thoroughly investigate the issue, and which would generate an appropriate legal response to the issue.

What research methodologies would you use?

What issues do you anticipate arising?

Use the rest of this of this page to make notes of your research program. When you come to class we will discuss your research program in small groups.

An Economic Analysis of the Rule Against Penalties

Andrew Ham ('The Rule Against Penalties in Contract: An Economic Perspective' (1991) 17 MULR 649, 654–670) offers the following economic analysis of the rule against penalties. Please read this extract and make notes to answer the questions which follow the extract. (All but the most important footnotes have been deleted from the extract.)

[649] .... The discussion here is in the context of fully bargained, arms-length agreements between parties of comparable bargaining power ...

[650] The basic philosophy of the economic analysis of legal rules is that individuals are rational agents aiming to maximize their well-being and make the best agreement possible, subject to the constraints imposed upon them by the law and the other party. My argument is that only the parties themselves have sufficient information at the time of forming the contract to be able to formulate the optimal damages clause taking all relevant subjective and objective factors into account. Therefore, in commercial transactions which are fully negotiated between parties of comparable bargaining strength, the optimal rule is to enforce all stipulated damage agreements. The courts still have an important role, however, in ensuring that the contract is fully and fairly negotiated and that one party is not taking unconscionable advantage of the other ...

[654] ... [M]uch confusion remains in the application of the penalty doctrine. The law does need to be reconsidered; the question is, what does economics have to offer in such a reconsideration? First, the rationale for the concept of freedom of contract and the proposition that it is sometimes better if agreements are not kept must be considered.

Freedom of Contract

Proposition 1: Agents should in general be free to bind themselves in any freely bargained exchange which they might choose.

Freedom of contract is one of the principles that underlies contract law, yet its rationale is seldom examined. It is based on the standard assumptions of economic analysis. To simplify matters we assume that all benefits and costs can be measured in dollar values, including 'non-economic' considerations. It is individuals themselves who determine the dollar values to be placed on the benefits and costs of an agreement. Furthermore, individuals will maximize the difference between their benefits and their costs; utility maximization. It follows that left to themselves, parties on equal terms will reach the agreement that maximizes the benefits to both sides. Such an outcome is desirable because it is efficient; that is, from a given pool of resources, the net benefit to the overall community is maximized. The problem of the efficient allocation of resources, the outcome of freedom of contract, is quite separate from the problem of the equity of their distribution which is a political decision. Legal intervention is justified if unfairness, dishonesty, or some other factor against public policy has led to a sub-optimal (ie inefficient) distribution of resources. 'Interference with freedom of contract is deemed justified when necessary to protect community interest not represented by the parties to a transaction: the law declares certain bargains void as in violation of public policy.'[10] The law will not intervene in voluntary agreements without good cause. The question that must be considered is whether the penalty doctrine is grounded in one such good cause. [655]

Optimal Breach of Contract

Proposition 2: Breach is optimal if it potentially allows a Pareto-improvement over performance.

Contractual obligations are enforced by the law at least partly because of the belief that a promise has inherent moral force which should be recognized. Also, business certainty requires that promises should be kept. However, breach should be encouraged when, relative to performance, it yields a net gain to the parties (ie a Pareto-improvement). Circumstances frequently change between the time of formation and the time of performance. If the situation becomes such that the opportunity cost of performance to one party is greater than the other party's gain from the contract, then there is clearly a net sum gain if the contract is not performed. Encouraging the breach of such inefficient contracts will not, in principle, deter the formation of future contracts because the victim of breach is always fully compensated and hence is indifferent between damages and performance. The breaching party is able to fully compensate the innocent promisee for losses sustained due to the former's breach, and still gain him or herself. Thus breach will benefit both parties and is 'efficient' ...

Whether this occurs in practice depends on how damages are assessed: to protect the innocent party's expectation interest and put him or her in the same position as if the contract had been performed; or to maintain the correct incentives and prevent inefficient breach by ensuring that the cost of breach to the party in default is as great as the cost of compliance. Thus damages should force the breaching party to include all the costs of breach to all parties in his or her decision to end the contract.

In most cases these two goals of compensation will coincide and will encourage optimal breach. By allowing recovery of an equivalent amount to the expected benefit lost when the contract is broken, the expectation measure of damages transfers the full cost of breach from the injured promisee to the promisor. Therefore a party has an incentive to break his or her promise only [656] when the gains from doing so are greater than the lost expectation of the innocent party which must be compensated. Breach will only occur when it results in an increase in the productive value of the resources in question. This is not always the case, as the optimal level of damages depends on the motive for breach.

Breach may be involuntary, to avoid greater loss, or it may be voluntary, motivated by greater profits (from a higher offer, for example) than those expected from performance. Thus, in a contract for the production of goods, costs may be uncertain until after the contract is made. In this case breach will be efficient if the seller's production costs exceed the value of the goods to the buyer. There may be uncertainty due to the chance of third-party offers; such as in the case of a contract transferring possession of existing goods. In the latter case there are two possibilities; (a) if bids are available only to the seller,

10 Birmingham, R L, 'Damage Measures and Economic Rationality: The Geometry of Contract Law' (1969) *Duke Law Journal* 49, 63.

the seller should not perform when the bid exceeds the buyer's expectancy, as above, and (b) if bids are also available to the buyer, it will always be efficient for the seller to perform because the buyer has the opportunity to resell to a higher bidder if there is one. Thus if there is performance the buyer benefits, or if there is a breach the seller benefits from the higher offer. However, unless the market is exceptionally well organized, buyers (a diffuse group) are less likely to have access to third party offers than are sellers who are specialists and dealers. Incentive-maintenance may dictate less comprehensive compensation for unavoidable breach than for voluntary breach in order to get the most efficient result. The significance of this will become apparent once we have considered the effect of damages on the allocation of risk.

DAMAGES, PENALTIES AND RISK

Damages Allocate Risk

Proposition 3: The measure of damages affects the parties' allocation of risk.

The standard of compensation employed will determine how the gains or losses from breach are distributed between the parties. As a corollary of the two motives for breach, there are two forms of risk to be allocated; market risk, that the market price will change, and casualty risk, that one party will be unable to perform his obligations due to unforeseen circumstances.

Under expectation damages, if all loss is compensated by the breaching party then of course all risk is borne by that party. The courts limit the risk that must be borne to that which *inter alia* is reasonably foreseeable at the time of contracting. This, together with the other limitations on what the courts consider to be recoverable loss, means that some of the risk of loss must often be borne by the innocent party. This may or may not be the optimal allocation of risk, depending on the parties' relative attitudes to risk and whether breach was due to the choice of the breaching party or was unavoidable.

Proposition 4: It may be optimal not to compensate some losses, which may lead to a conflict between incentive maintenance and the desired allocation of risk.

[657] Full compensation of all losses from breach, pecuniary and non-pecuniary, should only be allowed if breach results from the choice of the breaching party. This ensures the correct incentives for efficient breach. However, if breach is unavoidable due to some unforeseen event, the full cost of the breaching party's actions should not necessarily be borne by that party. Some kinds of loss should not be compensated because although the victim has been 'injured', he or she cannot replace what has been lost with inferior substitutes, as none exist. This applies particularly to subjective, non-quantifiable, non-physical loss. Attempts to compensate such losses may actually make the plaintiff worse off if he or she is in effect being 'insured' for losses that cannot be replaced, and which they do not wish to have insured. Sellers will adjust prices to allow for the added risk they must bear even though buyers have no use for this extra insurance and do not wish to pay the premium.

This result creates a conflict between insurance and incentives as less than full compensation means the cost of breach to the seller is less than to the buyer reducing the seller's incentive to perform. Although voluntary breach can be distinguished from involuntary breach, in the latter case a seller can usually take precautions to influence the probability of a random event (such as maintenance to prevent breakdowns). Such precautions cannot be observed by the courts in assessing what loss to compensate after the event. One solution to the conflict is for the buyer to compromise. As damages are the only means available to influence reliability, a liquidated damages clause must be drawn up such that the buyer is insured, if necessary to excess, to maintain the seller's incentive to perform.

The Effect of Penalties

Proposition 5: 'Excessive' liquidated damages may prevent breach even when such breach would be optimal.

The penalty doctrine aims to prevent unfair recovery in excess of justifiable and quantifiable loss and to prevent inefficient performance through fear of a penalty when breach is preferable.

Economists have developed models to show the ideal response to a change in circumstances assuming partial performance is possible. A penalty clause acts as a means of forcing inefficient performance as this is preferable (less costly) to paying a still larger penalty. So a penalty clause is analogous to an award of specific performance as both, whether by direct court order or by the deterrent effect of an '*in terrorem*' clause, result in performance of the contract that one party sought to breach causing the other party to initiate litigation. Specific performance is only awarded by the courts when ordinary money damages are [658] inadequate, and cannot substitute for performance. As a penalty has the same effect, it can be argued that similar criteria should be applied to their enforcement. That is, even when a stipulated sum has been found to be a penalty, the courts should enforce it if there is evidence that damages as assessed by the court would be inadequate.

If enforcing a penalty amounts to *de facto* specific performance then other writers' analyses of the latter can be extended to apply more widely. It has been shown[11] that specific performance is better than other remedies in minimizing 'excessive breach' due to the courts' undercompensation of loss. That is, breach occurs too often (ie contracts that should be performed are breached) because the party breaking the agreement does not take full account of the losses he or she imposes on others. 'Excessive performance' (ie contracts that should be broken are performed) will not be a problem if both parties have access to third party bids because the buyer can ensure the efficient result by reselling to a third party who offers more for the goods than their value to the original buyer. Performance of the original agreement only affects the distribution of the gains from resale. Hence specific performance is always superior to damages, given our assumptions, and therefore penalties that amount to specific performance should be enforced.

THE COURT'S ASSESSMENT OF DAMAGES

The Costs of the Penalty Doctrine

Proposition 6: Shortcomings in the court's assessment of loss may cause an optimal, efficient liquidated damages claim to appear excessive.

11 Shavell, S, 'The Design of Contracts and Remedies for Breach' (1984) 99 *Quarterly Journal of Economics* 121.

For a number of reasons the court's assessment of loss to the plaintiff may differ from that actually suffered. This may mean that a stipulated damages clause that would fully compensate is not enforced, and an inadequate court award is substituted. Thus the court's inference of unfairness in their attitude to agreed damages clauses for what they consider to be excessive amounts may not be warranted, and refusing to enforce such clauses may impose more costs than it removes.

Traditional damage measures provide quite adequate compensation in purely commercial transactions, as losses can be objectively evaluated either on the basis of lost profits from anticipated breach, or to reflect the difference between contract and market prices. The principles of compensation are harder to apply in two other possible cases. First, when the promised performance has a market value but the promisee attaches an additional idiosyncratic value to performance [659] and which he or she has contracted for by paying a premium on the market price. Evaluated after breach, such subjective loss is regarded as too speculative and uncertain to be recovered in the courts. Of course, such a limitation is justified where the costs of establishing idiosyncratic value exceed the costs of an inaccurate measure of damage. Secondly, limitations are imposed on the recovery of consequential loss and even reasonably foreseeable loss that is too uncertain to quantify. This avoids the difficult process of quantifying uncertain loss, but at the plaintiff's expense. Even when the parties have attempted to resolve the uncertainty with a stipulated sum, as efficiency dictates, the penalty doctrine increases transaction costs again by relating this sum to the maximum uncertain loss possible before enforcing the agreement.

Parties who know they may be disadvantaged by such rules can unambiguously gain if liquidated damages clauses that compensate fully are always enforced. 'In the absence of evidence of unfairness or other bargaining abnormalities, efficiency would be maximized by the enforcement of the agreed allocation of risks embodied in a liquidated damages clause'.[12] Efficiency is enhanced through minimization of transaction costs if agreements negotiated *ex ante* are enforced.

Apart from the limitations of compensation by the courts, such damages awards are not the best way of insuring against loss from breach because litigation is an inherently expensive and uncertain process. The seller already knows the probability of breach and could set the premium accordingly if he or she were to directly insure the buyer. A third party insurance company would have to devote significant resources to finding this probability out. Further, a seller may be able to influence the probability of breach for the best result. The penalty doctrine prevents parties from self-insuring idiosyncratic value like this.

More general enforcement of stipulated damage agreements would considerably reduce the time and expense of litigation. Proof of damage sustained, frequently a complex and expensive process, would no longer be necessary. In addition, if liability is not a major issue, then out of court settlements may be promoted due to the greater predictability of the outcome as the problem of valuation uncertainty has been removed.

12 Goetz, C J and Scott, R E, 'Liquidated Damages, Penalties and the Just Compensation Principle: Some Notes on the Enforcement Model and a Theory of Efficient Breach' (1977) 77 *Columbia Law Review* 554, 578.

The penalty doctrine undoubtedly increases transaction costs at the time of forming the contract. The threat of subsequent judicial review and non-enforcement of a clause means the parties must spend extra time and effort to frame their liquidated damages clause so that it fits the requirements imposed by the penalty doctrine and the courts will enforce it. These unnecessary costs are increased by the current uncertainty of the Australian law in this area. For example, transaction costs are increased by the court's refusal to allow the parties to specify a single damages provision for a range of contingencies. Parties cannot spread their risks by averaging potential loss over a number of transactions or a number of contingencies in one transaction. Each contingency must and will be [660] negotiated separately as long as the costs of such negotiations are less than the expected cost of litigation should a 'blanket' clause be challenged.

Finally, traditional measures of compensation are unsatisfactory because of their failure to distinguish breaches due to unexpected shifts in the profitability of agreements ('Voluntary Breach') from breaches in which there is no net gain to be allocated ('Involuntary Breach'). Under expectation damages the person in breach retains all the net gains from breach as the non-breacher is placed in the position he would occupy if he had received performance. These gains could be allocated between the parties (largely a simple case of wealth transfer) by a liquidated damages clause. The incentive to negotiate such a clause arises when the costs of negotiation are less than the expected costs of relying, in breach, on the standard damages rules of the courts. Compensation by the courts has a number of shortcomings, yet attempts by the parties to overcome the problems of uncertain loss, subjective valuation and the distribution of windfall gains are frustrated by the rule against penalties. Indeed, the penalty doctrine increases transaction costs in more cases than it reduces them, strengthening the case for enforcement of stipulated damages clauses. The argument is further bolstered by examination of the premise underlying the penalty doctrine that 'penalties' are 'unfair'.

The Presumption of Unfairness

Penalty clauses are assumed by the courts to be unfair or unconscionable because such an agreement could only have been reached by an abuse of the bargaining process. They assume that compensation in excess of actual loss is unjust and oppressive. This begs the question of whether the courts do in fact award full compensation and of whether such full recovery is always the best result. These issues have already been discussed but even if we accept the court's assumptions, there are problems. First, the reasoning in decisions assessing a stipulated damages clause often comes close to conflicting with the fundamental principle that the law will neither inquire into the adequacy of consideration nor, as a rule, offer relief from what has turned out simply to be a bad bargain. Secondly, the unfairness rationale is a post hoc judgment of the bargain which ignores the risk allocation made at the time of contracting. The entire bargaining process should be taken into account. The risk of breach should be recognized as a factor in determining the contract price. A premium may be paid by the buyer in order to get the seller to accept some of his or her risk in the form of an agreed damages clause for a sum greater than that the courts would award. To call an agreed remedy 'unfair' either neglects its role in shifting risk or implies inadequate consideration for the shift. Neither assertion is justified.

Stipulated damages clauses are often used where the real loss, including the subjective elements, is difficult to assess in advance but a pre-estimate can be [661] made which averages out the risks of over- and under-compensation. The question of whether a sum is coercive becomes irrelevant when the innocent party is indifferent between the money and performance. By inflating the measure of agreed damages the innocent party signals the other party that he or she values performance highly. By making a rational choice to minimize his or her own costs the breaching party will only breach when the cost of performance exceeds the agreed sum. To intervene at the time of breach is an unfair redistribution of contract risks and deprives one party of a benefit he or she contracted for.

OPTIMAL ALLOCATION OF RISK WHEN THE PARTIES' ATTITUDES TO RISK DIFFER

Stipulated Damages and Insurance

Proposition 7: It may be efficient to stipulate damages in advance to optimally insure the more risk-averse party.

As we have seen, a stipulated damages clause is the most efficient and reliable way for parties to share the risk of breach. One of the most important reasons for a stipulated damages sum exceeding actual loss is the differing attitudes to risk of the parties.

A party who is risk-averse is willing to pay more (as a matter of certainty) than the expected value of the risk in order to avoid the risk. For example, take a contract with a 50:50 chance of breach at some point before completion, and a potential profit of $100 to the buyer if it is performed and $10 if it is broken. The expected value of the agreement to the buyer is (0.5 x $100) + (0.5 x $0) = $50. Therefore if the buyer is risk-averse he or she will require a liquidated damages clause specifying more than $50 to ensure the contract is performed; just how much more depends on the buyer's degree of risk-aversion. In contrast, if the buyer is risk-neutral, he or she will require only the expected value as liquidated damages.

A risk-averse person will be willing to pay a premium included in the contract price in exchange for a liquidated damages clause that the courts would currently regard as excessive. Such an agreement reduces risk-bearing costs (ie the difference between the expected value of the loss and the largest amount the person forced to bear the risk would pay to avoid it) by transferring risk to the party more willing to bear it, but conflicts with optimal breach incentives because the breaching party must pay more in damages than the actual loss he or she causes. The effect of this can be seen by example. Assume profit is uncertain, the price is paid in advance and there is no market for the good. If only one party is risk-averse then the other, risk-neutral, party should bear all the risk [662] of breach. A risk-averse buyer should always receive an amount equivalent to his or her benefit; a risk-averse seller should always receive the contract price, passing any gain or loss to the buyer. Therefore the expectation measure allocates risk optimally only if the buyer is risk-neutral, the seller is risk-averse, and only the seller has access to third party offers because the seller needs only to return the buyer's expectation to him and can keep any gains from breach. If both parties have access to third party offers then the risk-neutral buyer should be returned to the position he or she would have been upon reselling to the higher bidder. That is, the seller should pay him or her an amount equal to the third party offer. Because the buyer keeps the gains such expectation damages would only optimally allocate risk if the seller is risk-averse and the buyer is risk neutral.

The seller is more likely than the customer to have access to other offers because he or she is a dealer and a specialist relative to the consumer. Before breach there is uncertainty and both parties have incentive to reveal their attitudes to risk and negotiate a clause that allocates the contract risk to the benefit of both parties (leaving aside the different problem of unfair conduct). After breach the situation is different and both parties, knowing the outcome of the transaction, direct their energies into gaining as big a share of the benefits as possible. Any binding executory contract will reduce uncertainty about the future. A fundamental part of making such agreements is allocating the risk of loss (or gain) between the parties should the agreement not be performed. The nature of the legal process is to intervene after breach when it is no longer possible to allocate risk and so the issue is ignored. The penalty doctrine prevents the parties from making any allocation that is significantly different from that of the courts.

Stipulated Damages as an Enforceable Interest

Most contracts can be characterized as consisting of a primary obligation, the subject of the agreement, and a secondary obligation in the form of a liquidated damages clause which, as we have seen, may exceed the expected value of performance. The primary obligation is protected by the court's award of compensatory damages, assuming this to be accurate. The promisee's interests in the promise to pay an agreed amount in excess of the court's award in the event of breach are not protected, on the basis that the bargain is actually for the base promise and not the secondary promise of damages.

This rationale must be rejected for two reasons. First, the measure of compensation used by the courts is often not fully compensatory. The perceived inadequacy of protection for a party's interests in the primary contractual obligation is the reason parties reason to liquidated damages in the first place. Secondly, an agreed damages clause is a protectable interest. Such a clause transfers the risk of undercompensation for breach to the breaching party. This transfer is reflected in the contract price because as the stipulated amount of recovery rises the promisor should demand a commensurate adjustment in the contract price to compensate him or her for the increased risk he is assuming. Therefore, as the promisee paid a premium for the higher than usual damages [633] clause, he or she has a substantial interest in seeing that the clause is enforced should the risky contingency eventuate, and that he or she gets the insurance bargained for. If the clause is not enforced the breaching party has in effect collected the premium without having to bear the risk. In other words, a risk averse person having paid a premium on the contract price to avoid the risk of breach is entitled to, and has an interest in, the enforcement of the secondary promise to pay an agreed sum in the event of breach.

Full Information and Wagering

Proposition 8: When there is substantial bilateral knowledge of risks, enforcement of liquidated damages is efficient and generates lower transaction costs and better incentives that a court award as long as actual cost is not less than the liquidated amount. This proposition leaves aside the problem of conflict between the incentives for optimal breach and the allocation of risk by the parties.

Rational choice requires adequate information on the alternatives available. If the parties have unequal information at the time of contracting then intervention may be justified. Without full possession of the facts by both sides, parties cannot properly allocate the risk of breach of 'price' the liquidated damages clause. The concept of reasonably foreseeable loss in the *Hadley v Baxendale* line of cases recognizes this. To be recoverable, the loss must either be injury normally to be expected to flow from the breach in question, or if there are special circumstances resulting from unusual loss, these circumstances must be known to both parties.

The penalty doctrine does not enforce agreed remedies on the basis of the information available to the parties at the time of contracting. The mere fact that damages are over liquidated is no reason to infer unequal access to the information. Those who accurately forecast or under-estimate loss are just as likely to be aware of the risks as those who over-estimate it. The penalty doctrine cannot be justified on the grounds that the parties lacked sufficient information to effectively allocate the risk of breach.

[664] Renegotiation as an Alternative to Breach

Proposition 9: Renegotiation may overcome the problem of inefficient performance and is an alternative to breach.

In considering the effects of the penalty doctrine on the efficient breach of contracts, it is often forgotten that the choice is wider than simply breach or performance. When enforcement of a penalty would lead to an inefficient result, there are incentives for the innocent parties to renegotiate their penalty rights. Thus, the parties can negotiate an efficient solution, and divide the gains between them rather than allow all the gains of the breach to go to one party or another. This could be done, for example, by negotiation a release form the contract which allows transfer of production to a more efficient market. Efficiency is not affected by the distribution of gains. This depends on factors such as bargaining power. Even if there is no penalty clause the parties will engage in renegotiation if the gains are greater than their joint costs. For example, if specific performance has been granted, the actual result may be that a compromise is reached under the shadow of the court's decision so that another solution, preferred by all, is reached.

Proposition 10: Such renegotiation may not be successful due to strategic behaviour in the bargaining process.

There are problems in relying on renegotiation as it can significantly increase transaction costs due to strategic behaviour by the parties. Circumstances may change such that the promisee no longer wants performance and so has incentive to negotiate with the promisor to release him or her from their obligations (the efficient result) and split the gain between them. The social costs of non-cooperation then increase as there are increased incentives for the promisee to induce breach by demanding performance and then to collect a premium, the stipulated penalty over and above actual loss.

The *incentive* to induce the other party to breach arises when the benefits of doing so exceed the costs, such as when a penalty clause provides for compensation in excess of actual damage. The potential breach-inducer also needs an *opportunity* as detected inducement may lead to non-enforcement and the loss of [665] any gain from inducing breach. Thus strategic behaviour is only a problem when it is difficult to detect, as for example when performance depends at least in part on the buyer's co-operation and assistance. Breach could be induced simply by withholding information at a critical time or by failing to cut 'red tape' thereby causing significant delays. There will also be increased transaction costs on the other side of the transaction as producers attempt to combat induced breach. This will entail both researching a potential inducer's previous record as a 'victim' of breach before entering a contract, and effort to detect breach inducement during performance of a contract. Thus, while the parties can be relied upon to renegotiate if strict enforcement of an 'overliquidated' damages clause would lead to inefficiency, additional transaction costs are incurred due to the danger of strategic behaviour.

Other remedies for breach also impose transaction costs. Undercompensation of the promisee's loss by the courts will cause the promisor to breach too often (excessive breach) as the promisee is not required to bear all the costs of the action, so that he or she gains by breaching without improving efficiency. Similarly, specific performance results in 'excessive performance' when contracts that should be ended are preformed at the promisee's insistence, even though his or her benefit is less than the cost to the promisor. If performance is substantially complete once the goods are produced, the potential cost of excessive performance is low as no further resources are required to simply transfer of ownership, for example, in the transfer of title or the sale of finished goods. The potential cost of excessive breach is low when the buyer can readily obtain substitutes for the subject of the contract.

Efficiency applies only to the means by which parties reach a certain wealth distribution relative to other ways of doing so; wealth distribution has no consequences for Pareto-optimality. Therefore, the relative efficiency of damage measures can be gauged by their relative transaction costs.

There is no reason for post-breach negotiation costs to be higher under a damages rule than under specific performance of a penalty. If specific performance is ordered, the parties will negotiate the buyer's share of the extra profit gained from the deal between the seller (promisor) and a third-party buyer. If expectation damages are ordered they will negotiate over what the original buyer's (promisee's) expectation was. This can be difficult (and hence costly) to quantify if no market and thus no substitutes exist. Therefore specific performance entails lower renegotiation costs than expectation damages. Specific performance and penalty clauses are thus preferable to ordinary damages and a 'penalty' which does not require litigation is more efficient than an order for specific performance, which does.

[666] Unconscionability and the Penalty Doctrine

In May 1988 the Law Reform Commission of Victoria issued a Discussion Paper[13] in which it was tentatively concluded:

> 'that the present rule against penalties should be abolished. A more flexible rule should be enacted in its place. The courts should be given

13 Law Reform Commission of Victoria, Discussion Paper No 10, *Liquidated Damages and Penalties*.

> a discretion to set aside an agreed damages clause which is unconscionable in all the circumstances.'[14]

A similar suggestion was made by Kirby, P in *Citicorp v Hendry*.[15] However, there is the danger that the drawbacks of an overly restrictive rule will simply be replaced by a different set of problems flowing from an overly general rule. It is on this issue, providing guidance as to what constitutes unconscionability, that the Commission's views are open to criticism. They suggest that

> 'In deciding whether an agreed damages clause is unconscionable, the court should have regard to the extent to which the agreed sum exceeds the actual loss which is likely to be suffered as a result of breach, not merely the extent to which the agreed sum exceeds the damages which would be legally recoverable in the absence of the clause. Even if the agreed sum appears unconscionable as judged at the time of the contract, the court should not set it aside unless it is unconscionable (that is, extravagant or substantially disproportionate) when account is taken of the loss actually suffered by the injured party.'[16]

Such a reform perpetuates one of the most basic objections to the penalty doctrine.

Penalty clauses are regarded as undesirable because the court assumes that such an agreement only came about through an abuse of the bargaining process, and that it is against basic justice to allow compensation in excess of actual loss because the benefits are all on one side. This justification is based on the presumption that the court award of damages is both fully compensatory and the moral standard by which justice is measured. It is inevitable that courts will invoke considerations relating to how fairly the bargain was negotiated. The question is whether one prefers this to be done covertly through the manipulation of technical rules or overtly through doctrines that make the real ground for the decision explicit.

> 'It seems obvious that the latter course best serves the ends of constructive judicial lawmaking, on the one hand, and rational independent analysis and evaluation of the aptness of legal rules on the other. In addition, cost-efficient utilisation of judicial resources argues for decisions which provide maximum feasible guidance to other parties in their actions, through rules that have some generality of application.'[17]

A number of classical defences, as well as the doctrine of unconscionability, have been developed by the courts to address the problem of unfairness in contractual relations. The defences of duress and fraudulent misrepresentation both examine the procedural fairness of the process by which the agreement was reached, not the actual substantive fairness of what was agreed. The former looks to the means by which consent was obtained, the latter looks to the conduct of the promisor.

14 *Ibid*, para 35.

15 NSWLR 1, 23 [*sic*].

16 Law Reform Commission of Victoria, *op cit*, para 36.

17 Trebilcock, M J, 'The Doctrine of Inequality of Bargaining Power: Post-Benthamite Economics in the House of Lords' (1976) 26 *University of Toronto Law Journal* 359, 384.

'[667] The process of formation provides the court with the information it needs to allow the promisor to escape from performance under the contract, and the court itself-can and must remain unconcerned with the substantive terms of the bargain.'[18]

These rules will be inefficient and impose error costs if well-founded and deserving cases cannot establish the necessary standard of proof to make out the defence. If the error costs of legitimate contracts being defeated by undeserving defences are lower, then the rules should be relaxed.

Epstein[19] argues that the proper role of unconscionability is to protect against fraud, duress and incompetence without demanding specific proof of any of them. To do this it looks at the subject matter of the agreements, the social positions of the parties who enter them and the perceptions of the stronger party. Freedom of contract does not require that all agreements are enforced. However the reasons for intervening and refusing to enforce an agreement must be either some defect in the process of contract formation, or some incompetence of the party against whom the contract is to be enforced. The doctrine of unconscionability (or any other doctrine, by implication), should not allow the courts to set aside agreements when they find their substantive terms to be objectionable. Rather it should be used only to police the process whereby agreements are formed, so as to facilitate the setting aside of agreements vitiated by fraud, duress and incompetence.

What is Unfairness?

The penalty doctrine is an attempt by the courts to draw an inference of procedural unfairness from the substantive terms of the agreement. This is not legitimate.

'When the doctrine of unconscionability is used in its substantive dimension ... it serves only to undercut the private right of contract in a manner that is apt to do more a social harm than good.'[20]

The question arises, if the penalty doctrine is not the way to supervise negotiation, then what is? In assessing the procedural fairness of a bargain, the absence of bargaining between the parties and the adoption of a 'take-it or leave-it' attitude by one party is

'evidence not of market power but of a recognition that neither producer nor consumer interests in aggregate are served by incurring the costs involved in negotiating separately every transaction.'[21]

The real measure of market power is the ability of a consumer if he rejects one supplier to turn to a workably competitive range of alternative sources. If a market is workably competitive, any supplier offering uncompetitive standard form terms will have to reformulate his package of price and contractual terms and conditions to prevent the loss of his business to competitors.

[668] Thus Trebilcock argues that the fairness of a bargain can be inferred not from the fact that there was bargaining and negotiation over terms between

18 Epstein, R, 'Unconscionability: A Critical Reappraisal' (1975) 18 *Journal of Law and Economics* 293, 296.

19 *Op cit* 302.

20 Epstein *op cit* 15.

21 Trebilcock *op cit* 364.

the parties, but from the fact that if the promisee decided to go elsewhere he had a real choice.

A second source of procedural unfairness arises because the weaker party is ignorant, in the sense that he has no information about, or understanding of the content of his obligation. This ignorance precludes reflection or a search for alternatives and results in unfair surprise which is a valid reason to intervene on legal and economic grounds.

> 'Where a contract is so worded or arranged that the supplier knows or should know that the other party does not understand its implications, and he knows or should know that the other party reasonably entertains other understandings as to its legal incidents, to allow him to sign the contract without correcting those misunderstandings is tantamount to misrepresentation and thus inducive to suboptimal allocative decisions.'[22]

Having found that there is no abnormal market power and no aberrations in the process of contract formation, the concept of substantive unfairness[23] poses 'conceptual problems' as almost by definition the outcome of such a process cannot be unfair.

It is my suggestion that the Commission's conclusions should be accepted. The penalty doctrine should be abolished and replaced by a general discretion to set aside agreed damages clauses when they are unconscionable. However, the doctrine of unconscionability must not be allowed to depart from its true purpose. Old habits die hard, and although it may remain as a secondary factor, the temptation to look at the substantive terms of the agreement should be resisted. The agreement reached by the parties should be enforced unless there is evidence that the bargaining process was defective in some way.

SUMMARY AND CONCLUSIONS

Contracts bring transactors together for their mutual benefit. In some cases changing circumstances may mean that a greater gain can be secured if the contract is broken. Liquidated damages are an attempt by the parties to pre-estimate, at formation of the contract, the amount of damages recoverable for breach. We have seen that a number of factors might induce the parties to negotiate a liquidated damages clause: (1) if expected damages are readily calculable but the parties believe that negotiation of a liquidated damages clause will save potential litigation or settlement costs should breach occur, (2) the expected damages are uncertain of difficult to establish and the parties may wish to eliminate the uncertainty of the amount that can be recovered and the expense of litigation to find it by setting liability in advance, (3) parties have different degrees of risk aversion and wish to negotiate liquidated damages so that the less risk-averse party at least partially insures the more risk-averse against loss from breach, (4) one party may attach unusual or subjective value to performance which would be rejected by a court as too fanciful to recover, (5) parties may [669] desire a different allocation of the risks of and gains from breach than that which flows from the court's approach.

If the parties are risk-neutral they will only provide for a given contingency (for example, by stipulating a liquidated damages clause in the case of that

22 *Ibid* 370.

23 Defined as judicially perceived non-equivalence of values exchanged by contracting parties.

contingency) if the adverse consequences of failing to provide for the occurrence of that event are sufficient to justify the sure costs of including such provisions and the expected cost of verifying the occurrence. Factors which must be taken into account are the difficulty of reaching agreement over an issue, the probability and magnitude of a particular loss occurring, the cost of verifying the occurrence of an event, and the importance of the transaction to the parties. The introduction of risk means that the allocation of the risk of loss due to this contingency must also be considered. In essence the issue is whether the costs of litigation and the risk of undercompensation exceed the cost of negotiating in advance.

The costs of negotiating a liquidated damages clause are greatly increased by the current uncertainty over what is required for a clause to be enforceable. Negotiation is more difficult as there are no clear guidelines and after breach there is almost always sufficient doubt for the breaching party to challenge the agreed sum on which the injured party seeks to rely. Much of this uncertainty is not due to the law itself-but to the judicial practice of applying the law to take other, possibly unenunciated factors into account – such as the relative culpability of the parties – in reaching their decision. The test of an agreed sum as 'extravagant and unconscionable in relation to the greatest loss that could be suffered' is sufficiently wide to allow a range of interpretations in order to reach a result desired on grounds other than legal doctrine.

The penalty doctrine is a longstanding principle of the general law originally developed to combat unfair bargaining and extortionate 'penalty' clauses. However, with the development of the unconscionability doctrine and the enactment of trade practices and consumer protection legislation, better ways have evolved to deal with such problems without the cost of striking out some fair and legitimate clauses. As with any attempt to correct a failure of the market the most efficient approach is to address the problem (ie unfair clauses) as directly as possible. In this case, this means examining the bargaining process and the relationship of the parties (via the doctrines of duress and unconscionability) rather than looking merely at the end product, the agreed sum.

The adverse effects of the penalty doctrine have been discussed at length. It runs against the principle of freedom of contract not to enforce the fairly bargained agreements and risk allocations reached by the parties. The penalty doctrine may remove the need to prove unfairness, but it also makes it necessary to show what damage could have been suffered, which may be more difficult. Perhaps more importantly, the measure of damage used by the courts may not be fully compensatory. Expectation damages do not allow for the parties' attitudes to risk as they are calculated after breach. Some loss may remain uncompensated or loss may be compensated that should not have been. For example, it is settled law that in an agreement for the payment of money it is a penalty to fix a larger sum as damages for late or non-payment. This not only fails to allow for [670] consequential loss due to the breach but also does not allow for the allocation of risk. In short, the parties themselves are in the best position to know what value they want to protect and how to allocate risk. Further reasons to enforce liquidated damages are the conflicting roles it plays and the frequently neglected factor that such clauses are 'paid for' in the contract price.

The conflict between the roles of incentive maintenance and the allocation of risk arises because differences in attitude to risk mean that one party can insure the other so that he or she is indifferent between breach or performance. Thus the costs of the breach are not borne by the party responsible for imposing them. Again, the parties can resolve this best among themselves by partial insurance through liquidated damages clauses, to compromise between the two roles according to their priorities. This is impossible for the court to achieve, after breach, because it lacks the necessary information and because after breach uncertainty is resolved and the parties have incentive to lie to maximize their gains.

In addition, as we have seen, parties wishing to be protected by an agreed damages clause in excess of what a court might award generally have paid a 'premium' on the contract price in return for this extra insurance. Hence they do have an interest in this secondary agreement to see, that if there is breach of the basic agreement, they get what they bargained for and the clause is enforced. Currently, of course, such premiums are heavily discounted by the probability that they will not be enforced.

The conclusion to be drawn from all the foregoing considerations is that stipulated damage should be enforced when the parties have comparable information unless there is evidence of duress of unconscionable conduct. That is, it can be shown that one party is at a serious disadvantage to the other and has been exploited by the stronger party in a morally culpable manner, resulting in a transaction that is not just improvident but overreaching and oppressive. This doctrine is a comparatively recent development in the law and addresses the problem much more efficiently and effectively than the penalty doctrine. The courts retain an important role in assessing fairness not only through doctrines such as these but also through their role in rendering agreements invalid in which one party in guilty of falsely alleging or inducing breach. It should be stressed that this conclusion is restricted to fully bargained exchanges between parties of comparable bargaining strength. Consumer transactions are a different situation, beyond the scope of this article, as for the most part they involve little or no negotiation.

Any rule for damages will 'influence resource allocation by affecting the probability that the parties will continue performance of an economically unjustified contract and by changing the way parties allocate the costs of covering various risks'. The best and simplest way to minimize these costs is, subject to the aforementioned policy considerations, to leave it to the parties concerned.

Analysis and Evaluation of Ham's argument

Summarise, as briefly as possible, Andrew Ham's economic analysis of the rule against penalties.

What assumptions does he make about contracting parties and the regulation of private contracting.

In note form, critically evaluate his analysis.

What does Ham's analysis add to your understanding of the court's construction of agreed damages clauses?

We will discuss your notes in class.

Evaluation of Law Reform Proposals

Ham discusses the Victorian Law Reform Commission's tentative solution to the issues raised by agreed damages clauses. What is the Law Reform Commission's tentative solution?

Is the approach of Murphy J in *O'Dea* an example of the approach advocated by the Victorian Law Reform Commission?

Do you agree with Ham's criticism of the Law Reform Commission's approach? Why or why not?

Does his proposed solution differ from the Victorian Law Reform Commission's approach? Explain your answer.

Does it provide an appropriate approach to a resolution of the issue? We will discuss your notes in class.

Drafting Problem 3

Have you taken the issues raised by Ham into account in drafting the agreed damages clause for Ms De Maggio? Redraft your clause now to take account of new factors that have occurred to you on reading Ham's analysis.

Explain why you have made your changes.

International Reform Proposals

The Victorian Law Reform Commission's Discussion Paper includes a discussion on international aspects of the rule against penalties. When you read these proposals as discussed in the Law Reform Commission's Discussion Paper consider whether these international aspects are relevant to Victorian lawyers?

UNIDROIT and International Financial Leasing[24]

46 Two international bodies have recently been involved in the development of draft uniform rules concerning the operation of rules against penalties. UNIDROIT has developed Preliminary Draft Uniform Rules on International Financial Leasing. Article 11 deals with the lessor's right on default by the lessee. Article 11(3) allows the parties to set their own terms for compensation. However, they must follow the basic principle in Article 11(2) that the lessor is entitled to:

> 'recover such compensation as will place the lessor in the position in which it would have been had the lessee performed the leasing agreement in accordance with its terms, except insofar as the lessor has failed to take all reasonable steps to mitigate loss.'

The parties' agreement is specifically made enforceable if the compensation which is set is disproportionate to that provided for by paragraph 2.

47 The simple general statement in articles 11(2) and (3) is confused by Article 11(4):

> 'Where the lessor has terminated the leasing agreement it shall not be entitled to enforce a term of the leasing agreement accelerating payment of the rentals.'

24 This extract of the Victorian Law Reform Commission's Discussion Paper No 10 entitled *Liquidated Damages and Penalties* is reproduced with permission of the Attorney-General of the State of Victoria, 200 Queen Street, Melbourne 3000. It is Crown Copyright Material, first published by the Victorian Government. The material produced here is not an official copy of Crown Copyright material and the Victorian Government accepts no responsibility for its accuracy.

Even if discounted acceleration were not performed (Article 11(2) is specifically subject to Article 11(1)), it is difficult to know how the lessor can be properly compensated for his or her loss. Apparently, Article 11(4) is not intended to prevent recovery of loss relating to future rentals.

UNCITRAL and the Rule Against Penalties

48 UNCITRAL has developed Draft Uniform Rules dealing more generally with clauses providing for the payment of agreed damages on default. The venture arose from difficulties created by the contrasting approaches of the civil law and the common law to those clauses. The civil law is more lenient towards agreed damages clauses. They are valid in principle, but the courts have power to reduce the amount in certain circumstances.

49 UNCITRAL's Uniform Rules on Liquidated Damages and Penalty Clauses apply only to international contracts – that is, contracts where the contracting parties have their place of business in different countries. They do not apply to contracts for supply of goods and services for 'domestic' purposes. The substantive provisions of the Rules are as follows:

> Article 5
>
> The obligee is not entitled to the agreed sum if the obliger is not liable for the failure of performance.
>
> Article 6
>
> (1) If the contract provides that the obligee is entitled to the agreed sum upon delay in performance, he [sic] is entitled to both performance of the obligation and the agreed sum.
>
> (2) If the contract provides that the obligee is entitled to the agreed sum upon a failure of performance other than delay, he is entitled either to performance or the agreed sum. If, however, the agreed sum cannot reasonably be regarded as compensation for that failure of performance, the obligee is entitled to both performance of the obligation and the agreed sum.
>
> Article 7
>
> If the obligee is entitled to the agreed sum, he may not claim damages to the extent of the loss covered by the agreed sum. Nevertheless, he may claim damages to the extent of the loss not covered by the agreed sum if the loss substantially exceeds the agreed sum.
>
> Article 8
>
> The agreed sum shall not be reduced by a court or arbitral tribunal unless the agreed sum is substantially disproportionate in relation to the loss that has been suffered by the obligee.
>
> Article 9
>
> The parties may derogate from or vary the effect of article 5, 6 and 7 of these Rules.

50 The precise effect of these provisions is far from clear. There is no rule against penalties. However, the basic principle appears to be preserved since the agreed sum may be reduced if it is 'substantially disproportionate'

> to the loss suffered by the relevant party. One of the central benefits of an agreed damages clause is gone. The clause does not prevent the relevant party from claiming damages for his or her loss in excess of the amount stipulated. Moreover, the parties can exclude the operation of most of the rules anyway.
>
> Conclusion
>
> UNIDROIT's work, like that of UNCITRAL, is limited to international contracts. The proposals being worked on by the two bodies do not appear to be of great assistance in reviewing domestic law relating to agreed damages clauses.

Summarise the differences between the position relating to agreed damages clauses in:

- the Australian common law
- civil law jurisdictions
- the UNIDROIT proposals
- The UNCITRAL proposals

Do you agree with the Law Reform Commission's conclusion that UNIDROIT's and UNCITRAL's proposals are not of much assistance to efforts to reform the law in Victoria? Explain your answer.

You might like to conduct your own research to check whether UNIDROIT and UNCITRAL have further developed their proposals outlined in the above extract.

Further Reading

The standard text books all have sections devoted to agreed damages clause.

See ....

There are a number of useful articles on the area. Some are referred to in the materials and in Ham's footnotes. See also ....

PART 5

CONCLUSION

In this book I have briefly surveyed the literature on teaching and learning to rethink the way in which we can use printed teaching materials in law teaching. The 'trade school' origins of Australian law schools have resulted in teaching methods which have focused principally on imparting to students the content of legal rules and which have emphasised knowledge of the positive law. I have argued that we should broaden our teaching methods away from the traditional classroom methods of the lecturing and the casebook method. We need to aim our printed teaching materials and classroom methods at ensuring that our teaching is more focused on developing all round student skills, interests and values, so that our students actively learn inside and outside the classroom, and take deep approaches to learning through activities such as discussion, experimentation, simulation, reflection, observation, intuition, as well as abstract thought.

We teachers need to tailor our printed teaching materials and classroom teaching methods to our students' interests and needs, and to a carefully selected range of learning objectives. Of course, we can only do this within the limits of our own skills, abilities and personality. These, however, are not necessarily fixed. We can learn new methods and new skills, and can reshape our teaching materials to promote active and independent student learning (particularly in relation to knowledge of the substantive law or of multidisciplinary perspectives) outside the classroom so that we can use class time to discover any misconceptions students may have of the subject matter, to ensure that students get feedback to help them improve their learning, and for activities which enrich their learning.

Our printed teaching materials should focus on enabling students to develop structured and principled knowledge which they abstract from activities in a range of contexts. The materials should provide students with frameworks or scaffolding to learn and internalise particular ways of thinking about law and problem solving. Students should be encouraged to learn how to learn, and to monitor their own learning, so that they can regulate their own progress. Materials should stimulate and inspire students to learn about legal phenomena – they should not become passive, inert teaching tools. However we design and structure our teaching materials and use them in the classroom, we should regularly evaluate our teaching to ensure that our methods and materials are playing a role in promoting deep approaches to learning in our students.

Developing printed teaching materials which improve student learning in law is time consuming and involves hard work. The benefits more than compensate – particularly the improvements in the way in which our students learn about law, and an increase in the enjoyment we get from our teaching.

BIBLIOGRAPHY

Alavi, C, 'Quality in Problem Based Learning' in Sachs, Ramsden and Phillips (eds) (1995)

American Bar Association Section on Legal Education and Admissions to the Bar, *Legal Education and Professional Development – An Educational Continuum*, Report of Task Force on Law Schools and the Profession: Narrowing the Gap, American Bar Association, Chicago, 1992

Anderson, R C, 'The Notion of Schemata and the Educational Enterprise' in Anderson, Spiro and Montague (eds) (1977)

Anderson, R C, Spiro, R J and Montague, W E (eds) *Schooling and the Acquisition of Knowledge*, Lawrence Erlbaum Associates, Hillsdale, New Jersey, 1977

Annis, L F, 'The Process and Effects of Peer Tutoring' (1983) 2 *Human Learning* 39

Baker, E L, and Quellmetz E S (eds) *Educational Testing and Evaluation: Design, Analysis and Policy*, Sage Publications, Beverly Hills, 1980

Bargh, H A and Schul, Y, 'On the Cognitive Benefits of Teaching' (1980) 72 *Journal of Educational Psychology* 593

Barrows, H S, and Tamblyn, P, *Problem-based Learning: An Approach to Medical Education*, Springer, New York, 1980

Bartlett, K T, 'Feminist Legal Methods' (1990) 103 *Harvard Law Review* 829

Bawden, R J, 'Problem-based Learning: An Australian Perspective' in Boud (1985) 44

Bean, K S 'Writing Assignments in Law School Classes' (1987) 37 *Legal Education Review* 609

Becker, M E, 'Obscuring the Struggle: Sex Discrimination, Social Security and Stone, Seidman, Sunstein and Tushnet's *Constitutional Law*' (1989) 89 *Columbia Law Review* 264.

Bereiter, C and Scardamalia, M, *Surpassing Ourselves: An Inquiry into the Nature and Implications of Expertise*, Open Court, Chicago, 1993

Bergman, P, Sherr, A, and Burridge, R, 'Learning From Experience: Non-legally-Specific Role Plays' (1989) 39 *Journal of Legal Education* 535

Berns, S, *Concise Jurisprudence*, Federation Press, Sydney, 1993

Biggs, J B, 'Individual Differences in Study Processes and the Quality of Learning Outcomes' (1979) 8 *Higher Education* 381

Biggs, J B, 'Approaches to the Enhancement of Tertiary Teaching' (1989) 8 *Higher Education Research and Development* 7

Biggs, J B, 'Teaching for Better Learning' (1991) 2 *Legal Education Review* 133

Bligh, D, *What's the Use of Lectures*, Penguin, Harmondsworth, 1972

Bottomley, S, Gunningham, N, and Parker, S, *Law in Context*, 2nd edn, Federation Press, Sydney, 1994

Boud, D (ed) *Problem Based Learning in Education for the Professions*, Higher Education Research and Development Society of Australasia, Kensington, 1985

Boud, D 'Problem – Based Learning in Perspective' in Boud (1985)

Boud, D, *Implementing Student Self-Assessment*, HERDSA Green Guide No 5, Kensington, 1986

Boud, D (ed) *Developing Student Autonomy in Learning*, 2nd edn, Kogan Page, London, 1988

Boud, D and Griffin, V (eds) *Appreciating Adult Learning from the Learners' Perspective*, Kogan Page, London, 1987

Boud, D J, Keogh, R and Walker, D (eds) *Reflection: Turning Experience into Learning*, Kogan Page, London, 1985

Boud, D J and Tyrie, A L, 'Self- and Peer Assessment in Professional Education: A Preliminary Study in Law' (1980) 15 *Journal of the Society of Public Teachers of Law* 65

Boyle, C 'Book Review' (1985) 63 *Canadian Bar Review* 427

Brown, A L, Campione, J C and Day, J D, 'Learning to Learn: On Training Students to Learn from Texts' (1981) 10 *Educational Researcher* 14

Brown, A L, Bransford, J D, Ferrarra, R A and Campione, C, 'Learning, Remembering and Understanding' in Flavell and Markman (eds) (1983)

Brown, J M 'Simulation Teaching: A Twenty Second Semester Report' (1984) 34 *Journal of Legal Education* 638

Brown, J S, Collins, A and Duguid, P, 'Situated Cognition and the Culture of Learning' (1989) 18(1) *Educational Researcher* 32 (1989a).

Brown, J S, Collins, A and Duguid, P, 'Debating the Situation: A Rejoinder to Palincsar and Wineburg' (1989) 18(4) *Educational Researcher* 10 (1989b)

Burg, E M, 'Clinic in the Classroom: A Step Toward Cooperation' (1987) 37 *Journal of Legal Education* 232.

Caffarella, R S and O'Donnell, J M, 'Self-Directed Adult Learning: A Critical Paradigm Revisited' (1987) 37 *Adult Education Quarterly* 199

Candy, P, 'Evolution, Devolution or Revolution: Increasing Learner Control in the Instructional Setting' in Boud and Griffin (eds) (1987)

Candy, P, 'A Climate of Intellectual Inquiry: The Ultimate Test of Quality in Higher Education' in Sachs, Ramsden and Phillips (eds) (1995)

Centra, J, *Determining Faculty Effectiveness*, Jossey-Bass, San Fransisco, 1979

Chene, A, 'The Concept of Autonomy in Adult Education: A Philosophical Discussion' (1983) 34 *Adult Education Quarterly* 38

Chesterman, M and Weisbrot, D, 'Legal Scholarship in Australia' (1987) 50 *Modern Law Review* 709

Chi, M T H, and Glaser, R, 'The Measurement of Expertise: Analysis of the Development of Knowledge and Skill as a Basis for Assessing Achievement' in Baker and Quellmetz (eds) (1980) 37

Chi, M T H, Glaser, R and Farr, M J (eds), *The Nature of Expertise,* Lawrence Erlbaum and Associates, Hillsdale, New Jersey, 1988

Clanchy, J, 'Improving Student Writing' (1985) 7 *HERDSA News* 2

Collins, A, Brown, J S and Newman, S E, 'Cognitive Apprenticeship: Teaching the Craft of Reading, Writing and Mathematics' in Resnick (ed) (1989)

Colloquium on 'political correctness' (1991/92) 16 *Bulletin of the Australian Society of Legal Philosophy.*

Coombs, I M, 'Crime in the Stacks, or a Tale of a Text: A Feminist Response to a Criminal Law Textbook' (1988) 38 *Journal of Legal Education* 117

Cotterrell, R, *The Sociology of Law: An Introduction*, 2nd edn, Butterworths, London, 1993

Crooks, T J, *Assessing Student Performance*, HERDSA Green Guide No 8, Kensington, 1988

Dahl, Tove Stang,*Women's Law: An Introduction to Feminist Jurisprudence*, Norwegian University Press, Oslo, 1988

Davies, M, *Asking the Law Question*, Law Book Company, Sydney, 1994

Dillon, J T, *Using Discussion in Classrooms*, Open University Press, Buckingham and Philadelphia, 1994

Duncanson, I, 'Broadening the Discipline of Law' (1994) 19 *Melbourne University Law Review* 1075.

Entwhistle, N, *Styles of Learning and Teaching*, David Fulton Publishers, London, 1988

Flavell, J H and Markman, E M (eds), *Carmichael Handbook of Child Psychology*, Vol 1, John Wiley, New York, 1983

Frug, M, 'Re-reading Contracts: A Feminist Analysis of the Contracts Casebook' (1985) 34 *The American University Law Review* 1065

Geertz, C, *Local Knowledge*, Basic Books, New York, 1983

Getman, J G 'Voices' (1988) 66 *Texas Law Review* 577

Gibbs, G, 'Twenty Terrible Reasons for Lecturing', Standing Conference on Educational Development, Occasional Paper No 8, Birmingham, 1982

Gibbs, G, Habeshaw, S, and Habeshaw, T, *53 Interesting Things To Do In Your Lectures*, Technical and Educational Services Ltd, Bristol, 1987

Gibbs, G and Jenkins, A (eds), *Teaching Large Classes in Higher Education: How to Maintain Quality with Reduced Resources*, Kogan Page, London, 1992

Glaser, R and Chi, M T H, 'Overview' in Chi, Glaser and Farr (eds) (1988) xv

Glaser, R, 'Education and Thinking: The Role of Knowledge' (1984) 39 *American Psychologist* 93

Glaser, R, 'Learning, Cognition, and Education: Then and Now', unpublished seminar paper, Centre for the Study of Higher Education, University of Melbourne, 24 April 1991

Goldschmid, M L, 'The Learning Cell: An Instructional Innovation' (1971) 2 *Learning and Development* 1

Gordon, J D, 'An Integrated First Year Legal Writing Program' (1985) 35 *Legal Education Review* 609

Graycar, R and Morgan, J, *The Hidden Gender of Law*, Federation Press, Sydney, 1990

Graycar, R and Morgan, J, 'Including Gender Issues in the Core Law Curriculum', a paper given at the 'Women, Culture and Universities: A Chilly Climate' Conference, University of Technology, Sydney, 19 and 20 April 1995

Greeno, J G 'Cognitive Objectives of Instruction: Theory of Knowledge for Solving Problems and Answering Questions' in Klahr (ed) (1976)

Higgs, J, 'Planning Learning Experiences to Promote Autonomous Learning' in Boud (1988)

Hunter, R, 'Representing Gender in Legal Analysis: A Case/Book Study in Labour Law' (1991) 18 *Melbourne University Law Review* 305

Hunter, R, Ingleby, R and Johnstone, R (eds) *Thinking About Law: Perspectives on the History, Philosophy and Sociology of Law*, Allen & Unwin, Sydney, 1995

Ingleby, R, 'Translation and the Divorce Lawyer: Simulating the Law and Society Interface' (1989) 1 *Legal Education Review* 237

Jacques, D, *Learning in Groups*, 2nd edn, Kogan Page, London, 1991

Johnstone, R, 'Evaluating Law Teaching: Towards the Improvement of Teaching or Performance Assessment' (1990) 2 *Legal Education Review* 101

Johnstone, R, 'Rethinking the Teaching of Law' (1992) 3 *Legal Education Review* 17

Johnstone, R, 'Improving Student Learning in Labour Law' in Mitchell (ed) (1995)

Johnstone, R and Malkin, I, 'Evaluating and Improving Teaching at the University of Melbourne Law School,' in Sachs, Ramsden and Phillips (eds) (1995)

Johnson, D W, Maruyama, G, Johnson, R, Nelson, D and Skon, L 'Effects of Cooperative, Competitive, and Individualistic Goal Structures on Achievement: A Meta Analysis' (1981) 89 *Psychological Bulletin* 47

Johnson, N, 'Introduction to Law: The Workbook Method' in Gibbs and Jenkins (eds) (1992)

Klahr, D (ed), *Cognition and Instruction*, Erlbaum, Hillsdale, New Jersey, 1976

Kurtz, S, Wylie, M, and Gold, N, 'Problem-Based Learning: An Alternative Approach to Legal Education' (1990) 13 *Dalhousie Law Journal* 797

Langdell, C C, *Preface to a Selection of Cases on the Law of Contracts*, Boston, 1871

Laurillard, D, *Rethinking University Teaching: A Framework for the Effective Use of Educational Technology*, Routledge, London, 1993

Le Brun, M and Johnstone, R, *The Quiet (R)evolution: Improving Student Learning in Law*, Law Book Company, Sydney, 1994

Lehman, D R and Nisbett, R E, 'A Longitudinal Study of the Effects of Undergraduate Training on Reasoning' (1990) 26 *Developmental Psychology* 952

Levine, J M and M Wang, M C (eds), *Teacher and Student Perceptions: Implications for Learning*, Lawrence Erlbaum and Associates, Hillside, New Jersey, 1983

Lockwood, F, *Activities in Self-Instructional Texts*, Kogan Page, London, 1992

Mack, K, 'Bringing Clinical Learning into a Conventional Classroom' (1993) 4 *Legal Education Review* 89

MacKinnon, C, 'Feminism, Marxism, Method and the State: Towards a Feminist Jurisprudence' (1983) 8 *Signs* 635

Marton, F and Säljö, R, 'On Qualitative Differences in Learning – I: Outcome and Processes' (1976) 46 *British Journal of Educational Psychology* 4

Marton, F and Säljö, R, 'Approaches to Learning' in Marton, Hounsell and Entwhistle (1984) 46

F Marton, D J Hounsell and N J Entwhistle (eds) *The Experience of Learning*, Scottish Academic Press, Edinburgh, 1984

McInnis, C and Marginson, S, *Australian Law Schools after the 1987 Pearce Report*, AGPS, Canberra, 1994

McKeachie, W J, 'Research on College Teaching: The Historical Background' (1990) 82 *Journal of Educational Psychology* 189.

Mitchell, J B, 'Current Theories on Expert and Novice Thinking: A Full Faculty Considers the Implications for Legal Education' (1989) 39 *Journal of Legal Education* 275

Mitchell, R, (ed), *Redefining Labour Law*, Centre for Employment and Labour Relations Law, The University of Melbourne, 1995

Mullins, G, Whittle, J and Mack, K, 'Law Students' Perceptions of Learning', paper presented at the Annual Conference of the Australian Association for Research in Education, Adelaide, 1989

Naffine, N, *Law and the Sexes*, Allen & Unwin, Sydney, 1990

Newell, A and Simon, H A, *Human Problem Solving*, Prentice Hall, Englewood Cliffs, New Jersey, 1972

Northedge, A, 'Learning through Discussion in the Open University' (1975) 2 *Teaching at a Distance* 10

O'Connor, P, 'Teacher Bids Good-bye to the Book' (1993) 24 (No 13) *ANU Reporter* 1

Oddi, L F 'Development and Validation of an Instrument to Identify Self-directed Continuing Learners' (1984) 36 *Adult Education Quarterly* 97

Ogden, G L, 'The Problem Method in Legal Education' (1984) 34 *Journal of Legal Education* 654

Parliament of the Commonwealth of Australia, Senate Standing Committee on Employment, Education and Training, *Priorities for Reform in Higher Education*, AGPS, Canberra, 1990

Patterson, E W, 'The Case Method in American Legal Education: Its Origins and Objectives' (1951) 4 *Journal of Legal Education* 116

Pearce, D, (chairman) *Australian Law Schools: A Discipline Assessment for the Commonwealth Tertiary Education Commission*, AGPS, Canberra, 1987 (the Pearce Report)

Pearson, M, and Smith, M, 'Debriefing in Experience-based Learning' in Boud, Keogh and Walker (1985)

Perry, W G, *Forms of Intellectual and Ethical Development in the College Years*, Holt Rhinehart and Winston, 1970

Pirie, A J, 'Objectives in Legal Education: The Case for Systematic Instructional Design' (1987) 37 *Journal of Legal Education* 576

Race, P, *53 Interesting Ways to Write Open Learning Materials*, Technical and Educational Services Ltd, Bristol, 1992

Ramsden, P, 'Student Learning Research: Retrospect and Prospect' (1985) 4 *Higher Education Research and Development* 51

Ramsden, P, (ed) *Improving Learning – New Perspectives*, Kogan Page, London, 1988

Ramsden, P, *Learning to Teaching in Higher Education*, Routledge, London, 1992

Ramsden, P, and Dodds, A, *Improving Teaching and Courses: A Guide to Evaluation*, Centre for the Study of Higher Education, University of Melbourne, Melbourne, 1989

Rawson, S L, and Tyree, A L, 'Fred Keller Goes to Law School' (1991) 2 *Legal Education Review* 253

Reed, R M, 'Group Learning in Law School' (1984) 34 *Journal of Legal Education* 674

Report of the Committee on Safety and Health at Work 1970-72, HMSO, 1972

Resnick, L B (ed) *Knowing, Learning and Instruction: Essays in Honour of Robert Glaser*, Lawrence Erlbaum Associates, Hillsdale, New Jersey, 1989

Richardson, J, 'Computers Mooted Ready to Lecture – the Law Students Set to be the Precedent' (1993) 3 *Campus Review* No 34, 1

Rowles, J P, 'Toward Balancing the Goals of Legal Education' (1981) 31 *Journal of Legal Education* 375

Rowntree, D, *Developing Courses for Students*, Paul Chapman Publishing Ltd, London, 1981

Rowntree, D, *Assessing Our Students. How Shall We Know Them?*, Revised edition, Kogan Page, London, 1987

Rowntree, D, *Teaching Through Self-Instruction. How to Develop Open Learning Materials*, Kogan Page, London, 1990

Rowntree, D, *Preparing Materials for Open, Distance and Flexible Learning*, Kogan Page, London, 1994

Sachs, J, Ramsden, P and Phillips, L (eds) *The Experience of Quality in Higher Education*, Griffith Institute of Higher Education, Brisbane, 1995

Säljö, R, 'Learning in the Learner's Perspective: Some Common-sense Conceptions', Internal Report, University of Gothenburg, No 76, 1979

Sampford, C J and Wood, D, 'Legal Theory and Legal Education – The Next Step' (1989) 1 *Legal Education Review* 107

Sampford, CJ and Wood, D 'The place of Legal Theory in the Law School' (1987) 11 *Bulletin of the Australian Society of Legal Philosophy* 98

Schirmerhorn, S, Goldschmid, M L and Shore, B S, 'Learning Basic Principles of Probability in Student Dyads: A Cross Age Comparison' (1975) 67 *Journal of Educational Psychology* 551

Schoenfield, A H, *Mathematical Problem Solving*, Mathematical Press, Orlando, Florida, 1985

Schon, D, *The Reflective Practitioner*, Basic Books, New York, 1983

Scheier, M F and Carver, C S 'Cognition, Affect and Self-regulation' in Levine and Wang (eds) (1983) 157

Thornton, M, 'Portia Lost in the Groves of Academe Wondering What to Do about Legal Education' (1991) 34 *The Australian Universities' Review* 26

Tobias, C 'Gender Issues and the Prosser, Wade and Schwartz Torts Casebook' (1988) 18 *Golden Gate University Law Review* 495

Tough, A, *The Adult's Learning Projects*, Ontario Institute for Studies in Education, Toronto, 1971

Tribe, D M, and Tribe, A J, 'Lawteach: an Interactive Method for Effective Large Group Teaching' (1987) 12 *Studies in Higher Education* 200

Van Rossum, E J and Schenk, S M, 'The Relationship Between Learning Conception, Study Strategy and Learning Outcome' (1984) 54 *British Journal of Educational Psychology* 73

Vygotsky, L S, *Thought and Language*, John Wiley, New York, 1972

Vygotsky, L S, *Mind in Society: The Development of Higher Psychological Processes*, Cole, M, John-Steiner, V, Scribner, S and Souberman, E (eds and trans) Harvard University Press, Cambridge, 1978

Washbourne, M, Lawrence, J, and Kurzeja, D, 'Training Problem Solving Skills in Children: Two Approaches to Adult Intervention', paper presented at Annual Meeting of Australian Association for Research in Education, Hobart, November, 1985

Watkins, D A, 'Depth of Processing and the Quality of Learning Outcomes' (1983) 12 *Instructional Science* 49

Whitehead, A N, *The Aims of Education and Other Essays*, Free Press, New York, 1967

Wildman, S M, 'The Question of Silence: Techniques to Ensure Full Class Participation' (1988) 36 *Journal of Legal Education* 147

Zarr, M, 'Learning Criminal Law Through the Whole Case Method' (1984) 84 *Journal of Legal Education* 697

Zimmerman, B J and Martinez-Pons, M, 'Construct Validation of a Strategy Model of Student Self-Regulated Learning' (1988) 80 *Journal of Educational Psychology* 284